Name___

Christ Chu

"Fathers... bring up your children in the discipline and instruction of the Lord." (Ephesians 6:4)

DAY BY DAY WITH JESUS

Original Christian Devotions
for Each Day of the Year

Companion Edition to
Daily Walk With Jesus
and
Daily Word From Jesus

by

Robert L. Tasler

AUTHOR'S NOTE

This book is published by "Bob's Books." <u>DAY BY DAY WITH JESUS</u> © 2015 is a companion to the author's first two devotionals, <u>DAILY WALK WITH JESUS</u> © 2013, and <u>DAILY WORD FROM JESUS</u> © 2014. All three, plus the author's books, are available at <u>www.bobtasler.com</u>.

This book is a collection of original devotions, many of which have been published in his regular free e-mailed weekly devotional, WEEKLY MESSAGE. Interested persons may subscribe to WEEKLY MESSAGE through the author's website.

The author is a retired pastor in the Lutheran Church – Missouri Synod and wishes to thank his good friend Marlene Dreier for her editing and proofreading, and he also thanks his loving wife Carol for her valued assistance with all the book's content.

NOTICE OF RIGHTS

Most of the Bible references used in <u>DAY BY DAY WITH JESUS</u> are from the English Standard Version, 2011 edition, although some verses are paraphrased by the author. The English Standard Version is an updating of the Revised Standard Version of 1971, and it is published by Crossway Bibles. The author will allow portions of <u>DAY BY DAY WITH JESUS</u> for use in various Christian outlets, but only with his written permission.

BOOKS BY THE AUTHOR
(Paperback and E-Book)

Daily Walk With Jesus
Daily Word From Jesus
Day By Day With Jesus
From the Cradle to the Cross
Spreading The Word
Reflections
Bobby Was A Farmer Boy
Fun and Games at Palm Creek
The Discipleship Bible Study Series (Paperback only)

(E-Book only)

Country Preacher
Small Town Preacher
Immigrant Son

TABLE OF CONTENTS

JANUARY............................... Page 1

FEBRUARY............................ Page 33

MARCH................................Page 61

APRIL..................................Page 93

MAY..................................Page 123

JUNE.................................Page 155

JULY................................ Page 185

AUGUST.............................. Page 217

SEPTEMBER........................... Page 249

OCTOBER............................. Page 279

NOVEMBER............................ Page 311

DECEMBER............................ Page 341

Author ....Page 373

PREFACE

I am grateful to the Lord and my readers for the success of my first two devotionals, <u>Daily Walk With Jesus,</u> and <u>Daily Word From Jesus.</u> It is my fervent hope that people of all ages and walks of life will be blessed by reading them and also this new one, <u>Day By Day With Jesus.</u> It is comprised of more original writings or adaptations of stories and thoughts that hopefully will aid people in finding strength and joy for each day God gives them.

The title, <u>Day By Day With Jesus,</u> is used with permission from Dr. Paul L. Maier, author and lecturer. Dr. Maier graciously wrote these words in his Foreword to my first devotional, <u>Daily Walk With Jesus</u>:

> *My father, Lutheran Hour founder Dr. Walter A. Maier, published devotions each year called "Day by Day With Jesus." They were leaflets for each day of the year with a message, an illustration called "Thought for the Day," a hymn verse and a prayer. Independently but happily, Robert Tasler has done much the same thing in title and content. Maybe, though, Tasler's is better for our hurry-up age since he combines all this material into one daily devotion. And done so with sparkling success!*

I am grateful to be allowed to use this title which evokes genuine Christian faith and trust, and because it is reminiscent of the fine daily devotions written by the sainted Dr. Walter A. Maier. May all who read this book be blessed by the hope and peace given by faith in our Savior Jesus Christ.

+ + +

Robert L. Tasler, AD 2015
Casa Grande, Arizona
Castle Rock, Colorado

Dedication

To the people of Christ Church - Lutheran and Christ Lutheran School, Phoenix, Arizona, its pastors, staff, leaders, teachers, students, members and all who seek to walk, talk and live Day By Day With Jesus.

DAY BY DAY WITH JESUS
in
January

+ + +

JANUARY 1

Happy New Year! I appreciate so many things as we begin this new year, including your willingness to read *Day By Day With Jesus*. May your New Year be filled with wonderful blessings and may nothing tragic happen in our world. May we be blessed like the man who prayed, *"Dear God, please grant this new year that I will have a fat bank account and a skinny body, not the opposite like last year."*

Time goes by quickly. Commentator Ben Stein writes with humor and common sense, making him interesting and worth reading. In a November, 2011, Newsmax article, he wrote, *"Of all life's mysteries, the most cruel and unyielding is that the moment, which seems to be permanent and fixed today, passes and is gone forever."* He concluded his comments, *"The only thing I can do about it is to cherish the time I have left and appreciate it while I still have it."*

"Tempus Fugit" - time flies. 1 Peter 1:24-25 says, **"The grass withers, the flower falls,"** and then gratefully adds, **"but the Word of the Lord remains forever."** Some seem to delight in speculating to us that each new year will be cataclysmic, that something will happen to change the course of human history. Maybe so, maybe not. But if you trust in God for your life, then **"No evil shall befall you, no scourge will come near your tent."** (Psalm 91:10, RSV) We cannot avoid all evil, but we need not be crushed by it.

We meet the new year trusting Jesus. He assured us **"Whoever believes in Me has eternal life."** (John 6:47) We know not the future, but Jesus will be there when it comes.

Cherish and appreciate your fellow travelers on the road of life.

JANUARY 2

It's good to approach a new year positively and with faith in God. Years from now the past year will be remembered for various reasons, most of which we do not know now. We do know the new year will bring surprises and struggles, but exactly what form they will take is known only to the Good Lord.

I recall once writing a sermon titled, *"What Do You Do When You Don't Know What to Do?"* Perhaps I wrote it because I didn't know what to preach about that Sunday. But I do remember the answer I put forward – *"Pray and Act!"* First, pray for God's guidance, then make a decision and follow through with it.

I once accepted a call to another congregation, and when we got there wished we had stayed where we were. All our worldly goods were packed in a U-Haul truck, and for four days that truck sat in the church parking lot while we looked for a place to live.

My wife and I were torn about our decision. What should we do, go back or stay? Amid the anxiety and fear, an older pastor gave me some advice. *"You'd better pray about this, and then either unpack that truck or else go back where you came from."* We prayed for guidance and then unpacked the truck. That was a long time ago.

Pray and Act! Another old friend once told me, *"Make your decision and don't look back. Nine out of ten times you'll have made the right one, and the other time will be a lesson you won't forget."* A wise man he was, my friend Roy! He's with the Lord now, probably smiling on his loved ones.

Pray and Act! I can't tell you how long to pray, but I can urge you personally to pray that God will show you plainly what is best for you to do. When you pray for that in faith, He is usually quite obvious with His answer. His prophet once told us, **"Commit your way to the Lord, trust in Him, and He will act."** (Psalm 37:5)

Today the Lord wants you to remember: "Pray and Act!"

JANUARY 3

Have you ever said, *"Oh my God!"* and considered what those three words meant? Are those three words a phrase of surprise or an expression of gratitude? How do we show our gratitude when we are truly grateful?

One night I viewed a marvelous desert sunset, with vibrant colors on fleecy clouds in a clear and changing sky with its deepening reds, yellows and blues. It was a sight only God could create in such grand fashion. I quietly said, *"Oh my God!"* because it was so beautiful and so fleeting.

I have often been critical when hearing those words flippantly spoken, yet they can have great meaning. Perhaps something worthwhile has caught our attention, and a connection was made with creation, so much that it caused us to cry out to our Creator, *"Oh my God!"*

One particular January day for me started out grey, wet and chilly, but ended with a display of warmth and brilliance that was hard to describe. Today is a gift, and these very moments are the only certain gifts we have. Today has such great value to our existence that gratitude should be our response, perhaps by saying, *"Oh my God!"*

Today you have life, your own life and the lives of those around you. Open your eyes and behold the sky and the weather moving through it. It is wondrous and changing. Look at the faces of the people you meet. They are unique, original, interesting, and you have eyes to see them with. Millions cannot see with eyes like yours, for their world is darkness.

Turn on the faucet with its clean water, hot or cold, and realize millions do not have this gift. Smile at someone and realize the value of that person smiling back at you. Whether they know you or not, what a gift your smile may be!

If you can count even small blessings in your life, let your gratitude overflow and then take time to say to your Creator, *"Oh my God!"*

"Give thanks to the Lord for He is good." (Psalm 107:1)

JANUARY 4

Things surely can take a sudden turn in life when you least expect it. Moses discovered this when he met the Lord in a burning bush, and Jonah did when God told him to take a trip to Nineveh. Paul found this out as he was traveling the road to Damascus, and Luther did during a raging storm.

Carol and I discovered this once, also. She went to visit a friend, missed a step, and broke her leg. We thought it wasn't serious until the doctor said it was a complete break that would require surgery. She laughed when the doctor said this, but then realized he wasn't just "pulling her leg." When she had the surgery, life was different around our home for many weeks.

I'm sure I'd have yelled a whole lot more than she did when they moved her to a gurney and the broken bones rubbed together. Her weeks of rehab in the nice new facility did help, though. They helped me, also.

Things surely can take a turn in life when you least expect it. You plan a fun day outside and wake up to clouds and rain. Or you train for a life occupation and find you dislike the kind of life it brings. Or you plan a good family life and end up in a divorce court. Or you plan a winter of activities and break a leg.

Of course, not every unfortunate event carries the same result or requires the same effort to overcome it. Legs can heal more easily than marriages, and impatient husbands can learn more easily than dissatisfied students. The world is not as bad it may seem with many ideologies in conflict.

The Bible says it so well: **"I praise You, O Lord, because I am fearfully and wonderfully made; Your works are wonderful, and I know this full well."**(Psalm 139:14) Our loving God made us, and He doesn't make junk.

Carol and I grew closer during the healing process. I again found my sweetheart and she discovered her hubby. Even a bad event can have a good blessing if we look for it.

I hope you don't have to break your leg to find out.

JANUARY 5

Prayer changes things, but not everyone thinks so. Even some Christian people believe prayer only benefits the one praying, giving peace of mind but not changing anything. They think God has things already worked out, so prayer doesn't change what He will do. But I agree with the words on the wall plaque: *"Prayer Changes Things."*

During the week after my wife broke her leg, she said she felt comforted that so many people were praying for her. Dozens of emails, cards and flowers helped her realize that *"Prayer Changes Things."* We can't prove that God did things any differently than He might have, but a Christian knows the blessings of prayers offered to God.

In Isaiah 38, King Hezekiah became sick and was at the point of death. So Isaiah the prophet told him, **"Set your house in order, for you shall die, you shall not recover."** But Hezekiah prayed, **"Please, O Lord, remember how I have walked before You in faithfulness and with a whole heart, and have done what is good in Your sight."** Then the Lord told Isaiah to tell him, **"I have heard your prayer; I have seen your tears, so I will add 15 years to your life."**

Some might say God knew what Hezekiah was going to pray, so He did what He was going to do anyway. But the Bible tells us God heard his prayer and changed what He'd planned to do. We can believe that actually happened.

God answers our prayers in several ways, depending on what He knows is best for us. He can also have us wait. Parents do this all the time. Our child may ask for something that seems good, but we know the child is not ready for it. One day that request may be granted, but not now. When the time comes and she is ready to receive and use it best, the parent will give the child what she asked for.

It was that way when God sent Jesus at Christmas, **"When the fullness of time had come, God sent forth His Son Jesus."** (Galatians 4:4)

Yes, prayer does change things.

JANUARY 6

Nearly one-third of the world's population is Christian. January 6 is recognized among most Christians around the world as the Festival of Epiphany. It marks the end of the twelve days of Christmas and celebrates the visit of the Magi, those highly educated astrologers, to the baby Jesus.

Matthew's Gospel tells us the Magi brought valuable gifts of gold, frankincense and myrrh to honor the baby. Gold is a valuable metal usually associated with a King. In giving gold, the Magi were recognizing the newborn child as the new King, for they had come to Jerusalem announcing their search for a child whom they believed was born "King of the Jews." Aged King Herod was understandably disturbed when he heard of this.

Frankincense is the white hardened gum from the African Boswellia tree which when burned gives off a fragrant smell. It was burned in worship to God and was quite valuable, often worth far more than gold. This gift is recognized by Christians to mean the child would be a priest on behalf of God's people.

The third gift, myrrh, is also a tree sap and comes from the thorny Commiphora Myrrh tree of East Africa. It was used for healing, but mostly as a burial compound to delay bodily decomposition in the grave. The "spices" which the women took to Jesus' grave would have included myrrh. Christians believe this gift indicates Jesus would be God's prophet, because most of them suffered untimely death.

Eastern Christians have adopted January 6 as their Christmas and celebration of Christ's birth. Among western Christians, Epiphany is the end of Christmas celebration and decorations are removed. The Epiphany season lasts until Shrove Tuesday, the day before Ash Wednesday.

No matter where Christians live, they rejoice at the birth of the one sent from God in the Bethlehem manger.

"Where is He who is born king of the Jews? We have seen His star in the east and have come to worship Him."
(Matthew 2:2)

JANUARY 7

The Church of the Nativity in Bethlehem is said to be the oldest church in Christianity. Christians have been conducting worship services there since it was built by Emperor Constantine at the encouragement of his mother Helena. The massive structure in Bethlehem was started in 327 AD and completed in six years. It has undergone much change and addition over the years, but still contains many stone fragments of the original building.

The most famous item inside the church is the Grotto, the cave where Jesus was supposed to be born. It is located under the altar in this great church beneath a silver and gold star on the floor. Today persons wishing to enter this famous church must bow low as they walk through the "Door of Humility" which is less than four feet high.

There is a reason for the existence of this small door. In 614 AD, Persian soldiers destroyed most of Bethlehem, but they left the old church alone. When the enemy commander went inside and saw a depiction of the Magi dressed in Persian clothing, he ordered the building spared.

Later when the city was rebuilt, the large front door was reduced in size to keep enemies from riding their horses inside, a practice that continued throughout history by the enemies of the Christian Church. Napoleon used European churches as stables for his horses during his destructive campaigns. Luther's grave in Wittenberg's Castle Church was the resting place of horses for nearly a year!

Despite their places in history, churches are only buildings. We value them, but they are not holy. The true Church, the one we call *"Holy Christian Church"* in our creeds, is invisible and unseen, for it is the holy assembly of all the saints throughout the ages who have believed Jesus is their Savior. All who accept Jesus of Nazareth as Lord are members, including you, me and all who read this, and its members will receive God's gift of eternal life.

The Church's one foundation is Jesus Christ her Lord. *(from the hymn)*

JANUARY 8

A local newspaper carries an advice column, one we've probably all read a time or two. A column in January contained quite a number of things people were advised to do at the start of the new year.

Her column could have been titled, *"Just For Today,"* since it was a list of commendable things such as, *"Just for today I will eat better,"* or *"Just for today I will correct no one's life but my own."* Here is my list offered a week after January 1:

-- Just for today I will take a moment to pray for the strength to face each moment God gives me with courage.

-- Just for today I will not think of how bad things are in the world, but how good we have it.

-- Just for today I will tell my loved ones I love them – several times, for no reason other than that I do love them.

-- Just for today I will smile at most people I meet, especially those assisting me in the checkout line, in the doctor's office or even someone walking past on the sidewalk.

-- Just for today I will be grateful for the weather, no matter whether it's sunny or rainy, cloudy or snowy, or hot and muggy. It is a gift from God that I can experience it.

-- Just for today I will call or write someone I have not contacted in awhile and tell them I am thinking about them.

-- Just for today I will take out my Bible and read a chapter from the Psalms or the Gospels and pray about it.

-- Just for today I will give thanks that God has created such a wondrous planet on which we can live, for it is unique in all creation to support complex life as it does.

-- Just for today I will give God thanks for His Son Jesus and the eternal blessings we have because of Him.

-- Just for today I will select five of the things on this page and actually do them! Maybe tomorrow I will select five more.

People often seek to begin again in a new and better way. May your new year be one of joy as you seek new and better ways of living your life.

"Rejoice in the Lord always!" (Philippians 4:4)

JANUARY 9

Lately I've been reading on a couple of subjects I don't know enough about. One of them is our earth, specifically its origin and placement in the universe. Two books I read on this both agreed that the earth exists in a "Goldilocks Zone" where all necessary ingredients – its star, distance from other planets, moon, chemical elements, gravity, radioactive field, plate tectonics, etc. – make everything *"not too hot, not too cold, but just right."* All these lead to the existence of complex life, the animals, plants and human beings. No other such place in the universe is known that has what our earth has.

The difference in the books was in the origin of life. The authors of <u>The Privileged Planet</u> believe life requires an Intelligent Being, a creator God, to arrange it all. The authors of <u>Rare Earth</u> believe life evolved over time in space, and that there is no such as thing as a creator God. Physicist Stephen Hawking agrees with the latter idea. He says the vast amount of ingredients needed for complex life might lead some to believe in God, but he does not.

But where did it all come from? To me, it's not whether there was a Big Bang. It's about who lit the fuse.

The Bible gives an incredible amount of information when it says, **"In the beginning, God created the heavens and the earth,"** and again, **"God said, 'Let there be light'."** (Genesis 1:1, 3) The origin of time, space and matter is no longer a matter of Sunday School faith but of scientific evidence.

More and more scientists now admit that life as we know it could not have just emerged by chance. The possibility for the trillions of needed elements to somehow randomly assemble themselves together in perfect order is too high. Something or Someone had to be involved.

Even atheist Richard Dawkins admits, *"It could have been something from outer space."* But how did "outer space" get everything in perfect order for it to happen? Come to think of it, God is out there in space, too, isn't He?

"I praise You, for I am wonderfully made." (Palm 139:14)

JANUARY 10

The debate between science and religion is most often framed in whether a true scientist can support the claims of Christianity. But seldom is it asked if a Christian can support science. All of us are expected to support scientific findings, but few expect science to support faith.

Putting the debate another way, must science and religion necessarily conflict with one another? The answer is yes and no. Yes, a Christian can trust much of what science tells us, and yes, a scientist can be a Christian. But, no, science and religion do not have to conflict. Scientists also have faith, even if it is only in their findings.

We can approach the debate another way, from the perspectives of reason and faith. Can faith support reason, and can reason support faith? For example, reason says Jesus was born, but faith says He was born of the Virgin Mary by the power of God. Reason says Jesus was a Rabbi from Nazareth, but faith says He was also the Messiah sent from God. Reason says He was crucified, but faith says He arose again from the dead. Can these two be reconciled?

They can be if we keep an open mind. Reason might lead us to think, *"If it's not provable, I cannot accept it."* Faith can lead us to think, *"No matter what evidence exists to the contrary, if I believe it, then it is true."* Both of these statements come from closed minds. An open mind says, *"I should examine the evidence of science."* It also says, *"Being unproven doesn't mean it is necessarily wrong."*

Reason can lead to both truth and falsehood, and faith can do the same. There was a time the church leaders made martyrs of those who said the world was round. Many scientists today say there is no God. Both are wrong.

A Christian can believe scientific findings, but can also know new findings can change accepted truth. A person of faith accepts those findings are from God. Both faith and reason are good, for both come from God.

"Come, let us reason together." (Isaiah 1:18)

JANUARY 11

My wife and I enjoy watching football and one January Sunday were thrilled to see our favorite team win the AFC championship. They were a great team and we hoped they would win the Super Bowl later that month. The quarterback was a remarkably talented athlete and student of the game.

We also watched the NFC championship game. After the game one of the players shocked the interviewer with insulting words, words he later wished he had not spoken.

After that game we watched a short video which contained surprising Christian witness from several young players and one of their coaches. In the video they were asked, *"Who is Jesus?"* Here are some of their comments:

"Jesus is everything, He'll meet you at the lowest time of your life and or at your highest." "He's the Alpha and the Omega." "Jesus is love and He comforts us." "He is the Son of God, who humbly came to earth, and all He gives us is free." "He's the greatest treasure in the universe." One comment drew smiles from the others. *"Jesus is better than the Super Bowl. When the Super Bowl is over and behind us, Jesus will still be there for us."*

Well said! Our world adulates the celebrity, the rich and famous, the successful athlete and the movie star. People mimic them, wear their fashions and emulate their life styles. But the life of the rich and famous can also lead us to the temptation of narcissism and self-centeredness. So when we hear Christian witness coming from the mouths of professional, public people, we are surprised.

In our increasingly secular world, it is surprising to hear public praise for Jesus. In a culture that denies and defames God, we are grateful for those who give Him honor, publicly or in private. We are thankful that amid money and power and success, people give glory to God instead of self. **"Let your light so shine that people may see your good works and give glory to your Father in heaven."** (Matthew 5:16)

When we have faith in Jesus Christ, we are all winners!

JANUARY 12

If you walk around our Arizona park in the winter, you may notice that every Monday and Thursday there are trash bags sitting in the street. One of the perks of living here is curbside trash service. We bag our garbage, trash and disposable things we don't want and put them outside for the maintenance men to pick up as they drive by on their motorized carts hooked to small wagons. Folks do well here at recycling, but there's still a lot of trash.

I am always glad when the trash man comes, since he hauls away all the unwanted stuff I don't want anymore. Several times in my preaching I've likened trash to our sins and Jesus as the Divine Trash Man who takes them all away and buries them on the landfill of sin called Calvary.

Sometimes if I use this example or one of my other favorites too often in a sermon, I can expect my wife to roll her eyes in a *"There it is again"* expression. But she is an understanding person and has often told me, *"If you have a good story, tell it."* That's helpful since she also an editor for my books.

While taking my daily walk one morning on trash day, I noticed one of the maintenance crew pick up a small bag and wince, and jerk his hand back, shaking it. I knew right away what the problem was. The sack was filled with cactus cuttings and some thorns had pierced his gloves. Picking up other people's trash can be a dangerous business.

Jesus found that to be true when He died for our sins. Getting rid of the trash of our sins cost Him His life. Even though He knew ahead of time that it would be painful, He didn't pull back and stop doing it. He stayed with the task God had given Him and removed all the deadly trash that could separate us from God and others.

Jesus paid the price we should have paid. I don't understand why God took such a hard way to do it, but sin is dangerous and deadly. We cannot trifle with sin. It must be removed so we won't spend eternity regretting it.

Give thanks today that Jesus has hauled away your trash.

JANUARY 13

Today is a special day among the Swedes, Finns and Norwegians. It is St. Knut's Day. My dear sister once wrote me a note about this day that is worth passing along. Here is what she said,

"Even in my dotage and decline, I can still learn something new. Here it is: St. Knut's Day is soon to be upon us! This is the day the Nordic people take down their trees and end the Christmas season. After much dancing and singing the last Christmas songs, the Christmas tree is taken out. In old times, it was thrown out the window. This celebration is called 'Julgransplundring,' plundering of the tree."

My sister is still learning new things and posted this on Facebook. I learned a few other things about St. Knut's Day among the Scandinavians. January 13 is also the Twentieth Day of Christmas *(I thought they quit counting on the Twelfth Day, Epiphany, January 6)*

Canute Lavard was a Danish Duke assassinated on January 7, 1131, by his cousin who usurped his throne. A civil war followed, after which Canute was declared a saint. In 1680, St. Knut's Day was moved to January 13, the 20th day of Christmas. In honor of this day, sweets and cookies are shared by all, and possibly even coffee and some nice Danish sweet rolls!

Swedes and Norwegians joined the fun, but Finns added a twist. The "Nuttipukki" (a scary young man dressed as a goat with mask and horns) visited houses and demanded food and alcoholic drink. Some Finnish areas still observe the Nuttipukki tradition, but he is now played by a happy little child demanding cookies and cocoa.

God made people to enjoy life. The holidays are given to help us celebrate the seasons of life. Old Testament Jews established holidays to recall God's blessings such as the end of creation (Sabbath), the Exodus (Passover) or being spared annihilation (Purim with Queen Esther).

"This is the day the Lord has made; let us rejoice and be glad in it." (Psalm 118:24)

JANUARY 14

In February, 1504, Christopher Columbus was in a bad way. In the course of his fourth visit to the New World, his badly leaking ships had left him stranded on the island of Jamaica. The inhabitants, initially hospitable, had grown hostile at the crew's brutish ways and had threatened to cut off the crew's food supply.

While consulting the charts that show the positions of astronomical objects at given times, Columbus realized that astronomers had predicted a lunar eclipse that would be visible in a couple of days. The day before the eclipse, he told the local leaders if they didn't change their minds, the moon would disappear. They scoffed at him, but when the eclipse covered the moon as he had predicted, they relented and gave him food. His ships were rescued and returned to Spain, but Columbus never returned to the New World.

Columbus' actions were deceitful, but he did what was needed to save the lives of his crews. We should always seek to do the right thing, realizing that many of our choices will involve risk. A desperate parent will do things for family that (s)he might otherwise condemn (i.e. Rebekah, mother of Jacob and Esau). Life is not always a clear choice between right and wrong. Sometimes it is the lesser of two evils. The sinfulness of mankind is evident everywhere. That is why we need a Savior to rescue us from ourselves.

The complex situations we face in the world today - immigration, gun ownership, free speech, and helping those in need - all require wise choices with limited resources. Such struggles should move us to trust God and seek guidance from His Word. To rely only on human wisdom is foolhardy. We need God to help show us the way.

I pray our civil and church leaders will seek the Lord's guidance as they act, because human wisdom alone will not solve what lies before us. It would be wise for us all to **"Seek the Lord while He may be found; call upon Him while He is near."** (Isaiah 55:6)

Let us turn to the Lord, and He will have mercy on us.

JANUARY 15

On January 15, 2009, the people onboard U.S. Airways Flight 1549 were in trouble. During takeoff from New York's LaGuardia airport, their plane hit a flock of geese and it stopped both engines completely. In a most amazing feat of piloting, Captain Chesley Sullenberger, a former fighter pilot, maneuvered the powerless plane over the densely populated area of New York and told his passengers and crew, *"Brace for impact!"*

A little over a minute later, the crippled plane made a water landing on the Hudson River where boats and ferries successfully rescued every one of the passengers and crew. When all were taken away in boats, the plane sank. Newspapers called it the "Miracle on the Hudson" and praised the pilot and crew who were later awarded the Master's Medal of commendation. One of the grateful passengers simply said, *"We have a second chance in life."*

In times of crisis or emergency, people naturally reach out for every possible thing to help them stay alive and rescue them. When it is all over and we are safe once again, our *"second chance in life"* is waiting for us.

Every day is a second chance. When we make it to the dawn of another day, we do well to realize it is a new beginning to life. As the plaque on the wall reads, *"O God of New Beginnings and Second Chances, Here I Am Again."*

The prophet Jeremiah wept for his people, praying and urging them, to turn from their evil ways. He promised them that if they did repent, they would see how God would give them a second chance. **"His mercies are new every morning,"** he wrote in Lamentations 3:22. Sadly, his people did not repent and were carried into exile.

God does not give up on us. He wants us to live by His commands, not only because it is His will, but also because His ways are so much better than ours.

Two years after the Hudson River landing, US Air was fined for "littering" in the river. The charges were later dropped.

JANUARY 16

It can really be cold on a January morning. I grew up in snow country, so I learned to respect the cold. Whether it is the puffy white clouds of a bright sunny day or the rolling black clouds of an approaching thunderstorm, I learned to respect the weather and the power it has over us.

Consider what cold and snow can do to some parts of our country this time of year. I spend my winters in Arizona, but it sometimes gets cold enough here to freeze plants at night. Then we hear our hometown in Colorado is getting a winter storm. The temperature there can drop thirty to forty degrees in one day and the melting snow on warm streets makes driving dangerous. Sudden weather changes can move a person to say a prayer for loved ones back home.

Our Colorado home is 6,200 feet above sea level, and that makes winters snowy and cold. It doesn't get as cold as in the Upper Midwest where I was born, but bad weather can still give us a hard winter in Colorado. Cold temperatures might lead us to think the earth is farther away from the sun in winter, but it's not. In the northern hemisphere, we are closer to the sun in winter than we are in the summer.

The reason for this is because the earth is tilted away from direct sunlight. Because of the angle of the sun, its rays aren't absorbed and winters are colder. To be warm, the earth must be in a more direct line so it can absorb the sun's rays, even though it might be farther away.

Isn't it also like this with God? If we turn our heads away from Him, He will seem distant and life will be colder. But if we turn our faces in faith toward the light of His love, we will be strengthened and spiritually warmed, no matter how far away from Him we may have been.

Storms of life may cause us to say, **"Save Us, Lord, or we'll perish!"** like the disciples shouted to Jesus on the stormy sea. (Matthew 8:25) Hopefully we'll then hear Him say, **"I'm right here. Why are you afraid?"**

Lord, help me when I am afraid of life's storms. Amen.

JANUARY 17

I love taking a daytime nap. A short rest can renew my energy for what lies ahead. My father was a lifelong farmer and took a nap almost every day. I can still see him stretched out on the sofa after dinner (noon meal on the farm), his arm under his head and eyes closed for a half hour or so. He did this almost every day, working hard and living to be ninety-seven, despite an irregular heart in his latter years. I don't take a nap every day like he did, but when I do, my day seems to go better.

I have a friend my age who refuses to take a nap in the daytime. He says he has too much to do and feels naps are a waste of time. No amount of urging him or joking with him about it has changed his mind so far. His family has urged him to take a nap, too, because they love him dearly.

Everyone needs rest. Isaiah the prophet had something to say about this. **"Even youths shall be weary and young men shall be exhausted."** (Isaiah 40:30) My friend says he gets enough sleep at night, so why take a daytime nap? It seems to work well for him, but I still like a daily nap.

The Bible, however, doesn't stop with those words from Isaiah 40. The prophet continues, **"But they who wait for the LORD shall renew their strength. They shall mount up with wings like eagles; they shall run and not be weary; they shall walk and not faint."** (Isaiah 40:31)

Isaiah wasn't telling us to take a nap, but he was saying we all need renewal for our weariness, no matter what time of life we are in. If we wait on the Lord, trusting Him to show us how to take our next step, He will renew us with strength we wouldn't otherwise have.

God renews our strength through His true Word, the Bible. When we read the Psalms or the Gospels, we have strength for the day ahead. When we trust that Christ's death on the cross has forgiven our sins, we can forge ahead to do what He gives us to do each day.

"Rest in the Lord; wait patiently for Him." (Psalm 37:7 KJV)

JANUARY 18

Did Jesus exist? I lead a Bible Class on this topic recently, and when the pastor announced it in church one Sunday, I heard a few chuckles in the audience. When he led in the opening prayer, saying, *"Dear Lord, who really does exist,…"* someone giggled. Of course Jesus exists! After all, we'd just celebrated His birthday.

My presentation that day gave evidence not usually known, for it was based on historical references to Jesus and the early Christians from non-Biblical sources. The Bible gives us "insider" information, but is there evidence of Jesus outside the Bible?

I spoke of writings by pagan Roman historians, Tacitus and Suetonius, who both despised Christianity, as well as the Jewish historian Josephus who is well known among scholars but was not a believer in Jesus. There is even a letter to Jesus from the King Abgar V of Edessa recorded by Christian historian Eusebius in his 3rd century history book. All of these referred to a man called "Christos" and his followers.

A striking fact of non-biblical references is that ancient secular sources have never denied or disputed the fact that Jesus lived. It wasn't until the 18th century and the "Age of Enlightenment" that secular philosophers began penning doubts that Jesus existed. "Mythicists" like Arthur Drews, Bruno Bauer and Bart Ehrman challenged His existence.

We may not be able to prove Jesus is the Son of God or that He did miracles or arose from the dead, but only a fool would believe He never lived. Only someone filled with human pride would think it was all made up.

Jesus of Nazareth did exist, and two and a quarter billion Christians today do believe He arose from the dead and is the living Savior of the world. It is still true today what Paul said when he wrote, **"No one can say 'Jesus is Lord' except by the Holy Spirit."** (1 Corinthians 12:3) There should be no doubt that He lived His life for all mankind.

May the Holy Spirit lead you to trust in Him.

JANUARY 19

2014 was a bad year for airline safety. Despite its having the lowest number of air crashes since 2005, there still were 111 plane crashes resulting in major loss of life that year. In March, Malaysia Airlines 370 disappeared off the radar in the Far East with 239 people on board. No trace of the plane was found for years. In July, Malaysia Airlines 17 was shot down by terrorists near Ukraine, killing all 299 aboard. Three days after Christmas, Air Asia 8501 went down with 155 onboard and there were no survivors.

While all this loss of life is tragic, flight 8501 had a unique feature. Forty-one members from the same congregation died that day. Over one-fourth of flight 8501 were members of the same church, Mawar Sharon Christian Church of Indonesia.

Having conducted several hundred funerals during my ministry, I cannot imagine what it must have been like for Rev. Philip Mantofa and the other pastors of this large congregation. Ministering to loved ones of more than one death at the same time is difficult. Ministering to the hundreds of people connected with those forty-one deaths at the same time would be unimaginably difficult.

Pastor Tejo Bunarto told CNN, *"Some things happen in our lives, and sometimes we just don't understand what God really intends. We just put our trust, and everything, completely in His will, because He's going to bring about everything that is the best in our life."*

It is estimated that 6.5 million people in the world fly each day, so we give thanks there aren't more fatalities. God has given us the wonderful gift of rapid transportation, and each time we step onto a plane or get into a car, we trust His grace that we will be kept safe.

God keeps track of earthly travelers because He loves and cares for us. We thank and trust our Lord Jesus and take heart in His promise, **"Do not be anxious about tomorrow, for tomorrow will be anxious for itself."** (Matthew 6:34)

May we all travel safely today in the arms of our loving Lord!

JANUARY 20

Our five senses are amazing. We depend on them constantly and without thinking use our sight, hearing, touch, taste and smell. Some people add a sixth one – a sense of humor. All are important for our earthly life.

In the morning as I get dressed, I add things to my body to make it work better – clothing, eyeglasses and hearing aids. I also take medications every morning to supplement my diet and give me better health. I may get along okay without glasses and hearing aids, but I'd better not forget to take my pills!

I taste the good water that comes from the tap and smell the fresh coffee ready to drink. I taste the buttered toast carefully, avoid touching the hot pan where I've made ham and eggs. I sit at the breakfast table with Carol and we use our tongues to speak, our eyes to read the newspaper and our ears to hear each other as we converse. We use all our senses every day, in every way, and they help us live the wonderful life God has given us.

Then we add the ability to speak and muscles to help us move and eat. Taste buds make food enjoyable and a night of rest gives us strength for the day ahead. All this we take for granted and assume will happen every day. But isn't this the way for all of us.

There are many today who will need help with basic things. They may be able to see or hear, but they cannot dress or feed themselves. They require help even taking medicine or standing up. Some have little strength and can barely breathe without a mechanical devise. Many would give all they own for a few more days of a normal life.

God is gracious to grant us our senses and the strength to use them. He gives us our *"three score years and ten"* to live and perhaps more. For this earthly life we are grateful. Knowing Jesus forgives us and gives us life with God by faith, we are eternally grateful.

"Oh give thanks to the Lord, for He is good!" (Psalm 106:1)

JANUARY 21

Last Friday someone in the park tried to drive inside his neighbor's house. Good thing there was a brick flower planter or he would have hit a wall. People driving by saw the damage and clucked their tongues that someone must have had too much to drink. Until the damage is repaired, the damage will remain. The wall will not repair itself.

A man came to church wearing a leg brace. It was protecting a broken bone as a result of a missed step. The difference between the brick wall and the man's leg was that the leg was healing itself. The moment he broke his leg, millions of pot-hole repair cells called osteoblasts began attaching themselves to the fracture to make new bone.

Those cells hadn't been waiting around for that break. Billions of them had already been diligently replacing old bone cells all through the year. About 20 percent of our bones are replaced in this way every year by the osteoclasts, the demolition cells that clean out the old cells so the osteoblasts can replace them with new ones.

If I tried to repair that broken brick wall by removing a line of bricks in a horizontal row, the rest of the wall would collapse. But if I replaced a brick here and there, keeping the wall basically intact, I'd eventually have a new wall. That's how our body fixes itself, depositing new fiber here and there until the bone is repaired. The "blasts" and "clasts" work together, without our permission. We don't have to call them to start working. They just show up.

Our body is an amazing creation. There are hundreds of types of cells inside our bodies that do their work to grow us, repair us and keep us alive and healthy. Some say the Bible conflicts with science, but it speaks truly when it says, we are **"fearfully and wonderfully made."** (Psalm 139:14)

It is easy to dismiss the notion of a Creator God, but our bodies are not products of chance. God made us this way. It takes more faith to think it all happened by accident than that a Divine Creator is made us His way.

Stay healthy, use your head and drive safely today!

JANUARY 22

Someone once said, *"When God solves our problems, we have faith in His abilities; When God doesn't solve our problems He has faith in our abilities."*

God is accurate and even in how He has made His creation. Consider the hatching of eggs: A canary egg hatches in 14 days; a barnyard hen in 21 days; domestic ducks and geese in 28 days; a wild mallard duck in 35 days; parrots and ostrich eggs hatch in 42 days. They are all divisible by seven, the number of days in a week.

God is wise in how He makes His creatures. Consider the elephant: The four legs of this great beast all bend forward in the same direction, unlike any other quadruped. The horse rises from the ground on its two front legs first. A cow rises from the ground with its two hind legs first. God made the elephant with a huge body, too large for two legs to lift it, so He gave it four fulcrums so it can rise from the ground more easily. How wise the Lord is in all His great works of creation!

He creates our food in even numbers: Each watermelon has an even number of stripes on the rind. Each orange has an even number of segments. Rows of corn kernels grow in even numbers and stalks of wheat have an even number of grains. Bananas grow with an even number in one row, then an odd in the next, then an even number, all so the bananas grow in bunches and the fruit is preserved. Amazing!

Flower blossoms open at specific times during the day. Carl Linnaeus, 18th century botanist, wrote that if he had a conservatory containing the right kind of soil, moisture and temperature, he could tell the time of day or night by the flowers that were open and those that were closed!

Nature is ordered by our Lord in a beautiful way to show His glory. Even the waves roll in to shore twenty-six per minute in all kinds of weather. If we entrust Him with our life, He can help us use them for a purpose.

"God's works are marvelous in our eyes." (Psalm 118:23)

JANUARY 23

We have a hummingbird feeder in our backyard in Arizona that gets many visits from those tiny feathery fliers. I've always enjoyed watching "hummers" and have learned a little in how they live and fly through the air like little helicopters darting back and forth. Here are a few facts about this amazing creation of God:

There are 325 species of hummingbirds worldwide but only a couple dozen varieties visit the United States each year. An average hummingbird heart beats 1,200 times per minute, has 1,000 to 1,500 tiny feathers on its body (the fewest of any bird species) and weighs less than a nickel. It can fly up to 30 mph with its wings flapping 50-200 times per second, and can reach 60 mph during a dive. At rest it takes 250 breaths per minute.

A hummingbird eats half its weight in sugar daily, feeding 5-8 times per hour by licking food with its tiny fringed tongue. It has 97% efficiency with converting sugar into energy. Some varieties migrate up to 1,000 or more miles in groups of several dozen at a time, and they can cross the Gulf of Mexico in 500 non-stop miles. As tiny and fragile as they seem, hummingbirds can live from 3 to 10 years. Most tiny eggs are a half inch long and can represent up to 10% of the mother's weight.

Despite their size, hummingbirds are among the most aggressive bird species and will regularly attack jays, crows and hawks that infringe on their territory. Backyard birders often have one dominant hummingbird that guards all the feeders. Tough little birds!

The Bible says God knows al things, even when a bird falls to the earth (Matthew 10:29), so He must be busy keeping track of these tiny flying wonders of His creation. If He knows where the birds are, then He knows where we are, too. We may feel neglected, but we are never forgotten by God. He loves us wherever we are.

"You are of more value than many sparrows." (Matthew 12:7)

JANUARY 24

I enjoy a good breakfast. I probably consume more calories at breakfast that at any other meal in my day, and have done this for years. This might be because of a habit I developed years ago of not eating after 6 PM each night. I sleep better and keep my weight down with this practice I learned from a health magazine.

I may enjoy an occasional meal or snack someone offers later than that, but nine out of ten evenings I eat nothing after 6 PM. I even clean my teeth about that time which helps avoid snacks (I dislike brushing more than once a night). This helpful routine results in a morning hunger when it's time to "break the fast."

I like my coffee hot with something substantial to eat, so I have developed several breakfast menus which I prepare for myself. My dear wife has different morning tastes, so we have always fixed our own breakfasts, occasionally sharing a waffle or a coffee cake we've made. Science says a good breakfast is healthy. As the saying goes, *"Eat breakfast like a king, lunch like a prince, and supper like a pauper."* Words of wisdom!

It is remarkable that in such a rich nation as ours it is a sign of wealth to eat smaller meals and maintain leaner bodies. Still today in some nations, one's size is an indication of wealth and privilege. My wife and I do not work hard, so we require less food. I have a niece who eats twice as much as I do every day and weighs half as much.

God's blessings don't usually mean we have more, but that we have enough. When we have enough, then we can share of our bounty with others in need. This is true of our clothing. "Orphan Grain Train" is a ministry that shares extra clothing with those in need.

Many people eat no breakfast and large suppers. If it works for them, well and good. We all should thank God for His blessings, and then enjoy life He's given us.

"Everyone should eat and drink and take pleasure in all his toil—this is God's gift to mankind." (Ecclesiastes 3:13)

JANUARY 25

I have big feet and they come in handy. I need them to keep my balance and stand higher on my tiptoes. My big feet help me walk with more confidence and, as my mother once said with a smile, *"Big feet give you good understanding."* I like to wear a good pair of shoes and will often pay a little more to get them.

It's generally not known that one of my favorite actors, John Wayne, walked with mincing steps because he had such small feet. At six feet four inches and size nine boots, it's surprising he could stand up! Maybe that's why he disliked riding horses, a little known fact since he appeared in over a hundred westerns during his 200+ movie career.

I like keeping my feet in fairly good shoes and especially enjoy a new pair of slippers. I once ordered a pair of quality moccasins from a well-known Minnesota store and was irritated to find they were made in China. But I still wore them. The most expensive pair of shoes I ever owned cost over $350 new, but I got them from a second hand store and have gotten much fine use from them.

I once knew a pastor who wore sandals and socks the whole year around due to a foot condition, and he spent most of his ministry in North Dakota! I am told he had a pair of overshoes, however. It reminded me of the words of Isaiah 52:7, **"How beautiful upon the mountains are the feet of him who brings good news."**

No matter how large or small our feet are, they are a blessing from God that we usually take for granted every day, at least until they give us problems. Then we are reminded how much we appreciate healthy feet. We all probably should walk more than we do, but whenever we do, let's give thanks for our feet. God was especially wise in His creation of them.

I'll guess you never expected to read a devotion about feet today. Praise the Lord that you have them!

JANUARY 26

One cold winter a water pipe froze in the basement of our Colorado home while we were away. The resulting leak ruined a large portion of our basement walls and floor. We do not have a large home, but the basement is fully finished. So when we were told of the damage and saw photos of our basement all torn up, it was distressing. Fortunately we had friends who alerted us to the problem and helped us get the needed repairs.

After returning, I dealt with the problem, alternating between anger over the mess and gratitude over having good insurance. We located an excellent carpenter who knew just how to make the repairs, ordered new carpet and were pleased with the outcome. He also repaired a drain pipe that had caused a musty smell there for years.

That experience once again taught us a lesson from our Lord in the Bible and in life: *"Out of something bad can come much that is good!"* It just doesn't seem that way when all you see is the bad.

There once was a man who lost his wife and struggled with decisions he was forced to make. He moved to another city, took another job and enrolled his children in another school. Work kept him from attending the same church each week, but on one Sunday he dropped off his kids at Sunday School and went looking for a Bible Class. The room was packed but he saw an empty chair in the back row. He sat down next to a pretty woman in a green dress who smiled at him. He smiled back and six months later they were married.

That was 1986 and that fellow was me. I thank God for leading me to that chair next to Carol, and my boys do, too, because she adopted them and raised them as her own.

Out of something bad can come much that is good. We rarely see the good at the time, but if we keep our eyes open, we will see it one day. Life rarely turns out the way we plan, but it can turn out well if we let God have His way.

"Trust in the Lord with all your heart." (Proverbs 30:5)

JANUARY 27

There is a chain of hardware stores that has a special appeal to me and many other men. It offers free stuff! Not only do they have low prices on things to use in your shop and around the house, they give out coupons. Most of them require you to buy something to get the free item, but now and then their coupon can be redeemed simply by showing up at the store. A fun store!

There's one of these stores near where my son and his family live, so nearly every time we went up for a visit, I stopped in for some free stuff. I'd maybe buy a paint brush or a pair of pliers, but would also come away with a set of screw drivers or a tape measure. I have a half dozen small black flashlights from there in my home, shop and car. I don't know how the business does it, because they must give away thousands of free things to those who shop at one of these stores with their coupons.

Free stuff appeals to people, even in religion. One of the most attractive features of Christianity is that God gives us eternal life totally free. It costs us nothing to attain, but we'll want to show Him our thanks. We may want to give thanks *"with heart and hand and voices,"* but there's nothing we can do to earn what God gives us when we have faith in Jesus.

It's like walking into a store and leaving with something totally free, at no cost to us, and we didn't even have to buy something to get it. It is not a BOGO, a *"Buy One Get One"* coupon retirees enjoy using at their local café. It's just a GO, *"Get One"* - *free*.

The price of what we get from God, though, is costly to Him. **"God loved us people of the world so much that He gave us His only Son, so that whomever of us believes in Him certainly, even now, does have eternal life"** (John 3:16 RLT Version). He gave us His only Son, His all, that we might have all we need to be with Him.

That thought should make today special – right?

JANUARY 28

About this time of year in the cold northern winter climates, people begin to think of other places they might like to be, warmer places with blooming flowers and waving palm trees. A friend of mine and his wife travel by train when they can. Even as a child he was fascinated by model trains and he and his wife have boarded trains in several states to see the sights from an Amtrak Dome car across America and from Eurail trains across Europe.

I have enjoyed a few train rides also, and it reminds me of a story I heard from a friend about how our life is like a train ride. The story goes something like this:

"At birth we board the train and meet our parents, and we believe they will always travel at our side. However, at some future station our parents will step down from the train, leaving us to journey on our own. As time goes by, others will board the train, our siblings, spouse, children and friends. Many will step down and leave the train permanently. Others will go unnoticed until we realize they have vacated their seats. Some may return.

"Our train ride will be full of joys, sorrows, expectations, hellos, goodbyes, realities and fantasies. The success of our trip will be having a good relationship with most of the passengers, and it will happen only if we try to give our best each day. The mystery of the trip is that we do not know at which station we will leave the train. Thus, we must live the best we can, loving, forgiving, and offering ourselves to all we meet. When the time comes to vacate our seat, we should leave behind good memories for those who will remember us as they continue on their train ride of life."

The train by which we travel is powered by our loving Creator God who made us and gives us the ride. Our travel companion will be God's Son who walked the earth and shared in human life by suffering and dying for our sins. The trip we take will be in the presence of our Creator for eternity, where there will be no more suffering, no more pain, tears, sadness or fear. With Him there will be only contentment forever.

May God give you joy as you travel through life.

JANUARY 29

One of God's most amazing and frustrating creations is His Holy Christian Church. The Bible teaches it is given us by the Holy Spirit and called the "Communion of Saints," the Body of all the believers in Jesus who live now, who have lived in the past, and who will live in the future. The Church is the Body of Christ with its weaknesses on earth, but its perfection in the presence of God forever.

The Christian Church is Christ's Body, eternal and holy, but its earthly body is sinful and exists only so long it remains faithful to Christ and the Gospel of forgiveness through the cross. The heavenly Church is a place of joy eternally. The church on earth is filled with sinful people, usually trying their best and fully dependent on Christ's forgiveness for entrance and life.

The Holy Church is the place of eternal rest, but the earthly church can be a place of struggle. It may strive to be a haven of refuge, but it can become a council of misguided rebels. The leader of the Church, Jesus, has the power to grant salvation, but the earthly church does not.

People on earth should seek first to be in the Kingdom of God through faith in Christ. Then they should help others, whether inside the earthly church or not. If a person is hurt by the church, Christ is always there to help, to forgive or to repair what is broken.

We are saved by our relationship with Jesus Christ, not by our relationship with the church. If possible, we should strive to be part of that earthly body, but we first should be bound to Jesus Christ by faith in Him. There are far more people hurt by their relationship with the church than those hurt by their relationship with Jesus.

True, there are martyrs, too many of them these days, people who give their life for Jesus by forces of evil bent on His destruction. But faith in Jesus will not disappoint us. In fact, it is our salvation. We will be blessed in the earthly church, but we will also be disappointed. Not so with Jesus!

"Seek first His Kingdom, His righteousness." (Matthew 6:33)

JANUARY 30

About this time of the year the Super Bowl is being held. It is the championship game between the winners of the two conferences of the National Football League. After playing games nearly six months, only two teams are left, and millions of people across America and the world enjoy watching to see who will win.

Do you ever wonder who makes those footballs? Jane Helser of Ada, Ohio, does. She began working for the Wilson Sporting Goods company back in 1966, two years before the Green Bay Packers defeated the Kansas City Chiefs in Super Bowl I.

At the age of 19 she began working there because she wanted to buy a new car, and today her career with Wilson has become part of the football legacy. Ms. Helser had personally stitched more than one million official NFL footballs in her 48 years with the company when she retired in 2014.

Her mother taught her how to sew her clothes, so she found enjoyment in her new job back in 1966. "But," she admitted, *it's a lot different sewing clothes than sewing footballs."* There are 25 steps to crafting a single ball, three of which involve sewing the exterior out of four strips of Illinois cowhide (not pigskin). In a typical day she will sew 150 footballs, contributing to the ten thousand or more game balls used each year.

Helser has met some NFL players during her career and when she retired, she received a signed football from her favorite player, Peyton Manning. Naturally, it was a Wilson football, one of those she had sewn herself.

Our Creator God gives us a life to live and work to do, labor to help ourselves and also to help others. Jesus also calls men and women to labor in His Kingdom. He said, **"The harvest is plentiful, but the laborers are few; therefore pray earnestly to the Lord of the harvest to send out laborers into his harvest."** (Matthew 9:37-38)

Whatever work you do today, do it to the glory of God.

JANUARY 31

Here's a little more about football. My wife and I have long rooted for our "home team," the Denver Broncos, especially after they acquired one of the finest quarterbacks in the history of the game, Peyton Manning. Despite the fact that we he didn't win the Super Bowl as often as he wished, Manning set more records than any other quarterback, and his sportsmanship and personal life are exemplary.

Peyton Manning is a dedicated Christian, and his faith shows itself. In his autobiographical book, <u>Manning</u>, he stated, *"I pray every night, sometimes long prayers about a lot of things and a lot of people, but I don't talk about it or brag about it because that's between God and me, and I'm no better than anybody else in God's sight. But I consider myself fortunate to be able to go to Him for guidance, and I hope and pray I don't do too many things that displease Him before I get to Heaven myself. I believe, too, that life is much better and freer when you're committed to God in that way. Do I "pray for victory?" No, except as a generic thing. I pray to keep both teams injury free, and personally, that I may use whatever talent I have to the best of my ability. But I don't think God really cares about who wins football games, except as winning might influence the character of some person or group."*

He also states that the important things in his life are *"Faith, Family, Friends and Football. As important as football is to me, it can never be higher than fourth."* In this age of self-promotion and celebrity worship, it is pleasing to hear a successful athlete give God the credit. It is so easy to "strut your stuff" and give yourself credit for what you do, so it is refreshing to hear a man speak of faith and show it in his personal life.

This is what Jesus meant when He said, **"Let your light shine so that people can give glory to God."** (Matthew 6:33) We are what we are only by God's grace and mercy. Only He can give us success and the benefits that come with it.

Do you know a Christian athlete? Who is your favorite team?

DAY BY DAY WITH JESUS
in
February

+ + +

FEBRUARY 1

I read the newspaper most every day and always look forward to reading the "funnies." Perhaps you also get your daily paper, read your favorite sections and comics or do your puzzles. It's a daily ritual for us. We've tried going without a print copy and reading the newspaper online, but we always come back to the printed copy.

In a recent "Family Circus" comic strip by Bil Keane, the father is reminding his growing little boy that he needs to know things will change. *"You never know for sure what's going to happen, Jeffy,"* he tells him. Little Jeffy responds, *"That's okay, Dad, as long as YOU do."* Artist Bil Keane during his lifetime was a Christian and his artwork showed it.

In the coming year we will often realize that each day is filled with some kind of insecurity, perhaps a painful injury, a bump on the road of life, or even a major incident. We never know for sure what's going to happen, but that's okay because our Heavenly Father does.

God reminds us of this fact in the Bible. Examples: **"The Lord knows how to rescue the godly from trials."** (2 Peter 2:9) Or, **"Call upon Me in the day of trouble; I will deliver you, and you shall glorify Me."** (Psalm 50:15) On my computer monitor I have these words, **"Be strong and courageous. do not be frightened, or dismayed, for the Lord your God is with you wherever you go."** (Joshua 1:9)

This year, this week, maybe even this day something will happen to remind us we don't know what is going to happen. But whatever it is, it will be okay, because God knows, and little Jeffy's words can be our prayer:

"That's okay, Dad, as long as YOU know."

FEBRUARY 2

Where is your treasure in life? What would you like it to be? "Treasure" usually refers to money and possessions, but it can be whatever we value and think about. For some, their treasure is knowledge or a strong faith in Jesus.

However, if our treasure is only money or the goods we can acquire, then that's where our heart will be also. Jesus once said, **"For where your treasure is, there your heart will be also."** (Matthew 6:21) That treasure seems to disappear quickly, however.

It's hard not to think about money if you never have enough. It's hard not to think about love if you feel unloved, or being content if you're always worried. We tend to think about things we don't have. If our health is poor, we wonder how to become healthier. If we have a poor relationship with someone, we long for it to be better. If our children or other loved ones disappoint us, we focus on what we should do differently.

Jesus says where our treasure is, there our heart will also be. He is not saying that if we value something highly in this world, that it is wrong. But He is saying that our heart will be in what we treasure. If we treasure Him and doing His will, our heart will be in a more peaceful place, a place of safety.

Hearts are frail. Hoping desperately for something we don't have risks our getting a "broken heart," the sadness from not getting what we desire. Jesus can replace what we don't have with something even more precious, faith in Him and a trust that won't be shattered by broken dreams.

Our Lord Jesus understands us human beings better than we think. He walked the earth and experienced human pain, suffering and rejection. He endured the cross that we might we forgiven.

Today, consider what is truly important to you, and try to determine why. Pray God will give you a contented heart.

What might be getting in the way of your contentment?

FEBRUARY 3

One of the joys of having more free time is reading topics of interest that I may have avoided or not had the time during my working days. I have always been interested in the weather and other aspects of our planet earth, as well as facts about our solar system.

One thing I have certainly learned and re-learned – our earth is a privileged place. The amount of elements required to produce either simple or complex life on our earth is astronomical – literally! Having our planet in its absolutely correct place among the other heavenly bodies is a miracle in itself.

Consider our moon, for example. Without it, our earth could not sustain life. If it were larger or smaller, earth's weather would be chaotic and life would not exist. We base our measurement of time on the moon. The moon completes one rotation on its axis every time it orbits the earth, which occurs every twenty-nine and one half days. The moon controls our ocean tides and contributes in large part to life on earth as we know it.

The moon has no light of its own, but it reflects the sun's light. Lunar reflective light helps plants and animals grow in warm climates and aids navigation on oceans and in colder climates. The moon stabilizes the earth's rotation and keeps it from going so fast that it would spin away into space. The moon's size (one-fourth the size of the earth) and distance away (240,000 miles) helps sustain the life we experience here.

And it didn't just happen by accident. The Bible tells us **"In the beginning, God created the heavens and the earth."** (Genesis 1:1) Physicist Stephen Hawking admits there are only two possible sources of complex life: evolution or God. He chose to believe in random evolution, but Christians believe it was God. I plan to keep reading on scientific topics, and I am quite sure I will find God behind them all.

The moon and the heavens show us God's glory.

FEBRUARY 4

It is said, *"Man makes his plans and God laughs."* We don't always know how life is going to turn out, but God does. This is true of my friends, Darrell and Wanda.

After High School, Wanda went to Key West, Florida. There she met Darrell and they were married. He had his degree and had planned to teach Florida youth, but a decade later I met them in North Dakota where I instructed and baptized him and they were great helpers in my church.

Darrell planned to be an investment counselor, but God had different plans. He soon attended a seminary and was ordained a Lutheran pastor. His first church call was to a mission in the Bahamas, and later to people with developmental disabilities. Then he was pastor in Texas and eventually went to the Caribbean working with LCMS World Relief. He returned to Texas, where part of his ministry was to a prison for illegal immigrants. There Pastor Darrell had a successful Bible Class to the inmates.

He once wrote me of how God changed their plans. They were returning home from a trip one evening when the cold weather forced them to take a different road. Along the way they came upon a rollover accident involving a mother and four small children. They stopped to help, prayed with them and called for EMTs to come. If they had driven their normal route home or at the normal time, they'd have missed assisting the victims. Darrell said, *"Was this a coincidence? Absolutely not!"*

Their life in ministry hasn't been easy. Darrell has endured financial problems, heart attack, vision problems and now he has cancer. Yet he stays positive in his outlook. He told me, *"The next time your plans are changed, remember that God is still in control. He knows what needs to be done and He protects His own."*

Darrell has taught me more in his faith life than I ever taught him in those instruction classes many years ago.

Praise God for His good plans and His dedicated workers!

FEBRUARY 5

On some Monday nights during the winter I am the "Bingo Caller" in our Retirement Park. Two to three hundred people gather at tables with hopes of winning money. Only a few win so I often tell them before the game they can double their money right now by folding it and putting it back in their pockets. It's an old joke but true when it comes to games of chance.

Bingo can be fun. Even when players lose, they still feel like winners. Each time they mark a number, they feel like they've gotten something right. We play twelve games each night, sometimes having multiple winners on one game. Most who come enjoy the fellowship plus the thrill of possibly winning. Bingo is quite popular at our park.

The excitement rises when the jackpots are big. The Caller must keep the crowd calm and interested. When the winner shouts "BINGO!" the game is over. The player's card is checked and if it's a winner, the player gets some cash. The rest are glad some of their numbers were called, and get ready for the next game.

It is tempting to think going to heaven is like that. If we get most of our actions right, we will win the heavenly prize, correct? If we do a majority of good deeds during our lives, God will award us the prize, right?

Sorry, but no. Without Jesus there'd be no winners. No matter how good a life we may have lived, or how close we come to winning, it takes Jesus to get us there. No *"near-perfect"* life will win. Everything has to be correct.

Heaven requires a winning card with a perfect score, and only Jesus can get that for us. On Calvary He won the Big One, and He offers to share His eternal prize with every man, woman and child who trusts Him as Lord and Savior. When we trust Jesus as our Savior, we win the "Big One." One of His disciples, John, said in John 6:47, **"He who believes HAS eternal life."** That's the plain truth.

When Judgment Day comes, believers will shout, HEAVEN!

FEBRUARY 6

It was afternoon when the young man exited the freeway. It had been a busy day at work and he was taking sandwiches to his fellow workers who had missed lunch. An older vehicle in front of him was also taking the off-ramp and had stopped in the right turn lane. The young man waited for the light to change, but when it did, the vehicle in front did not move. Another light change happened and still there was no movement. After the third light change, drivers behind were honking horns, so the young man got out and approached the vehicle and tapped on its window.

Opening a truck door, the young man caught the elderly driver as he fell out. Something was very wrong, because there was no response from the driver or his elderly passenger. The young man found no pulse on either of them, and police and EMTs who came immediately pronounced both occupants dead! Somehow the driver had stopped for the signal light and died.

A coroner said the woman had died of a stroke and the driver of a heart attack. He surmised the woman had a stroke first and died in the car. When the driver, her husband, realized she was dead, he suffered a fatal heart attack right there at the signal light. The couple both were dead, and the young man who found them was shaken.

Do you know what is going to happen to you today? Are you sure about your plans? Do you even know what will happen in the next hour? James writes in 4:14-15, **"What is your life? You are a mist that appears for a little time and then vanishes. Instead you ought to say, 'If the Lord wills, we will live and do this or that'."**

Life can seem like a mist that vanishes, but to God, we are His beloved creatures. That's why He sent Jesus to save us. If we were only a dying animal along the roadside, He would not have gone to such great lengths to create us, forgive us, teach us or prepare an eternal place for us.

The young man is my son. God had a reason for that incident.

FEBRUARY 7

On February 7, 1867, Laura Ingalls, was born in a cabin near Pepin, Wisconsin. She lived as a pioneer girl in southern Minnesota and South Dakota. In 1885 she married Almanzo Wilder and later was a school teacher, journalist, and author of the "Little House" books.

I first heard of these books in elementary school, a one-room "Country School" three miles east of our farm. One of my teachers, Mrs. Maude Sylvester, had visited Mrs. Ingalls on her Rocky Ridge farm in Mansfield, Missouri, where she lived most of her life, passing away in 1957.

Although her books seem idyllic, Laura Wilder's life was quite difficult. Crop failure, illness and the death of a child all left a mark on her life. She disliked the sewing, cooking, moving and hardships, but when her husband was left lame from diphtheria, she began to write for magazines to supplement their income. It was from this necessity that she became the author of many well-loved books.

One story comes to mind. She was newly married and had to cook meals for a group of harvesters. Left to do this alone, she had few recipes besides those she'd memorized. The meal went well until dessert. One of the men put a piece of her fresh apple pie on his plate, ate a bite and then he reached for the sugar bowl. He lifted the crust and sprinkled a large spoonful on the apples. As he did he said, *"I always appreciate it when a woman allows me to sweeten the pie just the way I like it."* She had forgotten to put sugar in her pie! But instead of embarrassing her, the kind man complimented her, making her obvious error seem like a wise act, and also alerting the other men of the sour taste!

Proverbs 15:1 tells us, **"A soft answer turns away wrath."** There are all kinds of ways to deal with mistakes. At times we want to run away, and other times, we're rescued by understanding and kindness. Mistakes can either push us down or build us up. If we resist their humiliation and learn from them, everyone will be better for it.

What soft word can you give someone today?

FEBRUARY 8

I ordered a pair of moccasins from Minnesota, my native state. I had heard they sold authentic footwear in this catalog, shoes made in the USA. It took awhile for the package to come, but I wasn't worried. They would be good and made by my kind of people.

Imagine my reaction when I saw a tag on each moccasin saying, *"Made in China."* How could this Minnesota business do this? How could the Chinese make moccasins? Who told them how to make ones Americans would buy? Who told them what to make and how to do it? Just about everything today is *"Made in China."*

Most of their items are okay, but some are cheap plastic. Some, however, are very well made from good materials. But how did someone ten thousand miles away know the kind I wanted to buy, how to make it, how many to make, and what sizes or colors? I mentioned this to a friend and he said, *"Here is my Smart Phone. If you want I can order you just about anything on it, from anywhere. It's a very good phone, durable and dependable. I believe it's made in China."*

But unless we happen to be Chinese citizens, you and I are not made in China. We are created by the God of the universe who knew us before we were born. Even now He knows our every need and every deed. He made us each unique, not stamping us from a sheet of humanity to look and act all the same. I think some governments or even churches would like us all to think and act alike. We'd be easier to handle, like a herd of cattle.

The Bible says, **"I praise you, for I am fearfully and wonderfully made."** (Psalm 138:14) God created us and all the things of this world, giving us the abilities, feelings, shapes, intellects, sizes and all that makes us human. When we come into the Christian faith, we are given a tiny label that says, *"Made by the Father"* or, *"Saved by the Son"* or, *"Baptized by the Spirit."* And we are all made perfect.

God made us all, including the Chinese who make things for us.

FEBRUARY 9

One of the sad things I've discovered about living in a retirement community is that some people go home in the spring and never return. When we return for the new winter season, we generally hear that one or two of our friends has been seriously ill or even died during the summer and will not be with us this year.

This is especially evident when someone decides to return home in mid-season due to some health issue. I once attended a coffee being held for an old friend who, like myself, had discovered the enjoyment of writing in retirement. Russ had an interesting life and discovered he had a gift for writing fictional novels, often working his personal experiences into his writing.

At the coffee I approached him and said, *"I hear you're going home, old friend."* He looked up at me with a grin and said, *"Be careful how you mean 'going home,' Rev. Bob."* That drew some chuckles. I said, *"I guess we can take that both ways, can't we?"* In his mid-80s, Russ hadn't lost his sense of humor. I asked if he'd finished a book he'd been working on, and he said, *"I'm getting there. I've decided to let the other guys win this time."* He'd also said that day, *"Non-fiction is a lot more crazy and interesting than fiction."*

"Going home" can have a different meaning to a Christian. The longer Christians are on earth, the more we realize our real home is with the Lord. I think about this often, what it will be like to leave this earth for the life God promises. In that life, will we be awake and aware, or will we be asleep until the resurrection?

There's no clear answer for this in the Bible because it speaks of both kinds of life after death, asleep and awake. It speaks of new life, and that believers will be with God. We won't die and *"rot along the roadside like an old telephone pole,"* as a country western song says. That's very Good News! We're not junk to be discarded as useless.

God made us and He doesn't make junk!

FEBRUARY 10

Do you ever dream at night? We all have personal dreams of what we would like to accomplish, but most people also dream when they sleep. Hopefully yours will not be unsettling or cause you loss of sleep.

There are many theories as to why we dream, but there are a few facts common to all. All people dream, but not all dream in color. We tend to forget most of what we dream and dream of people or facts that we know. Dreams are symbolic and some are recurring. Men and women dream differently, with men being more aggressive in their dreams. A quarter of those interviewed say they have dreamt about an event which actually happened later on.

Martin Luther wrote that we must not get too concerned about our dreams, since they spring from an unconscious mind that cannot be held accountable for what it does in our sleep. He says we may dream of sinful things, but it is not a sin to dream them, for we have no choice in the content of our dreams.

The Bible often treats dreams as visions from God, and many Old and New Testament characters learn things from God in their dreams. Both Joseph and Daniel interpreted dreams for kings, and many of God's people have learned His will through their dreams. I agree with Martin Luther that we must not be too concerned with what springs from the unconscious mind.

Praying when we wake up from an alarming dream can help. Reciting Bible verses can take away our night fears. Giving our fears to Jesus in prayer is most beneficial for our peace of mind. If we feel bothered by Satan in our dreams, tell him in the name of Jesus to be gone! Jesus has defeated him, so he holds no sway over us.

God says one day He will **"pour out His Spirit on the world and our children shall prophesy, the old shall dream dreams, and the young shall see visions."** (Joel 2:28) Then we will know for sure what He is telling us.

May all your good and beneficial dreams come true.

FEBRUARY 11

My wife often asks me to repair an item that has broken or stopped working, and sometimes I am successful. Over the years I have fixed so many things that it is impossible to recall them all.

I have repaired electrical switches, broken trinkets, lamps, minor auto problems, computers, bicycles and power tools. I have found ways to make repairs to our home, yard, motorized items, broken cups and even a smashed cuckoo clock. Neighbors and friends know this and sometimes call to see if I can fix something they've broken. All this is probably why I rarely buy a lot of new things, since I try to keep the old ones running if they still have value.

But I can't fix people. I think during my ministry I tried to do this a time or two, but I soon learned that wasn't my calling, nor anyone else's either. One of my brothers told me I thought I was the *"Family Fixer."* I understood some of what he was saying, but I'd never considered being that. He didn't say I really was the Family Fixer, only that I thought I was. There he may have been correct.

But people can't fix other people, only ourselves and then not always. We can repair some self-caused damage and fix some personal behavior. But to be fully repaired in body and soul requires the intervention of God. Only He who made us can repair the damage of sin we have caused ourselves in life.

Years ago my daughter-in-law had a collectible angel break in several small pieces. I offered to fix it for her, but opted instead to get her a new one. But I did glue the broken one back together and put it in our hutch as a personal reminder that we may be cracked, but by the grace of God, we can still be repaired.

The Bible says, **"God heals the brokenhearted and binds up their wounds."** (Psalm 147:3) That's very good to know, since we are frail people who so often need major repair to body or soul.

"Create in me a clean heart, O God." (Psalm 51:10)

FEBRUARY 12

My wife loves to go shopping and I often go with her, sometimes to help pick out something, and most often to carry what she has bought. It's enjoyable so long as it doesn't take too long. Or cost too much!

A large clothing chain store near us has an annual sale on January 1 with very low prices, so one year we went. The packed parking lot told me this was no ordinary sale. Inside we joined hundreds of eager shoppers as they ravaged racks of tops, slacks, jackets and anything else men and women like to purchase on sale days.

The clerks at the register were having a heyday. Their hands flying, removing hangers, flashing price tags over the laser price readers and stuffing treasures into bags as fast as they could. People grabbed and bought things they'd passed up before, because the prices were so low. One of the clerks told me that sale helped make his monthly sales quota. He wished they did it every month, not once a year.

At one point my wife handed me a blouse on a hanger and told me to go stand over by a men's table while she shopped. I was dressed fairly neatly and the table held several mannequins, so I decided to become one! I stood up straight, hung the item she'd given me on my collar and looked straight forward, not moving a muscle. A few people looked at me and smiled, and a couple of women actually came up to look at my outfit before they realized I was alive. It was great fun and it passed the time quickly!

Sometimes people treat others like mannequins. We notice them there, but don't really look at them or take them seriously. We don't bump into them, but we don't talk to them either. To us they're just standing there like imitation people, store mannequins.

But Jesus sees us all as real people. He looks at us and knows what is in our hearts. He wants us to trust Him and rely on His guidance. He also wants us to treat each other as the valued persons God has placed in our lives.

Today try to see other people with the eyes of Jesus.

FEBRUARY 13

The penitential season of Lent will soon be here which begins on "Ash Wednesday." The day before it is called "Shrove Tuesday", also known as "Fat Tuesday" or "Pancake Day." In some Christian cultures pancakes are eaten because they are made out of the main food items - eggs, sugar, butter, flour - whose consumption was often restricted during the fasting of Lent.

Pennsylvania Dutch call the day "Fastnacht Day," and Portuguese, Spanish, and Italians call it "Carnival," from "carne levar" which mean "to remove meat." Carnival can include parades and fancy dress, like the Mardi Gras.

In Hawaii, Shrove Tuesday is "Malasada Day" which dates back to sugar plantations when workers used up their butter and sugar prior to Lent by making fried pastries called malasadas. In Iceland it is called "Bursting Day," marked by eating too much salted meat and peas. The Scandinavians observe it with sweet pastries.

Some English towns hold Shrove Tuesday football games and a Pancake Race which dates to a time long ago when a housewife ran to get to church on time while still carrying her frying pan. The children of Whitechapel, Lancashire, go around asking *"Please a pancake?"* hoping to receive oranges or sweets, a practice from days when peasant workers visited manor houses to ask for extra food.

This is only a partial list of celebrations for Shrove Tuesday. Do you have a special way to celebrate any of the days before Lent? Do you observe Lent at all?

God told His covenant Jewish people, **"Three times a year you are to celebrate a festival to me."** (Exodus 23:14) Those were the Festivals of Harvest, Weeks and Pentecost. It is still a good thing to join together with other Christians and celebrate the goodness and providence of God, especially when it comes just before a time when we are more somber and reflective in practicing our Christian faith.

On Shrove Tuesday, make some pancakes for yourself.

FEBRUARY 14

I hope all who read this will have an enjoyable Valentine's Day. I wish I could tell you a story of the original Valentinus as a man who was kind or martyred in ancient Rome for his Christian faith. But historians say there may have been as many as 14 martyrs named Valentinus during that era. History gets rather complicated trying to separate one Valentinus from another, as well as explain about the churches dedicated to them.

February 14 is set aside to honor St. Valentine, but the date of its first use is. Early believers took over Lupercalia, a pagan festival on February 15 to honor the Roman god of agriculture, as well as Romulus and Remus, the founders of Rome. They moved it to February 14 and dedicated it to exchanging expressions of Christian love.

The oldest known written valentine still in existence today is a poem written in 1415 by the Duke of Orleans to his wife while he was imprisoned in the Tower of London. Several years later, King Henry V hired poet John Lydgate to compose a valentine note to Catherine of Valois who later became his wife. So began a practice still enjoyed today.

"Home is where the heart is," we often say. Home for many of us is where we were born or lived our early life, but it has probably changed so much it's no longer recognizable. Grown trees make the old house look smaller, and changes makes it unfamiliar. Home ought to be wherever you are, where you enjoy the blessings of God and the love He gives that you cherish.

Psalm 68:6 says, **"God places the lonely into families."** I've always treasured that verse because it shows how He cares for us in such a practical manner. Families are great blessings. If we don't have one of our own, God will give us one, perhaps in His Church. God's love is very precious and helpful to all, especially those in the Christian family.

What kind of family are you part of? Have you shown your loved ones your appreciation?

FEBRUARY 15

Carol and I enjoy watching sunsets. Both Arizona and Colorado sunsets are often spectacular, so we are treated to an array of colors, sky paintings and changing shades that are thrilling. Both our homes face the west, and sunsets are part of the reason.

Sunrises are nice, too, but they generally come a bit early in the day to appreciate their artistic display. They also come at a cooler time of day. I rarely stand in awe outside in my bathrobe and slippers watching the sun come up. Maybe I should try it some day.

In one of my favorite musicals, Fiddler On The Roof, there is a lovely song by Tevia, the grumbling but tender Jewish father who realizes his little daughter has grown up and has a boyfriend. So he sings:

> *"Sunrise, Sunset, Sunrise, Sunset,*
> *Swiftly fly the years.*
> *One season following another,*
> *Laden with happiness and tears."*

Sunrises and sunsets mark our years on this earth. With each passing day we are given blessings from our heavenly Father who has created us and sustains us through life. The seasons of life follow us: Spring with its newness and growth, Summer with its heat and hard work, Autumn with its maturity and changing colors, and Winter with its snow on the roof and tendency to sleep.

Which season of life are you in right now? Which season would you like to be in? Often the young wish they were older, and the old wish they were younger. Jesus is our Savior for all seasons of life. He is with us now in spirit, and one day we will see Him bodily in eternity. Until then, God's people will enjoy the changing seasons of the calendar as well as the changing seasons of our lives.

"Sunrise, Sunset, Swiftly fly the years."

Stay with us through them all, Lord Jesus.

FEBRUARY 16

Today my youngest granddaughter was born. She is a bundle of smiles and energy, active all day until she finally falls asleep. She makes us all laugh, and loves to talk. Ours is a world of talk, talk, talk - on the street, in the store, on the news, in politics and among friends. There is a lot of talking in our world, but maybe not a lot of listening.

Much of our talking has been silenced through the use of social media, e-mail or cell phones that carry "text messages" from one person to another. A man once told me with all the cell phone messages going around, people must really be lonely. He is right, but with all this talking, I wonder if there is much listening.

A parent lamented giving her daughter a cell phone. They discovered that during a one month period she sent out 5000 text messages to her friends. That averaged 1,200 messages a week and 170 a day, 21 days of which she was in school. And school was where her friends were!

How much do people listen? I was watching three people on a national news program discussing a current event. I liked the people and the topic, but one of them kept interrupting and didn't let the others finish. They were "talking over" each other, even shouting, so I turned it off.

How much have people listened to me? I estimate that in my years as a pastor I have preached over 4,000 sermons and taught thousands of Bible Classes. That's a lot of talking, but did anyone hear what I said? I believe every pastor asks himself that question. Yet he is also grateful to know that the results of his preaching and teaching are not his sole responsibility. The hearers have some, and also the Holy Spirit. God bids His people to share the Good News, and promises the Holy Spirit will help willing hearts to listen.

St. Paul said, **"How can they believe without hearing about Him? And how are they to hear without someone preaching? And how are they to preach unless they are sent?"** (Romans 10:14-15)

May God open your heart today to hear Him speak to you.

FEBRUARY 17

Americans enjoy a standard of living that nations have never had before. We have an abundance of things that a majority of people in the world can only imagine. Household conveniences, electronics, bank accounts, automobiles and fine clothing are enjoyed by most all. Some Americans, of course, are considered poor, but even they do not go hungry like people in some Third World countries do.

We can buy just about anything imaginable in our stores and it comes packaged and clean. This abundance has lead to problems, such as what to do with the packaging, as well as items that become old, broken or out of date. That's where re-cycling comes in.

Re-cycling is big business. Used clothing is sought by many companies. Trucks come around to collect various kinds of metal, plastic and paper. More and more of us are becoming conscious of our responsibility not to waste more than is necessary. One day perhaps even our unusable trash will be processed into something useful. But, of course, there will still be too much waste.

"Waste Not, Want Not" is a slogan our forefathers coined, not because they had so much, but because they had so little and wanted to make sure nothing useable was cast aside. Strangely, the one thing often cast aside, neglected and forgotten is humanity itself.

In their attempts to be environmentally responsible, people of developed nations have made unborn infants a throw-away option. Lesser developed nations value babies more than we do, protecting them and nurturing them, but in wealthy nations, babies become an item of cost. We hear, *"Can we afford to have another child?"* or *"Infants cause overpopulation."*

We who have been given much must take care not to toss out the baby with our biodegradable bathwater. God gives life and treasures His children of all ages. So should we, no matter how wealthy or developed we become.

"I am fearfully and wonderfully made, O God." (Psalm 139:14)

FEBRUARY 18

I enjoy an occasional hike, especially in the warm desert during the winter. It's refreshing and a great way to view nature up close. I have to admit, though, that my feet and legs enjoy hiking less these days. Hiking reminds me of a story.

A small ten year-old boy was the youngest, and all of his siblings had left home. He loved his home but often wondered when he would grow up and leave. One Saturday he decided to go for a hike along a small creek across the road. He took a sack lunch, his jacket, a book and his .22 rifle. It wasn't hunting season, but he wanted to be prepared!

The boy followed the creek bank, scaring up a pheasant and a rabbit. But then he walked too close to the edge and fell into the stream. The water was chest deep, and it was cold! The boy tried to make a small fire to warm up but his matches were wet and so was his lunch. All he could do was trudge back home, certain his folks would scold him. But his Mom smiled and told him to find dry clothes in the basement and then come up and have some fresh bread. The boy felt good to be back home that day.

Eight years later he left home for college and never really came back again. True, he lived at home a couple of summers, but he'd really left home after graduation. That's the way it should be. His folks didn't raise him to stay home, but to go and make something of himself. The boy eventually became a minister. You see, the book he'd taken along that day (and somehow kept dry) was his Bible.

We are all on a hike through life. Sometimes we know where we're going and other times we wander. We may stay on the road or fall in the water (like I did). We may take a wrong turn, but along the way we always have a loving Father who will show us the right way and give us a place where we can come home when we need to dry off.

"When our earthly home is destroyed, we have a building from God, a house not made with hands, eternal in the heavens." (2 Corinthians 5:1)

FEBRUARY 19

February 19, 1942, was a unique day in Canada. It was called "If Day" and simulated a German invasion and occupation of Winnipeg and surrounding areas. It was organized by the Greater Winnipeg Victory Loan organization, led by Winnipeg businessman J. D. Perrin.

"If Day" included a staged firefight between Canadian troops and volunteers dressed as German soldiers. There was internment of prominent politicians, a brief imposition of Nazi rule, and a parade. The event was a fundraiser for the war effort, and over three million dollars in War Bonds were sold that day. Winnipeg was divided into 45 sections, and when sufficient War Bonds were sold in an area, it was "reclaimed" for Canada from the "invading force."

Besides raising war funds, it was also a "wake-up" call to Canadians about the dangers of the Nazis. On "If Day," radio broadcasts dramatized the false invasion. Although it was advertised for days there and also in neighboring Minnesota, people were taken by surprise as painted "German fighter planes" flew over the city. A nearby small town, Selkirk, even held a one-hour blackout and mock bombing of the city. With 3,500 Canadian soldiers involved, it was the largest military exercise in Winnipeg's history. People were asked, *"What if this would happen?"*

Real trials and danger in life are not prefaced by *"What If"* but by *"When."* The greatest lessons learned in life are not merely observed, they are experienced. James, brother of our Lord, once wrote, **"Consider it pure joy, my brothers and sisters, whenever you face trials of many kinds, because you know that the testing of your faith produces perseverance."** (James 1:2-3)

Trials of all sorts, including wars, happen because we live in a sinful world where evil often prevails. When the "If" is gone and the "Real" is upon us, then we will discover if we have learned lessons God teaches us in life. Jesus is Lord of all our life, the real or the imagined one.

Are you ready for conflict in your life?

FEBRUARY 20

I am often asked where I get stories for my devotional books. When I say most of these are based on events that happened to me or stories I have heard, someone will ask, *"How can you remember all that?"* I really don't know how to answer except to say I just can.

Our memories are valuable gifts from the Lord. Events or words can jar a memory and thinking about it can reveal details, names and places. It can also help put them together into a lesson to learn. Our memory can be trained to look for certain things. Since I have been writing original weekly devotions for nearly twenty years, my mind is on the lookout for anything that might help make a spiritual example or story. I guess I trained it.

We can also train ourselves to forget. In my early ministry I struggled with the results of a few bad decisions, and some of them kept me up at night. I mentioned this to an older member who suggested I make a decision to forget some of those bad things. *"If they are gone and no longer affect anything, decide to forget them and you will. Don't wait for them to go away, you make them go away."*

What he said helped. If I know something I did couldn't be helped and it didn't hurt things in the long run, I forget it. I visualize mentally putting that memory into a box, putting the box in storage and forgetting it. I can almost guarantee I will forget about the box unless it is needed later. Until then it just stays in the box.

Christians believe that God never forgets because He is God. Yet some Bible passages tell us otherwise. **"I, even I, am He who blots out your transgressions, for My own sake, and remembers your sins no more."** (Isaiah 43:25)

Forgiveness is like forgetting. Because of the death and resurrection of His Son, God no longer remembers our sins. He knows we are sinners, but when we trust His Son, God forgets our sins and no longer counts them against us.

Now there's something to thank God for today!

FEBRUARY 21

Are you a worrier? Do you "sweat the small stuff" in life, or are you one of those who have learned not to worry about things? A wise person once said the only thing worry is guaranteed to do is shorten our life. Some of us might argue the opposite, saying that being anxious can lead us to take better care of ourselves and be more healthy. I tend to agree with the former – worry shortens life.

But we surely have much less to worry about than people of Jesus' time. Just having enough to eat or being safe from harm were their major concerns. Today it is rare for people in developed countries to be without enough to eat, drink or wear. We rarely worry about food, clothing or safety, but that's not all there is to worry about these days.

Today we can worry about paying our bills, mortgage, utilities, auto, school or medical payments. We might worry about the political direction of our nation. We may worry about our own or our child's marriage. Commercials try to make us worry about not having enough funds for retirement. No matter who we are or how much we have, we can find cause for worry.

But Jesus urges us to trust Him. My mother often said, *"Worry is concern without faith."* She meant we should be concerned about what we do and how much we have, but that we should give those concerns to Jesus.

I visited a man in the hospital who was gravely ill and given only a short time to live. After I prayed with him, he laid his hand on mine and said, *"Don't worry, Pastor. I'm okay because soon I'll be with the Lord. But you look worried. Is everything okay with you?"* And he listened as I poured out to him some minor trouble I was having. He died about a week later and after the funeral I got tears in my eyes thinking how he had ministered to me.

Life is a complex and wonderful thing God has given to us. We must value and cherish it, and help each other through the dark days of worry.

"Bear one another's burdens." (Galatians 6:2)

FEBRUARY 22

I would imagine just about every grandparent thinks his grandchildren are the cutest and most talented. I have five and their pictures adorn the walls of our home with their sweet smiles that we can see every day. We love our sons greatly, even as they have become adults, and their photos are on our walls also. But there is something really special about a grandchild, especially ours.

The more they come to know their grandpa and grandma, the more we can see them looking forward to being with us. It's their smiles that tell us their feelings. Our smiles show them our feelings, too.

If you look at old photos taken sixty or more years ago in black and white, just about all of them show people with a serious look on their faces. I don't know exactly when it happened, but somewhere in time people started smiling into the camera. Now a serious expression looks strange

A smile, even if it is forced, shows something of the heart of a person. Children smiling today will become serious soon enough. The cares and decisions of life will replace the carefree smiles with frowns of worry. I love seeing my grown sons smile and laugh. I know the cares of their workday life give them reason enough to be serious, but their laughter lights up my heart.

A smile can help someone who is troubled. I try to make it a habit to smile at the clerk who is counting my purchase. I smile and call them by name if I can, which surprises some. I once came into an office to sign mortgage papers, and I must have looked grouchy or worried because the receptionist said, *"Don't worry, God is good!"* And she gave me such a pretty smile that it brightened my day.

There is a benediction we often hear, **"The Lord bless you and keep you; the Lord make His face shine on you and be gracious to you."** The New Living Translation says, **"May the Lord smile upon you."** (Numbers 6:25 NLT)

May you also smile on others today.

FEBRUARY 23

Today is my parent's wedding anniversary. They spoke their vows before the pastor in 1930. They had "dated" (modern term, not theirs) eight years and finally got married when they realized they'd never have *"enough saved up."* They were married 64 years when Mom died.

I've conducted 300+ weddings during my ministry and some I remember well. One such wedding was held in February at ten thousand feet altitude in the Colorado mountains. There I heard the vows of a young woman and man pledge their love and faithfulness to each other. I had known the woman since she was three years old.

We all sat outside in a small amphitheater overlooking snow-covered treetops. The bride and groom had provided small read cotton blankets for the 30-40 people present, and they came in handy as snow squalls alternated with clear skies during the half hour ceremony.

Among the guests was a member of the Army's original Tenth Mountain Division, a man the bride had come to know through her work at a Museum. It was touching to see her dance with this ninety year-old war hero who had landed in Italy sixty years before to help free the world of Nazi tyranny. We are still close friends with the bride and groom who now have a small son.

The modern trend to downplay the need for marriage is disturbing and badly mistaken. I read it again recently, *"We don't need some paper to keep us together."* But marriage isn't just a piece of paper. It is a committed gift from God. It doesn't *"get in the way"* of a relationship, it *is* the way. `

Marriages are necessary building blocks in the wall of any society that wishes to be strong. Without committed marriages, the wall easily crumbles, and human lives will be the worse for it. Not everyone needs to be married, but couples who want the privileges of marriage should not ignore the God-given basic step. As the Bible says, **"It is not good for a person to be alone."** (Genesis 2:18)

Even if you're single, give thanks today for God's gift of marriage.

FEBRUARY 24

Most Americans have seen the Iwo Jima memorial from World War Two, whether in person or from a picture. Located in Washington, DC, it is the largest bronze statue in the world, and it depicts six soldiers raising an American flag on the top of Mt. Surabachi on the Pacific island of Iwo Jima on February 23, 1945.

The bitter fighting of the Allies to secure the island from the Japanese army is legendary and the memorial was created from a photo taken by Sgt. Louis Lowery. It is officially known as the Marine Corps War Memorial and is located near Arlington National Cemetery in our nation's capitol. The original mold for sculpture is located on the Marine Military Academy grounds in Arlington, Texas.

Iwo Jima was not originally a target for conquest. However, it was located halfway between Japan and the Mariana Islands where the American long-range bombers were stationed, and the Japanese were using it as an early warning station, radioing warnings of incoming American bombers to the Japanese homeland.

The fighting for the island was far more fierce than anyone expected, taking 31 days and costing 7,000 American lives before victory was achieved. Of the six soldiers who raised the flag, three later died in battle. The three survivors, Rene Gagnon, Ira Hayes and John Bradley, were sent home and hailed as heroes.

If you look carefully at the memorial, you will see six soldiers. But if you count the hands holding the flagstaff, you will see there are thirteen hands, not twelve. When asked of this, memorial sculpture Felix de Weldon said the thirteenth hand was the hand of God.

In the Old Testament, Ezra was given permission by the conquering king to return to Jerusalem, **"Because the gracious hand of the Lord his God was on him."** (Ezra 7:6) Are you in the Lord's hands? Are there times when you feel He is giving you an extra hand in life?

Watch how God gives you a hand today. Thank Him for it!

FEBRUARY 25

What is the worst possible sin we can commit? The worst sin would be the one with the worst consequences, and that would be the sin of unbelief. Without faith in Jesus, there is no forgiveness, because unbelief rejects forgiveness He has earned for us. The sin of unbelief is unforgiveable.

But next to unbelief, what is the worst sin? Contrary to what we may have learned, it is not sexual sin. Nor is it even murder or rape or child abuse or drug abuse. All of these are minor compared to the great sin called Pride. By pride I don't mean the pleasure we get in being praised, or leading the team to victory, or the pride we feel when our child does well. Those feelings are blessings.

Pride that is destructive is the attitude that we are superior to others. It is self-conceit that leads to wanting control over others. This kind of Pride is what motivates the tyrant or the intellectual elitist or religious snob.

This kind of Pride has been the chief cause of misery in families, societies and nations since the beginning of the world. Other vices can cause havoc and death, but Pride separates people from others and especially from God. As long as we have this Pride within us, we cannot know or trust God. A proud person is always looking down on things and people, and as long as that person is looking down, he cannot see God who is above him.

Can such a prideful person believe and worship God? Probably not because Satan is the source of Pride. Jesus commended the humble and repentant, but He condemned the proud. By nature we all have some Pride. It is easy to think we are better than, or at least "not as bad as" others.

Both the prideful and the humble need Jesus. We must be careful not to let Pride creep into our Christianity, for it will strangle our faith. The devil wants us to think we can control others, that only we can know the truth, and that all others are therefore wrong. But because of our sinful nature, we are all in need of Christ's forgiveness.

Give thanks that Jesus forgives us and shows us true humility.

FEBRUARY 26

Many people struggle with fear in their lives, but the real culprit is not fear. It is insecurity.

In 1843 Nathaniel Hawthorne wrote a short story called "The Birthmark." It is about Aylmer, a scientist, who marries Georgiana, a woman who is beautiful in every way except that she has a small birthmark on her cheek.

Aylmer is very proud of his lovely wife, but he soon realizes the birthmark makes her less perfect. He becomes obsessed with her imperfection and begins to dream of removing it. Georgiana is affected by his attitude and also grows to hate the birthmark and to wish it gone. Finally Aylmer says he will help them both by removing her birthmark with a potion he has developed.

As his lovely wife drinks the potion and falls asleep, Aylmer is pleased to see her birthmark slowly fading, but as it does, her life slowly fades away. When the birthmark is totally gone, his wife is dead and the story ends there.

Critics of this story have said it is about human imperfection and mortality, comparing the birthmark to the human condition of "original sin." Once the sin is gone, so is human life, and eternal life takes its place. Another critic said, *"No one on earth is perfect. The birthmark is sin, and once sin is removed, all that's left is heaven."*

I find it sad Aylmer could not be pleased with his otherwise perfectly lovely Georgiana. He must have been a very insecure man to think she must be absolutely perfect for her to be worthy of his love and acceptance.

Most married people don't have the problems this couple had. No one is perfect, and if we expect it in our spouse, we are foolish. Even the most talented and attractive person, such as yourself, also has flaws. It is wonderful that we have a beautiful Savior, Jesus, who accepts us as we are, imperfections and all. It is also a joy to know that in heaven, all of our human imperfections will be removed.

"Come, you blessed of my Father, and inherit the kingdom prepared for you." (Matthew 25:34)

FEBRUARY 27

When looking forward at life, we seldom plan for loss. We hope most of life will be gain, the result of our working hard and receiving due reward for our effort. Many people, however, find that life does not work as they'd planned.

Charlotte Elliott was born into a Christian family and like most young women, dreamed of achieving love and marriage. However, for her it was not to be. She struggled with a degenerative physical condition that resulted in her remaining single and an invalid all her adult life.

She also struggled with her feelings of unworthiness, and eventually met an eminent preacher, Dr. Caesar Malan, who told her, *"You must come to God just as you are."* These few words had an indelible effect on Elliott and would inspire her to write her best-known hymn:

> *Just as I am, without one plea,*
> *But that Thy blood was shed for me,*
> *And that Thou bidst me come to Thee,*
> *O Lamb of God, I come! I come!*

The poet Henry Wadsworth Longfellow expressed his thoughts about loss and gain eloquently when he wrote:

When I compare What I have lost with what I have gained,
What I have missed with what attained,
Little room do I find for pride.

I am aware How many days have been idly spent;
How like an arrow the good intent
Has fallen short or been turned aside.

But who shall dare To measure loss and gain in this wise?
Defeat may be victory in disguise;
The lowest ebb is the turn of the tide.

I am not a poet, but Longfellow as well as Elliott, who wrote 150 Christian hymns and lived to be 82, help us have a better understanding of how God's lessons of life are best.

What loss have you had that turned into gain?

FEBRUARY 28

February 28 is the last day of this month, at least most of the time. Every four years an extra day is added to correct a variation in our earth's annual journey around the sun. Because months and days do not come exactly every year, we need an extra day every four years to keep us on track.

Our earth revolves around the sun every 365 ¼ days, so every four years one extra day is added to correct our calendar. Our Gregorian calendar was adopted by Pope Gregory 13th in 1582. That calendar is used in most countries around the world, but not everywhere. The Chinese calendar and the Hebrew calendar have different years from ours, based on their unique histories.

In the 1990s an unsuccessful attempt was made to develop an international calendar by the United Nations. Some countries use two calendars, the Gregorian and one tied to their ancient culture. No calendar is perfect. All are based on the earth's irregular revolution around the sun and require periodic corrections to be accurate.

This is also true of humanity. People are not perfect and require correction to exist. No matter how carefully we may plan our lives, we all need this correction. No matter how perfectly we may set up our government or behavior or organization, there will always be imperfections. Only God is perfect and can establish perfect laws. People are sinful, and so we need corrections in life.

The Good News is that our salvation does not depend on us, but on God who has already made all the necessary corrections in Jesus Christ. God's Law requires perfect obedience, and He provides that for us in His Son Jesus.

This is why St. Paul tells us, **"For by grace you have been saved through faith. And this is not your own doing; it is the gift of God, not a result of works, so that no one may boast."** (Ephesians 2:8-9)

Have a great day, knowing God has made all needed corrections in Jesus Christ!

DAY BY DAY WITH JESUS
in
March

+ + +

MARCH 1

There is a story told to explain life that goes like this:

On the first day, God created the dog and told it to sit all day by the door and bark at anyone who comes in or walks by. For that God would give it a life span of twenty years. The dog said, "That's a long time to be barking. How about only ten years and you have the other ten?" God agreed and it was good.

On the second day, God created the monkey and told it to entertain people, do tricks, and make them laugh. For this, He would give it a twenty year life span. The monkey said, "Monkey tricks for twenty years? That's a long time. Can I give you back ten like the dog did?" God again agreed and it was good.

On the third day, God created the cow and told it to go into the field all day and suffer under the sun, have calves and give milk to support the farmer's family. For this He'd let them live sixty years. The cow said, "That is difficult for sixty years. How about just twenty?" God agreed and it was good.

On the fourth day, God created people and said, "Eat, sleep, play, marry and enjoy your life for twenty years." But the human said, "Only twenty? Could You give me my twenty, plus forty the cow gave back, the ten the monkey gave back, and the ten the dog gave back? That makes eighty, okay?" "All right," said God, "If that's what you really want."

So for our first twenty years, we eat, sleep, play and enjoy ourselves, for the next forty we slave in the sun to support our family, for the next ten we do monkey tricks to entertain the grandkids, and for the last ten years, we sit on the front porch and bark at life. Life has now been explained.

"To everything there is a season and a time for every purpose."
(Ecclesiastes 3:1)

MARCH 2

Bees buzz around my cactus plants all winter, except on cold days. Some come to the tiny sweet buds on the large prickly pear pads, but most come to my hummingbird feeder. Feeders attract the cute little hummers, but many also attract bees. They want to drink up the sugar water poured in it for the birds.

I heard something interesting recently, that bees lead each other to sweet flowers and other sources of nectar. Scientists say bees use a "waggle dance" to do this. The theory about this was not taken seriously at first when it was proposed by zoologist Karl von Frisch, but he later won the Nobel Prize, so people had to accept his findings.

Von Frisch's theory was that worker bees have tiny radar responders, and when they find a food source, they go into an intense "waggle dance" to signal to other bees the source of the nectar and even the distance to it. And here we thought bees just flew around until they found something sugary! They not only find sweetness, they attract other bees to it as well.

In John 4, Jesus met the woman at the well and offered her water that could change her life. She immediately went to tell others what she'd heard. She led others to the sweetness of His message. They were been drawn by His ability to tell things about her. **"Come, see a man who told me all things that I ever did."** (John 4:29)

Because of her "waggle dance" the Samaritan people came to see Jesus, the Living Water and the Bread of Life. Jesus of Nazareth is son of Mary and Son of God, and He has something people all want and need, the sweet forgiveness of God and His acceptance of the sinner who repents.

Jesus is still the Living Water and Bread of Life that nourish our souls. When we come to Him in faith and join Him in obedience to God, He will help us do the will of the Father who sent Him.

Honey is an amazing gift from God. Later I'll tell you about that.

MARCH 3

I am a child of immigrants. I am here because of migrations that began thousands of years ago when my ancestor Huns, Picts and Goths moved in search of a better life. A hundred years ago my parents and their families came to the United States, also in search of a better life.

People have been migrating over the earth for centuries to find more food, better weather or escape from a tyrant. Such a move is never easy. Relocation is difficult and there is always danger, but it's a chance they are willing to take.

Migrations today are more complicated because borders are more defined and nations more populated. Yet it is far safer than during time of the Vikings, Mongols or Vandals. "Migration" means large groups moving over many years, while "immigration" refers to legal or illegal movement of small groups across defined borders.

It's astonishing how complicated immigration has become. The more advanced our technology and laws, the harder it is to use them to work for us instead of against us. Peoples can have impure motives, be uncaring and not use common sense. Citizens rarely welcome immigrants, because by nature we're suspicious. We want our nation secure and don't like changes new people can bring. But eventually immigrants become citizens and our neighbors.

We may understand the cause of immigration, but we often doubt it will help us. *"Who will support them?"* we ask. What changes will they bring? Why should we foot the bill? Why give them benefits? Why not send them back? These are questions that must be faced today.

But this much is certain: people will always keep moving to a better life. We need to make the process orderly and yet secure our borders to stop any criminals who may come. But the long-range advantages of new people coming will outweigh short-term disadvantages. If our ancestors had been stopped, we wouldn't be here. Jesus said, **"I was a stranger, and you welcomed me."** (Matthew 25:35)

None of us are true "native Americans," are we?

MARCH 4

I read a true story about how a Bible saved an Ohio man's life. Bus driver Rickey Waggoner was fixing a mechanical problem outside his bus when three assailants approached him with intent to kill. It was a gang initiation meant to be brutal and "show courage."

Waggoner was shot twice in the chest at close range, but a contemporary version of the Bible he had in his pocket, The Message, absorbed the bullets that otherwise should have killed him. Upon hearing of this story in the Dayton Daily News, Eugene Peterson, age 81 and editor of The Message wrote, *"That's wonderful. I heard stories about things like that happening during World War Two."*

"There was obviously some kind of intervention in this case because Waggoner should probably not be alive," a Dayton Police officer told a reporter. Waggoner told police one of the assailants told another, *"Kill him if you want to be in this club."* Waggoner was shot in the leg and also stabbed, but was able to grab the gun and knife as the teenage suspects fled. He then called police from inside his bus.

While this kind of protection from a Bible is unusual, God's Word always protects those who read and have faith in it. It's one more way of God giving us life. The Bible's words are timeless and real, because Jesus Himself is the Word of God in human form. He died to give salvation to all, even those who wanted to kill Him or His people.

We give thanks to God that Waggoner was saved by The Message, and we give special thanks that Jesus Christ, the heart of The Message, has saved billions of people all over the world by forgiving them by faith through the power of the Holy Spirit.

The Apostle John wrote, **"The Word became flesh and blood, and moved into the neighborhood. We saw the glory with our own eyes, the one-of-a-kind glory, like Father, like Son, generous inside and out, true from start to finish."** (John 1:14, The Message)

Hopefully those two young men will "get the Message" some day.

MARCH 5

Sometimes our inaction can lead to a worse problem. I read a story about a man who decided to trap a woodchuck in his garage. He bought a live trap, baited it and the next morning found he'd trapped a skunk. He tried all kinds of ways to get the smelly critter out of the cage and finally called his son-in-law who calmly stepped up and coaxed the skunk out with a few light sprays from a garden hose.

Fear can lead us to inaction. We worry so much about what might happen that we fail to do anything. We fear giving offense by speaking against evil, so we say nothing and evil wins. We fear our kids will be angry with our rules, so we let them get by with bad behavior. We fear others will disapprove of us, so we fail to speak up for the truth.

But there's a time to step up and let the skunk out. The stink of doing nothing is far worse than doing something, even if others object. We've become so fearful that we think it's better to do nothing. But inaction only proves the adage, *"Stand for nothing and you'll fall for anything."*

If you hear God's name being trashed, tell the person to stop it. If you're fearful of hurting your teen's feelings by taking away privileges, remind yourself you're the parent. If our government has a skunk in the works, vote against him or her and tell others to do the same. If something needs to be done and you're there and able, step up and do it.

Jesus was gentle but He also stepped up and did what needed to be done. He was not always gentle with those who should know better. The Pharisees discovered that! Pilate found He wasn't afraid of authority. The High Priest found out Jesus would tell the truth in no uncertain terms.

The only time He was silent was when the shouting of evil was so loud that talking would have done no good. King Herod discovered this. Jesus always let His actions speak. He went to the cross and took our punishment. He said, **"Greater love has no one than that he lay down his life for his friends."** (John 15:13) And He proved it!

Don't be afraid to step up when something right needs to be done.

MARCH 6

Shrek the New Zealand sheep was lost for six years. Its owner said it hated being shorn and ran off and hid in some caves on the ranch. But Shrek had a problem. It could not shed its wool. When finally found, Shrek had six years of wooly growth and looked like a huge dirty snowball with tiny feet and a little nose. When shorn, its wool weighed sixty pounds, enough to make twenty suits. If it hadn't been found, its wool would have kept growing until its weight killed the sheep.

Unlike their wild cousins, domestic sheep have been bred to keep their coats so the wool can be used for clothing. It is impossible for domestic sheep to keep all their wool and live a normal life. Too much wool causes overheating, and its weight causes mobility problems. If an unshorn sheep gets wet and falls down, it will not be able to get up. Its face becomes so covered that it can't see or eat. It must be shorn.

After getting his haircut, Shrek was thin and weak, yet its owner said it lived sixteen years, a normal sheep life. But without its wool being removed regularly, it would have died sooner. The weight of wool can be deadly for a sheep.

So also the weight of sin can be deadly for people. We often carry a load of sin that weighs us down. Sins of rage, resentment and regret, things we have done and things we've not resolved, all can combine to make life too heavy. Without regular repentance, sin becomes deadly. The weight of unforgiven sin will crush us eternally.

Our Heavenly Father knows this, so He sent His son Jesus to take our sins upon Himself. He went to the cross so that we might not be overpowered by the weight of our sin. Jesus has removed that weight. Thus, St. Paul says, **"The wages of sin is death, but the free gift of God is eternal life in Christ Jesus our Lord."** (Romans 6:23)

Think what you'd feel like carrying an extra sixty pounds on your back, day and every night. Even the strongest of people would finally fall under its weight.

Give thanks you don't have to live like Shrek the sheep did.

MARCH 7

In the 1950's, singer Tennessee Ernie Ford popularized a song by Merle Travis titled, "Sixteen Tons." It was a coal miner's lament that no matter how hard he worked, he felt trapped and unable to change his situation.

Early coal miners worked long, hard hours deep in the earth under unhealthy conditions. They often lived in Company owned houses and were paid in "script" coupons that could only be used at the Company Store. Their children grew up in squalor and seemed destined to work in the mines also. They felt trapped by their world of work.

The Company in the song embodies the world's evil, and the miner feels possessed and unable to change his situation. Even if he was summoned to heaven, the song says the miner can't go because the Company "owned" him. The final line in the chorus went, "*St. Peter don't you call me 'cause I can't go - I owe my soul to the Company Store.*"

Sin traps us all. No matter how strong we may feel, we cannot remove its consequences. We may change, but we still need a Savior who can transcend the squalor of our sin and bring us cleansed to God. Jesus is that Savior.

People of all ages have struggled with hopelessness due to lack of money, poor health or a bad relationship. Sometimes the bondage is imagined, but most often it is real. Jews have struggled with bondage since the Egyptians enslaved them 3,500 years ago. Since the time of the Romans and Muslims, Christians have been enslaved and killed for their faith. Even today some believers are "owned" by cultures who believe they should be neutralized or killed.

But God does not abandon His people. He told the enslaved Israelites in Exodus 6:6, **"I will rescue you from your bondage and redeem you with an outstretched arm."** We may feel trapped, but God is there to rescue us. St. Paul said, **"While we were powerless to help ourselves, Christ died for us."** (Romans 5:6 - Phillips) We are not without hope when we have faith in Christ.

No one is hopeless whose faith is in Jesus.

MARCH 8

Sometimes the truth hurts. No matter what you may want to hear or for what reason, unwelcome truth can cut like a knife. Two instances come to mind.

I once officiated at the funeral of a "biker" whose friends asked the funeral director, *"Find some preacher for the service."* The parking lot was filled with as many bikes and pickups as the fifty or sixty attendees. I gently told them the Gospel of our loving Lord Jesus and His acceptance of all who came to Him in faith. At the reception no one spoke to me except a fellow who walked over and said quietly, *"Your zipper's open."* Not the truth I expected!

Another time came after singing and playing at a jam session with a bunch of old timers. I thought I'd done a good job leading the folks in singing, *"I'll Fly Away,"* but the only comment I got from a guy there was, *"Your guitar needs tuning."* Again, not the truth I expected.

Unexpected truths may not be what we want to hear, but they can help us do better. Those of us who work in public can expect some negative feedback. Writers often get criticized for grammar or typos, and although correction may sting, it is what is needed. How we react to it can determine our maturity and strength.

Then again, critics should make helpful remarks, not merely be critical. I doubt that biker or the old guitar picker intended to be hurtful - they just told the truth. Some critics seem to glory in pointing out mistakes and prove true the adage: *"Some do the work and others are critics."*

Jesus was gentle with most people, yet harsh with those who should have known better. His strong comments to the Pharisees were intended to help them wake up from their entrenched ways. Calling them *"hypocrites"* was a stinging rebuke. "Hypocrite" is the Greek word for "actor."

Jesus didn't come into this world to pick on us, but to fulfill God's plan of forgiveness. He said, **"You will know the truth, and the truth will set you free."** (John 8:32).

How can you show God's love to someone today?

MARCH 9

A scorpion, unable to swim, asked a turtle to carry him on his back across the river. *"But you will sting me and I'll drown."* said the turtle. *"My dear turtle,"* said the scorpion, *"If I were to sting you, you may drown but I'd drown with you. Now where is the logic in that?" "You're right,"* said the turtle, *"Hop on!"* The scorpion climbed on the turtle's back and halfway across the river suddenly gave him a mighty sting. As they both sank, the turtle asked, *"Why did you do that? You said there'd be no logic in your stinging me. Why did you do it anyway?"* The drowning scorpion sadly replied, *"Stinging is not about logic; it's just my nature."*

"That's just the way people are. It's human nature." How often have we said or heard that? It's the logic of a person who sees no possibility of change. Or it's someone who wants to be excused for wrong deeds. *"It isn't my fault - he made me do it!"* says the child. Some adults say that, too. Whether on the playground or in the courtroom, it's our nature to point the finger of blame. Yet if we're to blame, we need to accept the consequences and change our ways.

Early in my ministry I remember hearing an old fellow tell me, *"That's the way people are, Pastor, so you'd better get used to it."* But I never have. I've always wanted to be a part of change for the better. I always thought preaching or teaching the Gospel would help change people for the better. But I realize I can't change anyone except myself, and only with God's help.

People don't change people, but God does. He brings us experiences that change our lives. He takes away oldness of our sin and replaces it with newness of His love. He removes our sins, and seeks to make us more like Christ. Paul said in 2 Corinthians 5:17, **"If anyone is in Christ, he is a new creation; the old has gone, the new has come."**

God isn't satisfied with our old human nature. He wants to change us into something better than we are, and He can love us enough to make that change happen.

God loves us just as we are, but He won't leave us that way long.

MARCH 10

In life, there is a time to follow advice, and there is a time to follow your heart. Francis Ouimet grew up in Brookline, Massachusetts, next to the 17th hole of "The Country Club." At a time when golf was reserved for the wealthy, Ouimet started caddying at age nine. Using old clubs and balls he found on the course, he taught himself the game, eventually catching the eye of some members.

Although Francis Ouimet became the best high school golfer in the state, his father insisted he drop out of the sport and *"do something useful"* with his life. Francis tried working at a dry goods store and later at a sporting goods store. But he also kept playing golf and improving his game.

In 1913, Ouimet won a major amateur tournament and was invited to play in the U. S. Open which would be played on the course he knew best, "The Country Club." In what is considered the greatest golf match ever played, amateur golfer Francis Ouimet won that coveted tournament, besting favored British pro golfers, Ted Ray and Harry Vardon.

At the time, Ouimet was twenty years old and stood six feet two inches. His caddy, Eddy Lowrey, was less than five feet tall and only ten years old. Their story is the basis for Mark Frost's book, <u>The Greatest Game Ever Played</u>.

Ouimet remained in golf all his life, winning more amateur tournaments, being elected into several golf halls of fame and honored by his PGA friends. He served during World War One and his portrait is on a U.S. stamp. He is the only American ever elected captain of St. Andrew's Royal Golf Club of Scotland and yet he remained an amateur golfer all his life. The *"Francis Ouimet Scholarship Fund"* has given $25 million in aid to over 5,000 young caddies, including Arnold Palmer, Jack Nicklaus and Annika Sorenstam.

If Francis Ouimet had followed his father's advice to *"do something useful,"* he would have been just another unknown worker or soldier. Instead, he followed his heart and became a legend in the history of sports.

Give thanks we live in nation where we can use God's gifts.

MARCH 11

Martin Luther was a prolific teacher, preacher and writer. His explanation of the Bible has helped the Gospel to be known and believed all over the world. Several compilations of his writings have been published. One such collection, "Biblical Claims and Treasures," was published in German by Johann Schinmeyer of Saxony in 1925.

Rev. E. W. Merz owned a German copy of Schinmeyer's book and translated some of it into English. His son, Ed Merz, gave me one such translated "treasure" based on Psalm 62:8, **"Trust in Him at all times, O people; pour out your hearts to Him, for God is our refuge."** Here is what Dr. Martin Luther wrote about prayer based on Psalm 62:8:

> *"Are you ill-at-ease or heart-sick about something? Well then, for that there is good advice. Pour out your heart before Him and be free to complain to Him. Don't hold anything from God. Whatever it may be, cast it out in heaps before Him, as when you completely reveal your heart's concern to a dear friend. God likes to hear us and is glad to help and give advice. Don't be shy and afraid that you are asking too much. Think not that your request it too great or too much. Out with it! Ask confidently, even if it may seem a pack full of idle petitions. God is great and is content to do more than our weak minds can ask or think. Don't mince your plea with Him, for God is not like man who would grow weary of your much begging and asking. The more you ask, the more He likes to hear. Only pour it out clean, and all of it, without dribbling or trickling. He too, will in like manner, with His boundless mercy, pour out His super-abundant blessings that will submerge and overwhelm your sinful shortcomings."*

If you think Martin Luther is old-fashioned or out-of-date, think again. His explanations of passages transcend the ages and speak to people of every era. God's Word will never grow old if people will but take time to read it. Our modern translations are helpful in telling us His Word.

"Your Word is a lamp for my feet and a light for my path."
(Psalm 109:105)

MARCH 12

Many years ago a man and his wife took their young son Billy to a circus that had come to their Midwestern town. It was a small, run-down affair with a few mangy "wild" animals, some skinny horses, an old elephant and plywood booths set up around the main tent. For a few quarters people could pop some balloons with a dart, ring a bell with a big hammer to win a cigar, or loop the bottleneck with a wooden ring and win a trinket.

Under the "Big Top" people in the stands could watch several acts in its one center ring. Near the end of the show, the little family saw a trapeze flyer climb the steps high up to the top of the tent and begin swinging on her trapeze. The "lovely lady" swung back and forth and then let go, turned a summersault in the air and was caught by a strong man on another trapeze. The "catcher" swung her back to her platform, and they repeated the act a few more times. The lovely lady on the flying trapeze was the high point of the show and received the most applause.

The young boy thought she was amazing, and on the way home told his Dad she was the star of the show. But his Dad said, *"I think the catcher was the star. Good thing he didn't drop her!"* His mother added, *"God is like that with us, Billy. We have lots of ups and downs in life, even some scary loops. But in the end, God is there to catch us and bring us safely to heaven."*

Life is indeed a risky business filled with twists and turns. Jesus once told His disciples, **"I am going to prepare a place for you, and I will come again to take you there, so that you can be with me forever."** (John 14:1-3).

We do not know what all will happen today. We may be perfectly safe, or we may be injured an auto accident. Our loved ones may have a safe day, or one of them might be fall ill. Whatever the case, let us all be encouraged today, because Jesus the Divine Catcher is waiting to bring us safely home.

Here I come, Jesus - catch me!

MARCH 13

Life on planet earth is a precious gift from God. Every day we can look at ourselves in the mirror and give thanks that we are alive and able to experience the wonders of our life. No other planet has the kind of life we have. But some people believe our planet is overpopulated, causing great worry as they say we must not only limit the use of our resources, but also the number of people who use them.

Since the U. S. Supreme Court issued it's 1973 decision making elective abortion legal, there has been intense debate about the procedure. But instead of debating rights or legal precedents, let's consider the children involved.

Case #1: *A preacher and wife are poor. They already have 14 children, and now she is pregnant again. Considering their poverty and the welfare of the other children, do you think she should abort Baby #1?*

Case #2: *The father is ill, the mother has tuberculosis. They've already had 4 children. The first is blind, the second died, the third is deaf and the fourth has tuberculosis. Would you recommend they abort her fifth child, Baby #2?*

Case #3: *A white man rapes a 13 year old black girl and she becomes pregnant. If you were her parents, would you advise her to keep Baby #3 or get an abortion?*

Case #4: *A teenage girl is pregnant and unmarried. Her fiancé is not the father of the baby, and he's upset. He is thinking of leaving her. Should she let Baby #4 live?*

In case you answered "yes" to any of these situations,
**Baby #1 was John Wesley of the Methodist Church.
**Baby #2 was Ludwig von Beethoven.
**Baby #3 was Ethel Waters, great gospel singer.
**Baby #4 was Jesus Christ.

We do not know the life God has in store for us, despite how we arrive into this world. Giving a baby the chance to live is being far more merciful than taking away its life. It is a great responsibility to raise a child, but how can we not allow it the chance to live as we have?

Pray that all babies will have their chance to live.

MARCH 14

Sometimes so much trouble can come from so little. Misspoken or unintended words have ruined marriages, destroyed lives and even resulted in war. For example, just one word led to the split between millions of Christians in the Eastern and Western Christian Churches.

That word in Latin is *"filioque"* and means *"and from the Son."* In the 11th Century, the Western Catholic Church was centered in Rome under the Pope, while the Eastern Orthodox Church was centered in Constantinople under the Patriarch. The Nicene Creed had been the accepted Creed, an official statement of the Faith since the Council of Nicaea in 325 AD. But that one word, *"filioque,"* had been the center of controversy between East and West for centuries.

The phrase means that the Holy Spirit proceeds from the Father *"and from the Son."* Catholic Christians believed this, but Orthodox Christians did not, believing the Holy Spirit proceeded only from the Father. Just one small word, yet it had the power to divide millions of people.

For centuries the two bodies had agreed to disagree over the word until 1014 AD when the Roman Church officially made it a rule to use the word *"filioque"* in their Latin Creed. The Orthodox Church refused to do so, and in 1054 it officially broke away from the Roman Church. There were also other minor differences, but this was the big one.

Some attempts recently have been made to reunite the two Christian bodies, but that one word still remains in the Western Creed, but not in the Eastern.

I don't wish to demean either of the two bodies since they both believe the Bible gives credence to their stance on the subject. The Church has always attempted to understand what the Bible says, but sometimes differences persist.

All Christians are united in believing Jesus is the Savior, and that all who trust in Him are given eternal life by God. That is the heart and center of the Gospel, and all true Christians will agree to this.

"He who believes in Me has eternal life." (John 6:47)

MARCH 15

We all grow old in the same basic biological way, but we don't all age the same. Some of us remain young in heart long after our bodies have grown old. Others find our mind aging faster than our body. We cannot escape growing old, but perhaps we do have some control over how we do it.

As she celebrated her 100th birthday, Lenore was asked what was the "secret" for her long and active life. She said, *"Laughter, the Lord and little things."* Each day she said she found enjoyment by talking with people, taking a walk and reading the Bible. She said, *"I don't know how long the Lord will let me stay here on earth, but I surely thank Him for what He's already given me."* Gratitude is another of her secrets.

Few of us will live to be a hundred years old, but we can learn from Lenore how to enjoy the years we are given.

Laughter. In Genesis 21:6, Sarah said, **"God has made laughter for me."** She was referring to the delight she had in expecting the birth of a child as a 90 year-old woman. There is joy in the good things God gives us, because, **"A merry heart makes a cheerful countenance."** (Proverbs 15:13)

The Lord. Psalm 111:10 tells us, **"The fear of the Lord is the beginning of wisdom."** I chose that verse to be read when we were married, and I have always remembered it. When God is the center of our life, we can grow in all kinds of good ways.

Little Things. How can they help? Proverbs 13:17 tells us, **"Better a dinner of herbs where love is than a fattened ox and hatred with it."** Telling someone you love them, helping someone cheerfully or giving a smile unexpectedly – all these require only a small effort, but they bring joy to others. They are more important than great riches.

Harley, a lifelong friend of mine, died recently. We were the same age and both became Lutheran pastors. He served the Lord with sincerity and faith, doing the best he could among the people he served. Praise God He forgives us in Jesus and allows us the time we have on this earth.

Today may you find joy in "Laughter, the Lord and Little Things."

MARCH 16

During an annual physical examination, the doctor noted his patient's blood report was much better than the previous year. He knew the man had retired so he asked about his physical activity level.

The man said, *"I usually spent three days a week outside all day doing things."* *"What sorts of things?"* the doctor asked. The man replied, *"Yesterday was typical. I took a five hour walk through about seven miles of nature and some of it was through pretty rough terrain. I waded along the edge of a lake. I pushed my way through two miles of brambles. I barely avoided stepping on a snake and climbed several hills. I was so far from civilization that I had to relieve myself behind some bushes. Along the way I saw a bear and a bull elk. At the end of the day, I drank a beer and had a shot of bourbon."* Amazed by the story, the doctor said, *"You are a great outdoorsman!"* *"No,"* the guy replied, *"I'm just a really bad golfer."*

My golf game is nothing to brag about, but it does give me some exercise. How is your body doing? What kind of shape is it in? Are you surprised how it has changed in the past years? Has it given you any unexpected problems? Have you done anything to help it lately?

God gives you a body with its unique type, shape and characteristics. There is probably no other body like yours on the planet, and God wants you to take care of it the best you can, not abusing or neglecting it, lest your days on earth be even fewer than they could be.

In Luther's explanation to the Creed, he says, *"I believe that God has given me my body and soul, eyes, ears and all my members, my reason and all my senses and still preserves them."* Periodically it's good to take stock of what we can do to preserve the body He's given us. We can give thanks that He promises all who trust His Son will be given a new and "glorified body" in the resurrection.

"God created mankind in his own image." (Genesis 1:27)

I wonder what we will look like in heaven.

MARCH 17

I have a nephew who was a Firefighter and he once told me a little about his work. He said that Firefighters wear a helmet because they know it will keep them safer while they are trying to rescue others. The rest of their outfit is also designed to keep them safe.

He explained to me about their "search and rescue" technique. When Firefighters go into a room during a fire to search for people, the room is usually black with smoke. They will wear air masks and have a "hose line," their lifeline to the outside in case the fire turns on them.

Before going into the room, they decide where they will go, to the right or to the left. In a "right handed" search, the first Firefighter goes to the right and keeps contact with the wall. The other Firefighters also go in to the right and keep contact with the one in front. They all stay by the hose line in case they have to get out quickly, for it is their lifeline to safety as they work.

They search for missing persons by crawling on their knees and feeling with their hands. If a Firefighter's "low air" alarm goes off, the whole team leaves the area to the outside so another team can go in to continue their work.

My nephew said during his career he was fortunate to have rescued a person. He said they both learned a valuable lesson that day, that saving a life is far more important than saving a house or the things in it.

Christians can take a lesson from this. We can make sure we are equipped with God's Word and know how to use it, both to defend ourselves and to help others. The "hose line" of Holy Communion helps us remain close to others and to God. We need each other for safety as well as helping those in need. If we encounter "low air," (weariness, fear, doubt) others can help us do the work.

Galatians 6:2 says, **"Bear one another's burdens, and so fulfill the law of Christ."** My nephew took that passage seriously. He recently became a Lutheran pastor.

Give thanks for those who serve us physically and spiritually.

MARCH 18

A boy came to his grandpa, angry at a schoolmate who had been nasty to him. The boy was furious and wanted to know how to "get even" with his "mean guy" schoolmate. Grandpa listened awhile and then asked his grandson to sit down. He said, *"Let me tell you a story."*

The boy was tired of being angry so he listened. Grandpa said, *"I too, have felt great anger and even hatred for those mean people who didn't care what they did to me or others. But I found that hatred wore me out and anger did nothing to hurt my enemy. It was foolish, like swallowing poison and then wishing my enemy would die."*

Grandpa continued, *"Sometimes my feelings are like having two dogs inside me. One wants to be friendly and will only fight when it is right. But the other dog inside is full of anger. The littlest thing will make him fight for any reason. It's hard to live with these two dogs inside me because both of them try to dominate me."* *"Do you still have those dogs?"* the boy asked. *"Yes,"* said Grandpa. The boy asked, *"Which dog wins, Grandpa?"* Grandpa said, *"The one I feed."*

Perhaps you have heard that story before, but its lesson is always good to hear. Our anger can wear us out and really only hurts us, and it will continue as long as we feed and nurse it.

Forgiveness releases us from the urge to "get even." Forgiveness helps us regain our energy and directs us to better things. Feeding the dog of kindness has far better results for us than feeding the dog of anger.

It is not difficult to get angry when we hear of injustice or feel a hurt personally. It is far more difficult to let that dog lie than it is to feed it and cause more trouble. We see this often today in race relations, drug dealings, politics or immigration problems. The dog of anger is easy to feed.

It is better to follow Jesus' Word**s: "Whatever you wish that others would do to you, do also to them, for this is the Law and the Prophets."** (Matthew 7:12)

That Rule will always remain "Golden."

MARCH 19

There was one person who led or participated in every battle, training exercise or operation during WWII and the Korean War. You could always depend on this person, the one they called the "Super GI." He always got there first or always stayed behind when they left. This man was named "Kilroy" and somehow his eyes and nose peeking over the fence captured the imagination of GIs everywhere they went. That's why they left the message, *"Kilroy was here."*

There are many stories about who Kilroy actually was. The most probable person is James J. Kilroy, a shipyard riveting inspector during WWII who was accused of not inspecting a bulkhead correctly. So Kilroy began chalking those words and the small face with a big nose wherever he inspected the ship's riveting. The troops in those ships had no idea who he was, but they liked his face and began writing *"Kilroy was here"* wherever they went, and then claiming it was already there when they arrived.

It was a challenge to place Kilroy in the most unlikely places. He was said to have been atop the Statue of Liberty, under the Arch de Triumphe in Paris, on top of Mt. Everest and in the dust on the moon. An outhouse was built for the exclusive use of Truman, Stalin, and Churchill for the Potsdam conference. The first person to use it was Stalin who emerged and asked his aide, *"Who is Kilroy?"*

In March, 1946, a contest offered the prize of a genuine trolley car to the person who could prove himself to be the genuine Kilroy. Forty men stepped forward to make that claim, but James J. Kilroy brought along officials from the shipyard to help prove his authenticity. He won the trolley car and made it a playhouse for his nine children.

This reminds me of what the crowds said when Jesus came to Jerusalem on Palm Sunday. **"The whole city was stirred up, saying, 'Who is this?' And the crowds said, 'This is the prophet Jesus, from Nazareth of Galilee'."** (Matthew 21:10-11)

In the world today evidence everywhere says, "Jesus IS here!"

MARCH 20

The first sheep simply jumped to its death that morning. Then shocked Turkish shepherds watched as nearly 1,500 other sheep followed, each leaping off the cliff. It all began after the men had left the herd to graze nearby while they had breakfast. In the end, 450 dead animals lay on top of one another in a billowy white pile at the bottom of the cliff, the Turkish newspaper, *Aksam*, reported. Another thousand from the flock also jumped but were saved as the pile of the dead cushioned their fall.

"There's nothing we can do. They're all wasted," said a member of one of 26 families whose sheep were in that herd. The estimated total loss to the families in the town of Gevas in eastern Turkey, was 100,000 Turkish Lira ($75,000), a huge amount where the average annual income is $2,700 per person. *"Every family had an average of 20 sheep,"* another villager said. *"But now only a few families have sheep left. It's going to be hard for us."*

What caused this tragedy? Why did the sheep go over the cliff? The answer is simple and mysterious: Because the others were doing it. One jumped and the rest followed.

People and sheep have a lot in common. Most of us will follow a leader, as long as he or she seems to be doing good things for us. But if our leader leads selfishly and destructively, following him over the cliff is foolish.

The Bible refers to people as sheep (Psalm 100:3, Isaiah 53:6, Matthew 9:36). We are easily distracted and susceptible to group influence, often following the crowd rather than realizing it is going wrong and choosing a better way.

Jesus our Good Shepherd wants the best for His sheep and says, **"My sheep hear my voice and I know them and they follow me,... and I give them eternal life."** (John 10:14, 27)

Who are you following? A self-centered shepherd or a wise leader? We must daily hear the voice of the Good Shepherd and follow Him. He knows where He is going and will lead us safely through life and into eternity.

Who will you follow today?

MARCH 21

Today is the first day of spring, the Vernal Equinox. Scientifically-minded people of ancient civilizations often attempted to find special significance for the Vernal Equinox. At least forty sites have been identified in the world for this purpose, including Egypt's Giza Pyramids, Angkor Wat in Cambodia, Tikal Tower in Guatemala, the Stonehenge and the Great House in Casa Grande, Arizona.

These amazing ancient structures, built over a period of many years, all feature certain stones placed so the sun can shine through openings every year on this day. Ancient astronomers sought guidance on how this alignment would affect the year's harvest, rainfall, or even success in battle over their enemies.

Personally, I've always been more interested in how our Holy God can forgive sinful people than what happens on a certain calendar date. But the Vernal Equinox is interesting to scientists yet today, since it deals with the alignment of the earth with the sun and occurs so precisely the same from year to year.

Ancient astrologers have long attempted to discover whether the stars have any effect on human life. Today's scientific measurements show that the stars do, indeed, have a gravitational affect on human life, although they probably do not affect human behavior.

It was knowledge of the movement of heavenly bodies that caused the Magi to seek out a newborn king of the Jews. They believed bright stars were a "sign from the gods" that someone special had been born. They were right!

"We saw His star in the east and have come to worship Him." (Matthew 2:2) This was not good news to King Herod who wanted no challengers and even at death's door still tried to kill those he thought would take his throne. Today we continue to marvel at the heavenly bodies of the universe, and praise God for giving them to us.

"Praise Him, sun and moon! Praise Him, all you twinkling stars!" (Psalm 148:3)

MARCH 22

I have been privileged to preside at the burials of many veterans, including a dozen or more at Ft. Logan National Cemetery in Denver. A military funeral is a moving event. The casket is draped with an American flag resting silently in front of the mourners. When the pastor has spoken his benediction, a bugler is heard playing "Taps." Then three volleys of rifle fire are heard from a firing squad.

The firing of rifle volleys is a tradition meaning the dead soldier has been cared for. It is one of the highest honors given to a deceased soldier and originated from an old war custom of halting the battle to remove the dead and wounded. Once each army had cleared its dead and wounded off the field, it would fire three volleys to indicate that they were ready to fight again.

After the funeral volleys are fired, the flag is carefully folded in a triangular pattern and given to the next of kin with these words: *"On behalf of the President of the United States, please accept this flag as a symbol of your loved one's honored and faithful service to this country."*

Few people know that at some point one of those folding the flag will slip three spent cartridges into the folds. These can be from the shots fired during the volleys or others. It is important that they be there. The flag is usually not opened after burial, so the three cartridges will remain.

The shell casings inside the folded flag prove that the deceased and flag have been given proper military honors. They represent Duty, Honor and Country. Any remaining shell casings from the volleys may be presented separately to the next of kin as gifts for family or friends.

It is always proper for a Christian to honor military service. Our Lord urged His people to love one another as He has loved us. He said, **"Greater love has no one than this, that he give his life for his friends."** (John 15:3) Serving in the Armed Forces is a privilege. It is done to help the living by those who are willing to die for them.

For whom are you willing to give your life?

MARCH 23

I once saw a roadside sign with an interesting message. It was one of those signs on wheels with moveable letters, and the message said, *"Everything in life happens for a reason. Sometimes the reason is you're stupid and make bad decisions."* That message makes a point, no matter how crudely.

Every one of us can look back, sometimes not very far, and see the results of bad decisions we've made. Today in our society, calling someone stupid, dumb, lame-brain or other equally nasty invective, is frowned upon. *"It will make us feel bad about ourselves,"* we are told.

Perhaps that's reason enough to avoid such words. But sometimes we can't avoid the truth and we should feel we are a little stupid. How else are we going to learn from our mistakes? It's like the saying I read on a wall plaque:

> *Good Judgment Comes From Experience*
> *Experience Comes From Bad Judgment*

I don't advocate guilt as a way of life or a tool to control people. Too much of that comes from Satan, and we are all sinful humans prone to making bad decisions. But I'm not sure all guilt is bad. Sometimes we need a little to remind us of something we did wrong in the past. Maybe it will keep from repeating it again in the future.

But simple guilt doesn't stop us from doing wrong. We can know what is right but keep doing the wrong anyway. Sometimes we do wrong for its pleasure, and sometimes we just make foolish choices. Other times we can't seem to help ourselves.

The Apostle Paul had that trouble. He said, **"For I do not do the good I want, but the evil I do not want is what I keep on doing."** (Romans 7:19) *(Hey, brother Paul, we've all been there!)* He said a verse or two later, **"Thanks be to God [for forgiving us] through our Lord Jesus Christ."**

Ask God to help keep you on the right path today.

MARCH 24

Spring may be just starting in the upper Midwest, but it's already felt like spring for weeks in Arizona. After our annual "January chill", which is a few weeks of cold mornings and maybe even a few frozen plants, the days warm up during February and by March we already have some sweaty days in the nineties.

But right now in Iowa and Minnesota there's probably still snow out in the tree groves and maybe even some ice on the lakes. In Colorado, though, there will still be a couple of snowfalls left to shovel.

God has given us an amazing world, and I appreciate the change of seasons. Human life is made up of one change after another. Time makes us grow older and we cannot escape the changes it brings, no matter how well we may eat or how much we may exercise. We must be ready for life, taking each day for the blessings it gives.

Not every change is a blessing. A young man is driving to his office, a recent graduate from a university where he has studied medicine and become a doctor. A young woman has left her child with a sitter and is going out for groceries. Both of these people have good plans for their day and life, but their plans all change when their cars meet at an intersection in a terrible crash.

Sometimes small changes can lead to big problems. A man riding his bicycle hits a rock, strikes his head and has a light concussion. But instead of healing quickly as he's always done, complications set in and his morning ride becomes weeks in the hospital trauma unit. Change can be okay unless it is change for the worse.

God is with us in all our moments and days, those of carefree joy and those of fearful sadness. David often called out for God. **"Answer me when I call, O God of my righteousness! You have given me relief when I was in distress. Be gracious to me and hear my prayer!"** (Psalm 4:1)

God does answer us, and He will hear our prayers today.

MARCH 25

Yesterday's devotion was a bit discouraging. When someone talks to you about change, you really don't want to hear about change for the worse. You'd rather hear how a bad thing turned out good, like perhaps the doctor saved the woman's life, or maybe they were both single and later got married. But we don't want to hear that they both were killed in the car accident. Hey! Give us some good news!

Have you ever been in a situation that's life-changing, perhaps from a serious injury, divorce, getting fired or having a bad disease? Most of us have faced tough situations because we're weak or bad things can happen to us. I knew of a girl who has battled diabetes since she was two, and every day she must monitor her blood sugar. Yet she did well in school and had a cheerful attitude.

Whether we are a believer in Christ or not, all of us have been tempted to say, *"That may be good for you, but you don't have to live my miserable life. What did I do to deserve this? Can someone please give me some good news for this terrible life I have right now?"*

How can we overcome a bad situation? In John 16:33 Jesus said, **"I have told you these things, so that you may have peace. In this world you will have trouble. But take heart! I have overcome the world."** If Jesus has overcome the world, what have we to fear? Yet we do.

Our Lord did not have a chronic illness or a terrible childhood accident. He did not lose a spouse or child to the grave, but He did lose loved ones and He certainly suffered the pain of beatings and crucifixion. He died for sins He did not commit, your sins and my sins. **"He was pierced for our transgressions and crushed for our iniquities."** (Isaiah 53:5)

Jesus knows our every pain and weakness, and He hears our prayers for mercy. He will not leave us alone to deal with the changes and struggles we must face. We have His promise on that.

Others may leave us alone, but Jesus will not.

MARCH 26

A number of important things happened on March 26. In 1979, the Prime Minister of Israel and the President of Egypt signed a Peace Treaty at Camp David. In 1953, Dr. Jonas Salk announced the discovery of a successful polio vaccine, and in 1863, West Virginia passed a law granting slaves their freedom. All these events on March 26 have had lasting benefits for mankind.

One more event deserves mention. On March 26, 1872, Thomas J. Martin patented the first modern fire extinguisher. This may not have been so special, except that Thomas J. Martin was a black man, a former slave who some believe may once have lived in West Virginia.

Martin was an inventor. He had designed his fire extinguisher to be attached to a reservoir of stored water which was then used to spray burning fires. Although British Captain George Manby is credited with creating the modern chemical fire extinguisher in 1818, Thomas Martin's improved version is often regarded as the first practical fire extinguisher.

The events of life are often interlinked. A wealthy man's son playing in the Scottish hills becomes trapped in a bog. His cry for help brings a peasant farmer who rescues the boy. The farmer is rewarded by having his own son educated. The farmer's son becomes the famous doctor, Alexander Fleming, who discovers penicillin. Years later, the wealthy boy who was rescued and is now grown, becomes ill and is cured by penicillin. That man was Winston Churchill. Both men were knighted by the King of England.

God has marvelous ways of showing His love and mercy. The child born to Mary was threatened with death from the day He was born, and yet He became Savior of all who trust Him, including some Roman soldiers. **"This is love, not that we have loved God but that He loved us and sent His Son to earn the forgiveness of our sins."** (1 John 4:10)

How has God shown you His wonderful blessings?

MARCH 27

One evening several years ago while I was still in fulltime ministry, I received a phone call from a missionary friend in West Africa. He was coming to America and wanted to know if he and his group could come to my church for a fund-raising visit. I sat on my front step and spoke to him that morning on my cell phone. He said he, too, was sitting in his house and talking to me on his cell phone, only there it was already evening. We were 12,000 miles apart and yet connected by electronic devices small enough to fit in our hands. Amazing!

The word "connected" is used a lot these days and describes a lot of people. Most people rarely go anywhere without their cell phone and also have other "connectors" such as iPad, Laptop or iWatch. "Smart Phones" have amazing computer capabilities, as well as the capability to help us speak to each other over great distances.

Psychologists say the craving to be connected electronically can become an addiction so some are rebelling. After years of having the latest communication devices, they are throwing some of these things away. They are called "Tech-Nos," people saying "no" to technology and seeking more quiet time in their personal lives.

Psalm 23:2 describes this, **"He makes me lie down in green pastures, He leads me beside the quiet waters, He restores my soul."** Many Christians find that a daily time for Bible and prayer is essential for a balanced life. A gentle "disconnect" from the busy world helps us "re-connect" with God. The green pastures and quiet waters really do restore our souls.

Communion with God takes several forms. There is Holy Communion, received at the altar. There is the gentle communion of reading God's Word, and there is the quiet communion of prayer. All three are good and helpful. They are God's way of keeping us close to Him.

What will you do to stay close to God today?

MARCH 28

Today one of my granddaughters was born. She has been such a blessing to my son and his family, a true treasure of smiles and caring. Queen Elizabeth II once visited visit Trinidad and Tobago, islands off the northeast coast of South America. When the Queen entered one small town, many of the missionaries and their families joined with hundreds of others who gathered to greet her.

Adults and children waved small British flags and cheered as they watched as the Queen and her entourage came down the street. First came the soldiers, then the mounted guard and then the limousine from which the Queen waved to the cheering crowd. One young spectator later wrote that as soon as the Queen and her party left town, everything returned to normal. His exact words were, *"Royalty came to town and nothing changed!"*

When Jesus of Nazareth came to Jerusalem on the first Palm Sunday, He was met by a crowd large enough to be noticed by the authorities. People cheered Him as His "soldiers" cut palm branches and laid them on the road before Him. Some even put cloaks down for Him to cross as He rode on His "donkey limousine" with the shouting and cheering people. If anyone there could have seen what was ahead for Him in the coming days, they might have said, *"Royalty came to town and everything changed."*

Jesus continues to ride into the hearts of men, women and children, whenever they come to trust Him as their Savior. Paul said, **"Do you not know that your body is a temple of the Holy Spirit within you, whom you have from God?"** (1 Corinthians 6:19) Our bodies are temples where Jesus wishes to live and transform us into a Living Body that worships Him and serves mankind. When Jesus comes to us, everything should change for the better.

How we treat our work, friends, family, government and even how we treat our enemies should change because, *"Royalty came to town and everything changed."*

Has anything changed in your life because of Jesus?

MARCH 29

The Oregon Trail is a 2,200 mile emigrant trail that connects the valleys of the Missouri River all the way west to Oregon. Along the way, the Trail went through Kansas, Nebraska, Wyoming and Idaho before finally reaching the Oregon territory.

Near the present day town of American Falls, Idaho, is a large rock where travellers have carved their names or initials. It became known as "Register Rock" and is located in Massacre Rock State Park, on Highway 30 west of American Falls. Register Rock is listed on the National Register of Historical Places. Register Rock could be called "Guestbook of the Oregon Trail" that was inscribed with hundreds of names of travellers.

Another such place is "Register Cliff" located near Guernsey, Wyoming. Both sites in these two states were prominent enough to become key checkpoint landmarks for parties heading west along the Oregon Trail. They are often called "emigrant recording areas."

Travellers began inscribing their names on these rocks during the western migrations of the 19th century. An estimated 500,000 travellers used this trail between 1843 and 1869, with up to one-tenth of them dying along the way, mostly due to disease.

The Bible contains many accounts of those who have gone before us. Hebrews 11 lists important past travellers and pilgrims: Gideon, Barak, Samson, David and Samuel. There are also more recent pilgrims now with the Lord: Grandparents, parents, neighbors, teachers, pastors and Christian friends. We may not see their names in stone, but they are written in our hearts and memories.

Hebrews 12:1 says **"We are surrounded by a great cloud of witnesses."** These are God's faithful ones who have spoken and lived the Word of God among us so that we also may follow Jesus Christ. God willing, you and I will have our names recorded beside all those others.

And it won't even matter if they don't spell our name right!

MARCH 30

This time of year in Arizona, we are bidding farewell to friends who are returning home after the winter season. "Home" is always in another state or Canadian province. Some look forward to going home to family and neighbors, or just to start the yard work and see how the house survived the winter. One man even said he likes to shovel a little snow before it all thaws - imagine that!

One of my favorite musical compositions is Dvorzak's "New World Symphony" written after visiting America in the 19th Century. In it he incorporated the haunting melody from a spiritual called "Going Home." Its opening words are: *"Going home, going home, I'm just going home."*

This time of year some of us begin to wonder if our favorite baseball team players will cross home plate. We have seats at a few home games of the Colorado Rockies, but sometimes our team just can't bring a runner home.

At one memorable game, we were behind 4-2 in the seventh inning and people next to us decided to leave early. Things changed when the opposing pitcher walked three, gave up a hit and loaded bases with no outs. He walked one runner home, then another. When he hit a batter scoring another run, he was replaced. The new pitcher immediately allowed a long fly ball, the catcher threw high during a base steal, and one of our rookies hit a three run homer. Eight players made it safely home as the Rockies beat the Padres 10-4. It was fun seeing the umpire make the *"Safe!"* sign as player after player crossed home plate. It is always fun when more of our players cross home plate than theirs do.

"Safe at home." That has a good sound to it. Home is the place where you go and are welcomed by loved ones. We all need a home somewhere, a dwelling with others who love us. But our earthly homes are not eternal. Those are with the Lord, as He told us in John 14:2, **"In my Father's house are many rooms."**

Today give God thanks for your home.

MARCH 31

The older we become, the more we realize we may not see people we love that much longer. Especially if there is serious illness involved, every good-bye might be our last. With some people, I've adopted a new word of good-bye. Instead of *"See you next year,"* I tell the person, *"See you again, if not here, then there."*

Two men in the Armed Forces were being deployed to different assignments, and the first man said, *"See you on the other side."* The second man looked at him questioningly, so the first explained. *"I mean I'll see you next year when our deployment is over."* "Oh good," said the second man, *"I was afraid maybe you'd gotten religion and figured you may not come back."* The first man smiled and said, *"Actually, you're right on both accounts."*

"See you on the other side," can be a very appropriate comment when used between Christians, but it evokes some questions. Who of us will be here next year? What will the "other side" be like? None of us knows what the next year, next week or even the next day will be like. Although we need not make it the constant center of our words and thought, it is still good to face it realistically,

James, our Lord's half-brother, wrote in James 4:14, **"You do not know what tomorrow will bring. What is your life? For you are a mist that appears for a little time and then vanishes."** Such a thought is sobering, but it is also the truth. James was pointing out the foolishness of planning to prosper and make money without giving thought to what may happen to us. He plainly asks which is greater, earthly life or eternal life?

A Christian may find tension in living with joy for today while knowing there may be no tomorrow. Martin Luther advocated living for each day God gives. *"If I knew I would die tomorrow, I would still plant a tree today,"* he once said. What do you think he meant by that?

Luther's words provoke good thought!

DAY BY DAY WITH JESUS
in
April

+ + +

APRIL 1

Several years ago my son's father-in-law passed away. His sudden death at age 72 was a shock to all who knew him. A quiet man whose father was a Lutheran pastor, he and his wife had lived in Tucson over forty years.

I asked my son whether their small children knew their Grandpa had died. He said they knew because they'd heard their Mom crying on the phone and asked why. *"But I don't believe they understand what's really happened,"* he said.

A short time later their six year-old son asked him, *"Do you think Grandpa likes his new room?"* The question stopped my son in his tracks. He had told the boy some time before that when a person dies believing in Jesus, God gives him a new room to live in up in heaven just like he wants it. Thus his question, *"Do you think Grandpa likes his new room?"*

My son talked with him about this, and then asked him what he would like in his new room in heaven. He said without hesitation, *"Escalators, fans and lots of stuffed animals."* Those things had recently fascinated him, and he wanted his room filled with them.

What would you like in your heavenly room? How would you explain a Christian's death to a child? How would you explain to him the blessings of heaven and eternal life with Jesus? Are you ready for your new room?

Around this time we observe Holy Week, a time when we are assured that Jesus did all that was necessary so that we can all go to the new room God has prepared for us. Think of how much joy you'll have when loved ones are with you because of Jesus, our Risen Savior.

In my room I want a recliner and visits with my loved ones.

APRIL 2

Tsegay Kebede of Ethiopia is only 5 feet 2 inches tall, and he is also one of the best distance runners in the world. He is also glad to be alive. He was on his way to training with a squad of runners for a world-class marathon when the brakes failed on their vehicle and it toppled over a small cliff. *"We screamed for help because we were all crushed,"* Kebede said, thinking back to that June day in 2007. *"All the time I was praying, 'God, I came to Addis Ababa to change the life of my family. Are you going to end my life here? Please save my life.' My prayers were answered. I thought I would die for those few minutes but I think I was given another life."*

The fifth of 13 children, Kebede could not have dreamed he would achieve his success. As a boy he collected firewood for $1 a day to help himself and his family survive in rural Gerar Ber, 26 miles north of the Ethiopian capital. He used his meager earnings to pay for school and food for his family. *"I would buy bread and some tea and would have only one meal a day,"* Kebede reflected. *"After that, I had nothing left in my pocket. I had to wake up the following morning to go back to work in order to survive. If I didn't, there would be no food."*

Kebede began running at age 8. *"Sometimes, when I think back on how I used to survive with my family, it brings a tear to my eye. I thank God every day that I have the opportunity to help my family out of poverty. It is almost like a dream that I used to live like that. Now from the marathon, I have sent money home for my parents, brothers and sisters, to build a house. I have also bought them cattle so they can be self-sufficient. That is my aim – for them to be able to provide for themselves."*

Most athletes work to achieve success for themselves. If they become a professional, they will have fame and fortune. Few are those who do so to benefit loved ones. Jesus came to earth to benefit us, not Himself. **"For you know the grace of our Lord Jesus Christ, that though He was rich, yet for your sake He became poor, so that you by His poverty might become rich."** (2 Corinthians 8:9)

What you willing to do for your loved ones?

APRIL 3

What would happen if the lights went out? How would your life change if you no longer had electricity? We all are very dependent on the energy coming into our homes, but what would happen if it stopped? Would we have enough basic supplies even for a few weeks?

Jesus' death on Calvary's cross put the disciples' lights out. His death took away their Light of life. The death of Him who gave them purpose for life nearly destroyed their world of hope, but only momentarily.

What would life be like if God no longer was there to help us? Skeptics, agnostics and atheists like to repeat empty phrases such as, *"God is dead,"* or *"God does not exist."* What if that were true? Would we then be able to exist? Thanks be to God He is not dead but lives and gives us life.

Our daily life is based on electronics. Without them we'd have no communications, banking system or means to heat our homes or power our businesses. Governments, hospitals and factories would all change.

We don't think twice when we flip a switch for heat, lights or entertainment. Churches might not even know their membership and most would need to change their worship. Every part of our earthly life involves some kind of electrical impulse. Let's face it, we're hooked on electricity!

While electricity is an earthly blessing, Jesus gives us eternal blessings. Through His Word, Holy Communion and Baptism, we receive the Bread of Life and are cleansed of our sins so we can live each day. Jesus said, **"I am the Light of the World; whoever follows me will not walk in darkness but have the light of life."** (John 8:12)

We praise God each Easter that God gave the world back its Light in the resurrection of Jesus Christ. Even if our lights would go out due to some disaster, you and I would still have the Light of the World in Jesus Christ. He who created electricity will make sure we have what is needed for eternal life.

"Shine Jesus, shine, fill this land with the Father's Glory."

APRIL 4

Church organists are a special group of people. They usually begin their career on the organ or piano bench when they are young and unsure, often tiring of the constant lessons and recitals. Not all stick with it, but those who do find that all the practicing, lessons and performances are worth the effort. Pianists usually end up playing for others, accompanying groups, individuals or congregations.

While most may help with accompaniment for a few years, some remain at it a whole lifetime. And while each has certain skills, they all do the best they can. Organists do their best. Most people who complain about the organist also know they themselves could do no better.

At one church the organist finally retired after 46 years there. She was not a flashy player nor highly skilled, but she was a faithful, hard worker who was always there. *"They told me it would only be temporary,"* she said at her retirement. *"Temporary sure turned into a long time!"*

At another church the organist retired just before he died. A highly talented man, he served his Lord and his churches with great skill and vigor. In his youth people came from miles around just to hear him. In his seventies, his fingers were no longer as quick, but they still danced over the keys. He said his secret was never to stop practicing. It was a thrill to hear his offertories, postludes and songs of the Masters, as well as some of his own works. Worshippers often applauded at the end of the service.

God's people, whether musicians, pastors, teachers, ushers, altar guild, youth workers or council members, do the best they can. We rejoice that God accepts all our efforts. In fact, the Holy Spirit helps us and makes our "ordinary" efforts "extraordinary." We are always blessed when people use their talents to help churches do their important work in the Lord's Kingdom.

The next time you wonder why something happens in churches, consider who is doing it and why.

Then ask yourself if you could do any better.

APRIL 5

One morning in early April I walked around our RV park in Casa Grande, Arizona, and was struck at how empty it was. From January through March it's full with most of its 2,000 spaces occupied by 3,500 or more people. During those days people are everywhere, driving golf carts and cars, biking, walking, golfing and visiting.

But that morning, less than two weeks since people begin leaving for their northern residences, about two-thirds of the spaces and homes were empty. 2,500 people had left, and that left the park feeling really empty.

"Empty" is not a positive word to most people. An empty bank account can be terrifying, an empty chair means someone has left us, and sometimes we feel empty of emotions if the tears of death or loss have drained us. An empty relationship leaves us feeling hopeless. Empty nesters acutely feel the loss of children no longer home. In general, "empty" is not a word we like to hear.

Unless, of course, we consider Christ's tomb. The disciples found it empty because the body was gone. **"He is not here - He is risen,"** said the angel. **"Come and see the [empty] place where He lay."** (Matthew 28:6) Now "empty" is good, VERY good!

An empty home can leave us sad, and the emptiness at a burial can be devastating. But the empty grave of Jesus brings us hope and joy. **"Because He lives, we, too, shall live,"** said one of His disciples. There's nothing negative about "empty" when it means Jesus is alive.

The emptiness of an RV park will be temporary. God willing, another season will come, and in the fall hundreds of friends and neighbors will return. The enjoyment of a busy neighborhood will return once again. Meanwhile, God gives us each new day to experience His mercies and blessings.

May the empty tomb fill you with hope and joy because you know in your heart that CHRIST IS RISEN!

APRIL 6

Our world must be a lonely place because we have so many telephones to keep in touch. In America there are 311 million people and 330 million cell phones. Russia has 143 million people but more than 224 million cell phones! China has over a billion cell phones in use. Who is using all those phones? With so much communication, why are we still so lonely? Shouldn't the phones help us communicate better?

Jesus said, **"He who has ears to hear, let him hear."** (Matthew 11:15) That's a way of saying we should work hard to listen and understand what He is telling us. It is His way of telling us to look behind the words we hear to the real meaning of what is said.

We live in a sea of words, a sea that is too often stormy or polluted. Politicians spar with words crafted to influence people. Preachers try to persuade us with new ideas from the Bible. Adults teach the young, and youth tune others out with headphones. We all have ears, but we're not always using them to hear.

Good communication involves hearing and listening. Jesus' brother James wrote, **"Let every person be quick to hear, slow to speak and slow to anger."** (James 1:19) Most people have ears and can hear, but listening requires discernment, wisdom and the required interest to find out what is being said.

Many families suffer from poor listening. Companies have problems when workers are poor listeners. Nations require diplomats to filter the words and messages spoken by their leaders. Leaders can manipulate people with specially crafted messages.

Jesus wants us to be active listeners. The Rabbi of Nazareth was as good a listener as ever walked the earth. He still knows our hearts and hears our cries as we try to listen with ears plugged by sin. Do you have good hearing? Do you use your mind to help you listen? Today, try to listen carefully to others and may God bless your conversations.

Pray for help to listen today to what others say.

APRIL 7

The end of the winter season at an RV park often brings items left next to the garbage dumpsters. These discarded items may still work and are left for someone else to use. One day I dropped off some scraps of wood and picked up a small item sitting on the ground.

It was a nearly new red "Dirt Devil" hand vacuum. I took it home and as I suspected it just needed a good cleaning to make it work right. It even had an adapter for narrow spaces - just what I need for getting dust out of our window tracks.

A day or two later I drove past the dumpsters and there sat another vacuum, a nearly new upright model, also a Dirt Devil! Again I took it home, emptied the dirt chamber, cleaned the filter, and now we have a better upright than the one we've had. The next day I put our tired, old noisy upright vacuum by the dumpster and later that day it, too, was gone.

Both of these abandoned items had the same problem - their owners forgot to empty the dirt. This made me think of our need for spiritual cleaning by confession and absolution. If you and I don't get our sin dirt removed by forgiveness, soon nothing in our life will work well.

Calvary is God's eternal garbage dump. When Jesus died, He got rid of our sins there and the sins of all people. The Bible says He has removed our sins from us **"...as far as the east is from the west."** (Psalm 103:12) That makes Jesus our "Divine Garbage Man." What He removes is gone forever.

The next time your life seems out of kilter, check to see if you need to do some personal house-cleaning. John the disciple encourages us, **"If we confess our sins, He is faithful and just and will forgive our sins, and cleanse us from all unrighteousness."** (1 John 1:9)

Jesus empties and cleans our personal Dirt Devil - now there's an interesting concept!

APRIL 8

This time of year it can be over 100 degrees in Arizona, so it was no surprise that one year Carol and I enjoyed watching "Frozen Planet" on the Discovery Channel. Every program showed the amazing adaptability of God's creatures in the Arctic north and Antarctic south.

One show featured a mother polar bear and her growing cubs who flourished during the -50 degree winter days but struggled during the +50 degree summer days. Although my wife and I are from the Upper Midwest, such temperature extremes would be too great for us.

Another program showed a variety of Arctic birds teaching their little ones fly by flying underneath them and give enough "aerial lift" so they wouldn't land on the tundra and become lunch for a fox. The parent birds made sure the juvenile first made a water landing which would ensure its getting up into the air again to fly another day.

We are living on most a wonderful planet, despite what environmentalists may tell us. We are residents of a privileged planet that God has created where He allows humans to prosper and flourish as in no other era of time and on no other planet. Despite fears of global warming or a weakened America, we live in the most amazing time of history. For this we give God unceasing thanks.

We should also be unceasing in our efforts to share the story of Jesus. One Sunday in church we heard the President of Concordia Seminary in St. Louis urge us to do just that. *"Despite what others may lead us to believe,"* he said, *"it is a good time to be a Christian. It is a great time to be a pastor or a layperson and tell the story of Jesus,"* he said. *"It is an outstanding time to see the Holy Spirit bringing people to faith."*

Summer days in Arizona are usually hot and the nights can be cold. But sinners worthy of death are made living saints by the death and life of Jesus, God's Son, something almost unimaginable. Wherever we go we know God's amazing grace will go with us.

Thanks be to God!

APRIL 9

Holy Week in the church means special worship services, culminating in the joy of Easter Sunday. It also brings back memories of unplanned events that made their way into some of my Holy Weeks over the years.

During Holy Week, 1974, my youngest son was born. Another Holy Week I spent three days in a treatment center with a dear friend helping with his struggle to defeat the demons of alcohol. One Holy Week I had minor surgery. Some Holy Weeks brought funerals and one Palm Sunday my family got the flu. I barely got through the service before getting it myself.

Holy Week took on a different meaning after walking Jerusalem's Via Dolarosa. In 1999, we traveled to Israel with other Christian pilgrims. One of our participants had difficulty walking, so our guide took us over the *"Way of Sorrows"* in reverse order, to make it easier to walk the path.

This brought us to the Church of the Holy Sepulcher at a rare time when it was nearly empty. In a place usually jammed with people, echoing voices and flashing cameras, we were nearly alone. We quietly walked up to the Armenian chapel above the remnant of Calvary, went into the memorial tomb and saw details in the Chapel rarely seen. Instead of many hundreds, only a few were there.

Jerusalem was not empty that first Holy Week. Despite the mayhem of the Passover activities, Jesus' trial and crucifixion were noticed by the crowds. Many of the people saw Him carry His cross through the streets, but only a few heard Him speak His Words as He died.

The day Jesus died has become indelibly woven into the fabric of human history, and the events of Holy Week changed the world forever. Because He rose from the dead, the world's people have hope. Christians have a living Savior, not a dead hero. All who trust Him as the Son of God are blessed with a future in the joys of heaven.

"Behold the Lamb of God who takes away the sin of the world." (John 1:29)

APRIL 10

I wish you all a blessed Easter time this year. Have you ever been the "one in the middle," the one between two others? Perhaps it happened in a family quarrel, a work dispute, or trying to keep two people from physically fighting. Whatever the case, being the one in the middle can be uncomfortable and even dangerous.

On Good Friday Christians recall that Jesus died on the cross, the Holy One of God between two thieves. That was where He intended to be. On Calvary He was the Divine One between God and humanity, suffering and dying to bring people back to God. From the time of His birth He was destined to be the *"Man in the Middle,"* the One who would reconcile people and God.

Two thieves were crucified with Him on Good Friday, but only one recognized the *"Man in the Middle."* Most thieves see their surroundings, who is watching them and what is taking place. Both of those thieves knew they belonged on Calvary, but only one realized the *"Man in the Middle,"* shouldn't have been here. Despite his hopeless condition, the observant thief didn't want to die alone. He rebuked the unrepentant thief and reached out to Jesus, the One who did not belong there. Jesus offered him eternal life because of his faith, and He does the same for all who realize they need forgiveness and seek Him in faith.

Jesus came to earth to be the *"Man in the Middle,"* the Mediator between God and people. **"There is one God, and there is one Mediator between God and people, the man Christ Jesus."** (1 Timothy 2:5) A mediator tries to bring factions to resolution and peace, and no one has done it better than Jesus. **"He was put to death for our sins, but raised again for our justification."** (Romans 4:25)

Sin separates people from God, but Jesus' resurrection unites us. The resurrection of Jesus is proof He is God's Son who has done all that is necessary to restore people to God through forgiveness of sins. He is risen indeed!

Maybe being the middle is just where God wants you to be.

APRIL 11

Today is my youngest son's birthday. We brought him home from the Bismarck hospital in a cardboard box, and he has been a wonderful blessing ever since.

One spring Carol and I watched "The Bible," a miniseries produced by actress Roma Downey. Its final episode was about the betrayal, suffering, death and resurrection of Jesus and was aired appropriately on Easter evening. I had been wondering what others thought about the series, so I asked my "Weekly Message" readers to send me their thoughts. Nearly two dozen emailed their opinions.

Television can be a useful tool to share the Gospel. Some wish TV hadn't been invented because they say it has been a bad influence on people. But most of us know it has good and bad purposes, like the personal computer. When any kind of electronics can be used to broadcast the Truth of God in the Holy Scriptures into millions of homes, then we should rejoice in the good this can be for everyone.

Electronics are only one of the many ways through which the Gospel can be shared. Personal conversation is probably the best method, as it involves people sharing face-to-face with questions and answers. Next comes the written word, printed Bibles made possible by the invention of the printing press in 1450. But electronic methods give us additional ways of sharing information, and their use seems to grow every year.

When I asked about *The Bible* I got these responses:
1) *"It was a fresh approach to help us understand the Bible."*
2) *"It helped us see the reality of the biblical history."*
3) *"It may help some people see Jesus as our Savior."*
4) *"The actors were well chosen for the parts."*
5) *"Some parts were quite violent and difficult to watch."*

What benefits do you think the media can have in presenting the Gospel? Which form of sharing seems best? Jesus told His disciples of all ages to take the Gospel into the world and share it, teaching and baptizing all people.

Can you recall when you first realized you trusted Jesus?

APRIL 12

"**Christ is risen!**" Christians can say this with joy every day, not only at Easter! The joy Christians share during the time of resurrection is like none other. His resurrection is why we have any hope at all.

This is why St. Paul, empowered by the Holy Spirit, wrote, **"If Christ has not been raised, then our preaching is in vain and your faith is in vain... But in fact Christ has been raised from the dead, the first-fruits of those who have fallen asleep."** (1 Corinthians 15:14, 20)

The year *THE BIBLE* was aired, I asked my readers to share their responses to it. *"What did you think of The Bible?"* I asked them in my "Weekly Message." The History Channel's five-part miniseries finished on Easter Sunday. Some responses were brief, but some were quite detailed.

Of the 48 responses I received, only two were truly negative. They expressed disappointment about minor changes in the stories and a wish that more details of the Bible stories could have been included. Personally, I felt God was honored, and the actor who portrayed Jesus was quite believable. The New Testament stories were fairly accurate when compared to the Gospels.

The following week I asked another question: *"Is the Bible in electronic form still God's Word?"* I wanted to hear whether people thought reading the Bible on an iPhone App, a Kindle Reader or an online website is the same Word of God as that which we read in our printed Bibles.

About two dozen again responded with a resounding, *"Yes, of course,"* with a few adding that reading the Bible in electronic form *"Doesn't feel the same"* as reading it from a printed book. I agreed with both points of view. It's God's Word no matter what, but I like the printed words because I'm rather old-fashioned.

It is never out-of-date to be old-fashioned if what we hold to is the timeless truth that Jesus is the Son of God.

Are you sometimes old-fashioned about the Bible also?

APRIL 13

It's baseball season now and those who follow it have their favorite stories. During the 1986 post-season playoffs between the Boston Red Sox and the New York Mets, Bill Buckner, the Red Sox first baseman, missed an easy grounder that led to the loss of that game and eventually the loss of the series.

Buckner was vilified by the Red Sox fans who felt it was another sign of the "Curse of the Bambino," a baseball legend that the Red Sox were jinxed due to their 1918 trade of Babe Ruth to the Yankees. Despite his fine 20-year career that included 2,700 hits and other honors, Buckner is mainly remembered for that mistake.

The disbelief of the players and fans told the story. Once again, victory had been snatched from the jaws of defeat. Red Sox just couldn't win the Big One. The "curse" was broken in 2004 when the Red Sox won the world series, but Buckner still is remembered for his error.

Have you ever stood in disbelief when something slipped away from your grasp, when the "Big One" got away? Regret can be destructive. When it doesn't go away, it can harm your soul. Hell is filled with regret. It is very possible that regret is the primary terror of hell. When people make mistakes that affect their life and the lives of others with tragedy and loss, regret can pull us into the shadows and fill us with the blackness of failure and doom. Regret leads us into a valley we may think has no exit.

Satan loves regret because he can lead us to believe his black thoughts, not the pure thoughts of God. Satan tries to convince us we are failures, but our Lord Jesus calls Satan what he is: **"A murderer and Father of Lies."** (John 8:44)

In Christ, we are not failures. Trusting in Him, we have forgiveness of our sins. By faith in Jesus, regret need not drown us in despair. **"Even though I walk through the valley of the shadow of death I will fear no evil, for You are with me."** (Psalm 23:4)

Never give in to the devil's grasp of regret!

APRIL 14

Why does God allow bad things to happen to good people? Whether it is the needless tragedy of a child dying, or the pain of seeing a loved one suffer, or senseless killings by a deranged person, we wonder WHY. Whether it's the evil of a tyrant or death for refusal to believe in Allah, we are led to ask, *"Why did God allow that?"*

The cynic or unbeliever phases it differently, *"IF there is a God, why did he allow that?"* But even the most dedicated Christian will ask, *"Why, God, why?"*

There are few words to describe the pain that is behind those words. We are numb or in shock or in denial. *"No, no! It can't be?"* Yet we know it is real.

The question of why goes back thousands of years to Job, David and Jesus Himself. Events of the past century, the Holocaust, pogroms, genocides, drug wars, famines and ISIS slaughters, all may move us to ask why. If God is good, why doesn't He put a stop to all this?

But Jesus told us this would happen. In John 16:33, He said, **"In the world you will have tribulation."** If He had stopped there, this would not be Good News. But He also said, **"But take heart; I have overcome the world."**

This much is sure: we cannot fully know the mind of God or give a clear answer to why God allows suffering. We cannot see with God's eyes. St. Paul said, **"Now all we can see of God is like a cloudy picture in a mirror. Later we will see Him face to face. We don't know everything now, but then we will, just as God completely understands us."** (1 Corinthians 13:12, Contemporary English Version)

When we ask about specific events and want to know why certain things happen, we may not find the answer in the Bible, and we won't get an answer from the world. Now things are hard to understand, but someday we will see clearly. We cannot figure everything out from our perspective, but one day in eternity we will know, because He will tell us. We have His promise on it.

In heaven it will be good to have our questions answered.

APRIL 15

On "Tax Day," April 15, 2013, another senseless bombing occurred, this time at the Boston Marathon. Two homemade bombs by two self-made terrorists exploded two blocks apart, killed three and wounded 260. Besides damage to buildings and people, those bombs tore apart a little of the American soul. One perpetrator was killed and the other received a life sentence for mass murder.

I wish this kind of tragedy would be rare among us, but such vile, senseless events will probably increase. The message for today may not be what we'd like to hear, but it is a somber reality we need to face.

Once I said in a sermon, *"The worst is not behind us – it is yet to come."* It seems our world is speeding towards a crash that we are unable to stop. All this may be part of something of which the Bible has spoken called, *"Satan's Little Season."* It is a time of the rapid spread of evil in the world as the calendar speeds ever closer to Judgment Day.

Even as the Christian Church is gaining more members worldwide, the Evil One is tempting others to reject the God of the Bible. In the future we will undoubtedly see more cultural clashes and senseless disasters. We can only pray God will keep His people faithful to Jesus Christ in the coming years.

I once asked people if they appreciated having the Bible in many electronic forms and they responded affirmatively. They said how wonderful it was to have the Bible so close at hand as they worked and traveled.

I, too, give thanks to God that we have His Word in so many forms and so easily accessible at all times. I pray we will read and hear His Word and believe its message that Jesus is God's Son and our Savior. The Bible is the most important "App" we can have, because its message is life-changing and eternal. May God have mercy on us as we move into a very uncertain future.

"In all your ways, acknowledge Him, and He will make straight your paths." (Proverbs 3:6)

APRIL 16

America has a fine air travel system. Despite security clearances, cramped seats, extra fees and delays, these are nothing compared to the blessing of being able to board an aircraft and two hours later have travelled 1,000 miles in relative comfort. A century ago this would have taken 4 days by train or 2 months by covered wagon.

The day after a September flight I encountered an unexpected problem. Someone had "hacked" my credit card and run up some charges. But that was minor also. A quick call to Visa cancelled our account and a pair of new cards was delivered to our door the next day. A few hours on the phone and computer put the new card number into needed accounts - so simple! When it comes to our Visa, we *"Don't Leave Home Without It!"* All of us carry important items with us wherever we go.

How about our faith in Jesus? Do we have that with us? What about our hope for the future? That flight had taken me to a Men's Retreat in Wisconsin on the theme, *"A Hope and A Future in Christ,"* based on Jeremiah 29:11-14. Jeremiah prophesied at a time when the people of Judah were in exile in Babylon and his message to them was rather amazing:

"Settle down in your new land, build homes, plant crops, marry the locals and raise families, because God will bless you there. Don't listen to the complainers, but build and prosper in the land of your exile. And if you are faithful to God, after seventy years He will bring you home again." (Jeremiah 29:5-10, abbreviated paraphrase) Jeremiah told them, *"This is your new home, so make the best of it!"*

It's easy to grumble when things don't go our way, but it's better to trust God and follow Him faithfully. Jeremiah then told them: **"For I know the plans I have for you,"** declares the Lord, **"plans to prosper you and not to harm you, plans to give you hope and a future."** (Jer. 29:11). Those comforting words have been a blessing for all who trust the God of our salvation and His Son Jesus Christ.

Trust in Jesus – "Don't Leave Home Without Him!"

APRIL 17

All around the world, Christians today are under fire. To be a follower of Jesus is not easy, and while we know Satan is behind it all, most of his "front men" today seem to belong to a specific group that has been against Christianity from the day it came into existence.

I am speaking of the religion of Islam, and as you read this, Islamic militants are bringing death all over the world. In a recent newscast, a commentator said, *"Islamists seem to want to take us back to the 7th Century with a war against the infidel."* A little history can help us understand this.

In 610 AD, Mohammed had a vision and from it came the Koran which was the basis of a new religion he named Islam. Mohammed died in 623, but his followers rapidly took a militant stance that they must conquer the world for their deity, Allah, moon god of the ancient Babylonians.

Muslims quickly engaged armies and conquered surrounding nations. In just one hundred years, Muslims conquered most of the African rim of the Mediterranean Sea and the Arab nations to the Middle East including ancient Israel which they seized from their arch-enemy, Christians. Their motto was, *"Spread the word by the sword."*

In the 11th Century, the first Crusade was called to regain Israel from the Muslims. Other Crusades followed, each one seeking to liberate Christian lands which Muslims had taken. During the Middle Ages, Islam mellowed, but it still fought some battles until the 20th Century when "Holy Wars" were renewed against Christians.

These days it is considered wrong by many to speak in such general terms about Islam. But we must face the truth and realize there are millions of Islamic militants who want the destruction of America and Israel, as well as bringing Sharia Law everywhere. Corrie ten Boom once said, *"To win a battle, we must know who the enemy is."*

We pray God will protect us from our enemies, and we also pray Muslims will come to know the truth of Jesus.

Only in Jesus can the Truth set people free.

APRIL 18

On April 18, 1942, the United States staged an air raid on Tokyo. Sixteen B-25 bombers were launched from the USS Hornet aircraft carrier, targeting Japan. The raid was planned and commanded by Lt. Col. James Doolittle. All the aircraft were lost, yet all but three crewmen survived. The raid caused little damage, but it helped raise American morale and cast doubt on Japan's defenses.

Lt. Col. Doolittle had his doubts. He later wrote of his crash landing, *"My crew chief Paul Leonard and I went to the crash site to see what we could salvage... I sat down beside a wing and looked around at the thousands of pieces of shattered metal that had once been a beautiful airplane and felt lower than a frog's posterior. This was my first combat mission and I was sure it was my last. As far as I was concerned, it was a failure.*

"Paul tried to cheer me up. He asked, 'What do you think will happen when you go home, Colonel?' I answered, 'Well, they'll court-martial me and send me to prison at Fort Leavenworth.' Paul said, 'No, Sir. They're going to make you a general... And they're going to give you the Medal of Honor.' I smiled and he made a final effort. 'Colonel, I know they're going to give you another airplane and when they do, I'd like to fly with you as your crew chief.' Tears came to my eyes because it was the supreme compliment that a mechanic could give a pilot."

Leonard's predictions proved right. Doolittle's crew all received medals, and Doolittle was promoted to General, later receiving the Medal of Honor. Leonard, however, was killed in Africa in 1943. Doolittle lived to be 97 years old.

What we see is not always what it seems. Doolittle's raid seemed a failure to him, but it wasn't. He was sure he'd be punished, but he became a national hero. He wasn't even sure he'd survive the war, yet he lived a long life.

God has plans for each of us that we cannot see. He knows what we will do and how it will impact others around us. This is why He allows such a variety of events in our lives, because He knows how it will bless others.

How can you be a blessing to others today?

APRIL 19

Who are our real enemies? Yesterday's devotion spoke of a battle against an enemy in a great war of the last century. The devotion before that was about a current war with enemies who adhere to an ideology has been at war with Christianity for 1,400 years.

Who are our real enemies today, in this time of seeming peace and prosperity? It all depends on how we identify them. Who is it we battle with today, and how is the battle fought? Corrie ten Boom said *"To win a battle, we must know who the enemy is."* Who is it that is doing battle with us?

Our enemies today are not all seen. There is an enemy called Poverty that harms our society, and an enemy called Crime that makes our neighborhoods and schools unsafe. There is an enemy called Fear that keeps us up at night, and an enemy called Disease that harms our bodies and our homes. There is an enemy called Ignorance that creates suspicion and trouble, and one called Pride that makes us feel superior to others.

The real enemy, though, the Evil One who is behind all these, is Satan and he is at war with God and the people of God. Satan is the Arch Enemy who creates trouble all over the world and turns people against each other.

Jesus tells us to do something difficult. **"You have heard that it was said, 'You shall love your neighbor and hate your enemy.' But I say to you, Love your enemies and pray for those who persecute you, so that you may be sons of your Father who is in heaven. For He makes His sun rise on the evil and on the good, and sends rain on the just and on the unjust."** (Matthew 5:43-45)

How can we love our enemies? How is this possible when they want to kill us? Loving our enemies begins with prayer which will bring us a changed attitude. If we only hate as the enemy hates, both of us will be destroyed. But if we pray for our enemies, God can bring about changes of heart which will keep us from destruction.

Lord, help us show love to those who hate us.

APRIL 20

Do you have siblings? Perhaps a brother or sister, natural or adopted, who is living or with the Lord? My father had 8 brothers and sisters and my mother had seven. There were five in my family, four brothers and one sister, and three of my brothers are with the Lord now.

For nearly twenty years my wife and I hosted Singles Conferences and one of the songs the single men and women came to enjoy was called, *"Brothers and Sisters in Christ"* by Terry K. Dittmer. Verse two contains these words:

> *"Man walked alone and in need*
> *Without faith, hope or promise or creed;*
> *Wandering, aimlessly lost,*
> *Unaware of the staggering cost;*
> *That God in His mercy would save*
> *All His people from death and the grave.*
> *And assembled as one in the name of the Son,*
> *Lifting hearts, lifting hands, celebrating as friends,*
> *And proclaiming the Lord, all our praises afford.*
> *We are brothers and sisters in Christ."* (© T.K. Dittmer)

Men and women may not be married, but they still wish to be part of a family. That makes family important, whether it is biological or not. Most single people enjoy gathering, and not just to find someone to marry either. They seek the blessings of friendship, companionship and people they can trust and enjoy.

The Christian Church can provide some of those needed friendships. Whether it is through church worship, social events or work projects, God gives people the blessing of being with "brothers and sisters in Christ." This is also true of couples who find friends with other Christians.

Psalm 133:1 reminds us of this: **"Behold, how good and pleasant it is when brothers dwell in unity!"** With God's help and prayer, people can find good friends when they need more "brothers and sisters in Christ."

There's no need to walk alone in this life.

APRIL 21

On April 21, 1926, a girl child was born in a grand house in London. Princess Elizabeth Alexandra Mary was the first daughter of Albert, Prince of York, who later became George VI, King of England. Elizabeth was crowned Queen in 1952 after the death of her father. She is the oldest and also the longest reigning monarch today.

Elizabeth II is Queen of sixteen independent states known as the Commonwealth realms. She married Prince Philip, Duke of Edinburgh, in 1947 before becoming the Queen, and they had four children. She is honored and revered by people all over the world and today reigns over 130 million subjects in those countries.

Queen Elizabeth II reigns, but she does not rule. To "reign" means she holds a high office in a nation and is honored by those who live there. To "rule" means to have authority and control. Queen Elizabeth II does not rule England. The last English Monarch to both rule and reign over her people was her namesake, Queen Elizabeth I, who lived 1533-1603 and ruled England 45 years.

Over two thousand years before this, a boy child was born in a lowly stable of Bethlehem to a young woman named Mary. Her husband Joseph was not the father of the child, but he raised the child in obedience to God. The child grew up in Nazareth with the Hebrew name Yeshua, later known as Jesus. After his innocent death on a Roman cross, He was resurrected to life and crowned King of kings, ruling over all people of the world for all the ages.

Despite being Queen, Elizabeth II is subject to Jesus by virtue of her sinful humanity and her faith in Him. Jesus was born of His mother by power of the Holy Spirit, and He had brothers named James and Jude, and also sisters. Jesus rules over all, and His kingship will never end.

Jesus is King of kings and Lord of lords. His kingdom is eternal in the heavens and temporal in the hearts of people. We honor Jesus and worship Him as the Son of God.

"And He shall reign forever and ever." (Revelation 11:15)

APRIL 22

Can you remember your first job that earned your first paycheck? I was fifteen years old and worked 4 hours, stacking bales on the wagon behind a baler for a neighbor. He gave me a check for $6.00 - $1.50 an hour, good money for a boy in 1960. I don't recall how I spent it, but I did work for him a few more times, usually for the same wage. That was the best pay I received as a youth.

In Matthew 20, Jesus told a story about a vineyard owner who hired men to work in his vineyard for a denarius a day. The workers all agreed to work and get paid that amount. At noon, the owner hired a few more workers at the same wage, and an hour before closing he hired a few more, again at the same wage. When it came time to be paid, everyone was paid the same. This angered those who'd worked longer and felt they should get more.

The point of the story is about what God the Father gives to those who believe in Jesus. All who trust Him are promised the same eternal life, whether they follow Jesus all their days or just one day. Eternal life in Jesus doesn't come on a graded scale. All believers receive the same gift from God, because all have been promised it. We can be assured the gift is just as sweet for the lifetime believer as it is for the last-minute one.

Such a deal doesn't set well with our human nature. We may feel we deserve more if we have believed longer. But the gift is perfect for everyone, no matter how long they are in God's workforce of faith.

Our sinful nature wants more. It prods us to think the lifetime believer is worth more than the "Johnny-come-lately." But we are all equally in need of Jesus, and He will give eternal life equally to all who trust Him in faith.

Pride may whisper to us that we are worth more, but humility says, *"You need the same Jesus, for the same reason as everyone."* Life with Jesus is a gift. We don't earn it – but He gives it to us anyway.

Thank You, Jesus, for giving us heaven, despite our sins.

APRIL 23

Lisa Beamer, whose husband Todd Beamer died on United Flight 87 over Pennsylvania on 9/11/01, appeared on the "Good Morning America" show and told this story:

"I had a very special teacher in high school many years ago whose husband died suddenly of a heart attack. About a week after his death, she shared some of her insight with a classroom of students. As the late afternoon sunlight came streaming in through the classroom windows and the class was nearly over, she moved things aside on the edge of her desk and sat down there.

"With a gentle look of reflection on her face, she paused and said, 'Class is over, but I would like to share with all of you, a thought unrelated to class, but which I feel is very important. Each of us is put here on earth to learn, share, love, appreciate and give of ourselves. None of us knows when this fantastic experience will end. It can be taken away at any moment. Perhaps this is God's way of telling us that we must make the most out of every single day.' Her eyes began to water, but she went on. 'So I would like you all to make me a promise. From now on, on your way to school, or on your way home, find something beautiful to notice.

'It doesn't have to be something you see, it could be a scent, perhaps of freshly baked bread wafting out of someone's house, or it could be the sound of the breeze slightly rustling the leaves in the trees, or the way the morning light catches one autumn leaf as it falls gently to the ground. Please look for these things, and cherish them. For, although it may sound trite to some, these things are the stuff of life. They are the little things we are put here on earth to enjoy, the things we often take for granted'."

Memories of my childhood home are still vivid: The smell of Mom's fresh bread, the gold autumn leaves in the grove, crisp, blue sky over snowy winter trees, or the black and white framed photo of Mom and Dad in front of their house that hangs on my wall. It's the "stuff of life."

So are the many hours in church pews hearing the eternal truth of God's Word with its promise of eternal life in Jesus. That we can never take for granted.

"The earth is the Lord's and all that is in it." (Psalm 24:1)

APRIL 24

It's been said that the biggest lies come when the truth is slightly twisted to suit our own purpose. This is the case with some stories found on the internet.

One widespread story has a lady and her husband in plain clothing visiting Harvard and kept waiting by the President's secretary. They are finally seen by a snobbish man who rebuffs the idea of a memorial for their son who'd spent a year at Harvard, but tragically had died. The story ends with their telling the President they'll build their own university. That couple is Mr. and Mrs. Leland Stanford.

The real story is very different. It is true Leland and Jane Stanford lost their only son while traveling in Europe, but he was only sixteen and had never attended Harvard. On their return home they did visit the president of Harvard and also the presidents of Cornell, MIT and Johns Hopkins, all to seek advice on establishing a museum, university, or other memorial in honor of their son. It was suggested they begin with an endowment of at least $5 million, and the Stanfords agreed they could do that. They returned to California, purchased 900 acres near Palo Alto, and built Stanford University and Museum.

But they were not dressed in homespun, nor were they victims of snobbery. At that time Leland Stanford had already been Governor of California and was a wealthy railroad magnate. He and his wife were recognized wherever they went. That's the real story, but it isn't the one you will find rolling around the Internet.

In our age of instant communication we must not alter the truth to fit our own needs. It is always better to speak *"the truth, the whole truth, and nothing but the truth."*

The leaders of Jesus' day bent the rules to serve their own purposes, but He never did. He fulfilled the truth of God's Word in His mission to be Savior of the world, and He gave us words that will be associated with Him forever:

"The Truth will set you free." (John 8:32)

APRIL 25

Do you remember your first car? Do you remember how much it cost, its shape, model or color? I was thinking of this recently, and it led me to recall all the cars I've owned in my years of driving. Twenty-one cars may seem like a lot, but nearly all of them were used and didn't last long.

Recently there was a television series called "Strange Inheritance" in which each show told of the amazing things people have left to their heirs. One episode told of a wealthy man's collection of 3,000 cars, most of which were unique and valuable. Estimates were that this collection was worth over one hundred million dollars.

But the collector had requested in his will that the collection not be broken up or sold off piecemeal. So what could his heirs do with them? Even if you are wealthy, what do you do with 3,000 valuable cars? How could you care for them or even store them?

Over the years I have been asked by well-meaning people to do things after their death that I've not been able to fulfill. I have also helped a few people deal with a final request that has placed them in difficult situation. In nearly every case I have urged them to do what was best for them, not only for the deceased person.

It is best that people not place their heirs in a quandary after they are gone. The request of a dying person may seem a sacred thing, but if a certain special request presents major problems to the heirs, they should fulfill it only if they are able, or it is legally required, or in the best interests of all. Not all requests need to be fulfilled.

Jesus invited a man to follow Him, but he said, **"Let me first go and bury my father." Jesus responded, "Follow me and let the dead bury their dead."** (Matthew 8:22) Following Jesus is more important than following the wishes of someone who has died. When possible, honor your loved one's wish, but only when it does not endanger something more important.

What is the best way to honor those who have gone before us?

APRIL 26

In High School I tried competing in various sports, but my heart was not in athletics. Band and chorus were enjoyable, but I didn't care for competitive sports. It wasn't that I couldn't do the work, but sports seemed a waste of time and energy. Mostly I didn't like the workouts. I tried several sports - golf, basketball, track and cross country - but did poorly at each.

In my sophomore year a friend convinced me to run in Cross Country, and I found I disliked that sport most of all. Distance running hurt my feet, muscles, and lungs. It was monotonous and it was all I could do just to complete that season. One year of that was enough.

But one memory of a workout stays with me, the day I put on a pair of new red running shoes. They were light, fit perfectly and felt good. I felt proud having them. Those new shoes made me want to run fast and hard, and that day during practice I outdistanced everyone in the workouts. I felt so good my breathing didn't even hurt. Afterwards, our coach complimented me and asked why I had this sudden change. I said it must have been my shoes, but he just shook his head and told me to do it again.

But that was my only good day in Cross Country. It never happened again. The next practice it was back to the pain and drudgery. I wore the same shoes, but they were no longer new and now my feet hurt in them.

We cannot live every day feeling great. Most days are not spent on the mountaintop but in the valley or on the plain. Even our faith can be this way, one day flying high, and the next down low. The wear and tear of life or our limitations and sins will make our faith seem weary.

That's why every day we need to hear the newness of God's grace. Every day we need His strength. **"They who wait for the Lord shall renew their strength; they shall mount up with wings like eagles; they shall run and not be weary; they shall walk and not faint."** (Isaiah 40:31)

Will you run somewhere, for some reason, today?

APRIL 27

A few years ago I was going through a box of old things and came across a small wood and metal trophy. Seeing it brought back a pleasant memory long forgotten. It was a trophy for placing second in a collegiate pole vault.

(Now after yesterday's devotion about my dislike for competing in sports, you might wonder how I ever got a trophy for athletics in college. But sometimes you win a prize you don't really deserve. This was one of those times.)

In my first year at Concordia College, St. Paul, Minnesota, I gave in to a friend's urging and joined the track team. Actually, I went to only half the practices and not all the track meets, preferring to earn money as a dishwasher. One of my "kitchen scullery" friends was also on the track team and often scolded me for not coming to practice. Dave was a dedicated quarter-miler, one of the most difficult races because it is a long, hard sprint, a real gut-buster. He rarely missed practice and worked really hard.

One Saturday on the team bus to a track meet with several other small colleges, our coach stood up and asked, *"Can anyone here pole vault eight and a half feet?"* Not every track meet had pole vaulting, but he said they'd have it at this meet. *"Let me know if you could do it,"* he said, *"because there are only two other competitors for three places, so we'd earn a point if he could clear the minimum height."*

So I volunteered! I'd vaulted my junior year in high school and figured I could try. Wonder of wonders, I did clear the minimum height of eight feet six inches and came home with a second place trophy! My friend Dave who'd sweated in practice day after day, came in fourth and got a green ribbon for competition. He looked at my trophy and just shook his head. I agreed with him – I didn't deserve it!

But that's how it is with all Christians. None of us deserve heaven. Not a single one of us is good enough to get to there. Heaven is a gift Jesus has earned for us. **"It is a gift of God, not of works, lest we should boast."** (Ephesians 2:9)

Do you have any trophies? Remember how you earned them?

APRIL 28

"*God gave you a good voice, so you'd better use it!*" she said. Mrs. Owen was a farmwife and talented pianist who was driving a grumpy, sullen teenager to a farm meeting where she would accompany the song I was to sing as entertainment. I had been grumbling about going, but she put me in my place. "*God gave you a good voice, so you'd better use it!*" I never forgot those words.

Over the years her stern warning has reminded me to use what I've been given. It's not that I ever disliked singing. I agree with Martin Luther who said, "*Next to the Gospel, music is God's greatest gift.*" But sometimes we grumble about things we must do, even if they are enjoyable and helpful. Even a beloved hobby can become work if there is a deadline to meet or a task that's difficult due to its nature or our own limitations.

Jesus once told His disciples a parable about a wealthy man who gave three of his workers each a large sum of money. They were to use what he had given them and report back to him later. Two of them increased their talents and were praised for it, but the third did nothing with his talent and was reprimanded. Jesus' point was if God gives us something valuable, we should take care of it, but also use it for the good of others.

What "talent" have you been given that can be enjoyable and helpful? A pleasant personality? A strong body? Cheerful attitude? Working skills? Management? Teaching? Music? God has given each of us some talents and abilities we can use for our good and for others.

Years later, after the funeral of an uncle, I spoke with Mrs. Owen and asked if she recalled telling me what she did. Her answer was typical of a Christian servant. "*I don't remember, but then I said that to a lot of people.*" She had made it her task to remind others to use their gifts. I think I made her glad that at least one person had taken her words to heart.

How can you use your gift today?

APRIL 29

We hear a lot these days about "climate change" and "greenhouse gases," usually accompanied by warnings that humans are dangerously polluting the earth. Most of this is based on emotion, not fact. Facts can help us better understand the marvelous atmosphere we have.

Our atmosphere is a mixture of nitrogen (78%), oxygen (21%), and other gases (1% which includes carbon dioxide) that surrounds Earth. High above the earth and held in place by gravity, the atmosphere is more than just the air we breathe. It's also: 1) a buffer that keeps us from being peppered by meteorites, 2) a screen against deadly radiation, and, 3) the reason we have radio waves on earth.

It is divided into five layers. Most of the weather and clouds are in the first layer, the Troposphere, about 11 miles thick. Above this is the Stratosphere, about 30 miles thick. Then comes the Mesosphere for a distance of 50 miles, and then the Ionosphere goes up another 400 miles. The International Space Station and many satellites are in the Ionosphere, as well as the Northern and Southern Lights.

Lastly comes the Exosphere which dissipates into the airless outer space. Despite its severely cold temps (as low as -180 F), our atmosphere burns up incoming meteors and keeps the earth from looking like our crater-marked moon.

Scientists have detected no other atmospheres in the universe like ours. Without an atmosphere, earth could not sustain life. Ozone in the stratosphere screens out harmful ultraviolet light. Only down here in the Troposphere can life exist. Here the weather affects temperatures, rainfall, plant and animal growth and makes life pleasant.

It is a blessing we have the air we breathe, so we should treat it responsibly. God's creation continually re-circulates the air, removing pollutants and making breathing safe. When mankind took its first breath, God had everything in place to benefit our lives.

"God breathed into his nostrils the breath of life, and the man became a living creature." (Genesis 2:7)

APRIL 30

In 1977, the *Voyager I* spacecraft was launched on its way to the edge of our solar system and beyond. In 1990, almost four billion miles from earth and at the very edge of our solar system, scientists turned its camera around and took pictures that revealed the earth as a tiny blue speck among the innumerable heavenly bodies.

This photo became the basis for Carl Sagan's book, Pale Blue Dot. In it, his atheist view becomes evident as he describes how earth and mankind are specks in the cosmos. Despite its beauty and people, he said earth is insignificant.

But this "pale blue dot" is unlike all other bodies. It exists in a "Goldilocks zone," a place not too hot, not too cold, but "just right." It is not too far and not too close from other heavenly bodies, and its gravity, moon, atmosphere, magnetic field and molten center are all "just right." Because of this perfect placement among the planets, earth can support complex human life, something absolutely unique.

No other planet in our solar system is so well situated to its "home star" as the earth is to the sun. No other planet has life such as we have it here, with seven billion people living, working, learning and growing. No other heavenly body has people who write, sing, laugh, love, invent or introspectively think such as we humans do.

Most importantly, no other life forms have an Almighty God who cares for them as we do. At this time there is no proof that any other life forms are even possible, because no other planets are known to exist in a "Goldilocks zone." God has put us here, created life and sustained us. **"When I look at Your heavens, the work of Your fingers, the moon and the stars, which You have set in place, what is man that You are mindful of him?"** (Psalm 8:3-5)

The next time there's a clear night, look up at the moon and stars and wonder at God's creation. Then praise Him that He crowned you with glory through the mercies of His Son Jesus Christ.

Lord, thank You for caring for us, despite our doubts! Amen!

DAY BY DAY WITH JESUS
in
May

+ + +

MAY 1

How many store clerks do you think you have seen in your lifetime? How many of them have you talked to? Smiled at? Called by name? During a college course a sociology professor gave a pop quiz. It was not difficult and students breezed through the questions until the last one: *"What is the first name of the person who cleans your dormitory?"* What kind of question is that for a college quiz?

Students could visualize the guy pushing the big dust mop down the hallways or emptying trash. He was a tall, dark-haired student, but nobody called him by name because they were busy going here or there. Sometimes they spoke to him, usually to say something needed cleaning, then just kept walking. But nobody called him by name. He was just a guy with a campus job, like the dozens of others who had jobs to earn extra money to pay for college. Why should they know his name?

I wrote down the guy's name on the line and as I handed in my paper, I asked if the last question would count toward our quiz grade. *"Absolutely,"* said the professor. *"In your careers, you will meet many people serving you, in stores and businesses. All of them are significant. They deserve your attention even if all you do is smile and say 'Hello'."* I never forgot what the professor said because I knew the guy who cleaned our dorm. It was me.

Everyone needs recognition. We've all been given a name in our Baptism, and God knows who we are every moment. He cares about us, what we do, where we go, and who we are, because He loves us and knows our name.

"I have called you by name; you are Mine." (Isaiah 43:1)

MAY 2

What's more important - theology or practice? A man once asked me to give a sermon at a non-denominational chapel and advised me to be practical, not theological. *"People don't want theology,"* he said, especially not baptism or communion. *"Stick to the practical - God, love, Jesus, faith."* After our discussion I decided to decline his invitation.

That man was not giving people much credit. Theology is the "science of God" and most people want to know more about Him than just a thin layer of words. They want to learn more about God and that involves theology. A farmer once said he experienced more of God on a July day in a cornfield than he did in a Bible Class. It's true that God's presence can be felt in nature. But that farmer knows more about farming than just how a nice cornfield makes him feel. He must or he won't last in farming.

He may enjoy the feeling of seeing corn grow (practical), but he also knows what it takes to make it happen (theological). Farming is more than just digging in a field. It's all about the land, seed, weather and fertilizer. A good farmer learns all the details about crop rotation, financing, machinery and being a good steward of the soil. Enjoying a nice field is a reward, but it's not farming.

In the same way theology is about the details of God, who He is, what He says and how He does His work. We need to grow in our knowledge of God and learn His Word, His will, and His Commandments. Enjoying God's presence in nature is good, but our feelings are fickle and can change. God's Word does not.

Churches are not always good at giving people all they need. Too many are content to help people feel good when they're at worship and hope they'll return. Giving only the bare essentials of God is treating people like children. It's all frills and no work. Watching the wind blow in a lovely summer field is nice, but it won't pay the bills. **"Make me to know Your ways, O Lord; teach me Your paths."** (Psalm 25:4)

Learning theology is very practical.

MAY 3

One Sunday morning I was reading the paper with a good cup of coffee when Carol asked, *"Are you ready?"* Ready for what, I thought as I turned a page on the Op-Ed section. Then I realized it. Church! I had only five minutes to get ready for church! Good thing I wasn't leading it that day.

Are you ready? Carol and I once attended a presentation on "Preparedness." The speaker asked if we were prepared for a weather crisis, earthquake, terrorist attack or a lengthy stoppage in electricity. Few people are prepared with food and water for even a week or two.

Preparedness is important. We have set up a Family Trust to help those who survive us when we die, so our heirs will not be troubled with legal issues. We get prepared for many things. A young woman completes her residency so she can be ready to be a doctor. Pastors, teachers and other church workers finish college, ready to assume the tasks of fulltime church work. We start getting ready very young. Mom asks, *"Are you ready?"* hoping a child is finally dressed. One day she will ask if the child is ready for life.

Getting ready can be a constant thing. I often work on my sermons weeks ahead of time and have found it a habit hard to break. Some people wait until the last minute with many things. A pastor told me he works better under pressure, preparing at the last minute. He has probably done it for so long that he has become good at it.

Thankfully, our loving God didn't wait until the last minute to prepare His plan of salvation for us. The Bible tells us our salvation was prepared at creation. After Adam and Eve's first sin, God made a plan to correct the evils of Sin. He took time to prepare the world for the Savior.

We know Him as Jesus of Nazareth, **"He was delivered up for our offenses, and raised again for our justification."** (Romans 4:25) In Jesus, God the Father was ready with a plan for our salvation, but are we ready to meet Him? Are we prepared by faith to receive blessings He has for us?

Are you ready?

MAY 4

In 1949, British author George Orwell first published his well-known book, _1984_ which featured a chilling view of life in a futuristic society where everything was regulated by powerful rulers who allowed few freedoms for people in a totally structured world. Although the year 1984 came and went with little fanfare, some of Orwell's prophesies have taken hold, including the power of language to persuade people. People joked about what could happen when 1984 actually arrived that might change the world forever.

On May 4, 1984, my own personal world changed forever. My wife and I had moved to Utah to begin ministry at two small congregations. On a Friday afternoon we were driving to Salt Lake City for a "Welcome to Utah" gathering when we were involved in a one-car rollover in which my wife Sandra was killed. I was only slightly injured but she was ejected from the car and died a few hours later while being transported via Life Flight to Salt Lake City.

Nothing can prepare a person for such an event. Gratefully our sons, ages 10 and 12, were not with us. The next days, weeks and months brought confusion and hurt as well as some bad decisions. I still wonder how we ever got through those days, but by the grace of God we did.

While there were blessings, there were mostly fears of facing life without this fine Christian woman, the wife of my youth and mother of my sons. I learned much from the experience, but I would never wish it on anyone.

I learned that faith in Jesus does not let you down and that God does not give you more than you can handle. I learned the sustaining love of family and friends, and also that I was weaker than I ever thought. I learned that, **"With God, all things are possible."** (Mark 10:27)

A few years later God brought another wonderful woman into our lives. Carol became not only wife, mother and partner, she filled the emptiness created that fateful day in 1984 with her heart and soul.

"Give thanks to the Lord, for He is good. His love never ends."

MAY 5

There are certain phrases of three words people may enjoy hearing. Consider these: *"I love you"* or *"Thanks so much"* or *"Tests are normal"* or *"Can I help?"* Can you think of other three-word phrases that are pleasing to hear?

One that I am considering today is *"Paid in Full."* I just got a statement from my mortgage company that says I have paid off my house. And it only took 31 years! I recall when my father said he had finally paid off his farm loan and I promised myself I wouldn't wait as long as he did for that to happen. But now I am nearly as old as he was when he also saw those wonderful words, *"Paid in Full."*

The ease of gaining credit can bring the burden of debt. What is borrowed must be repaid. If someone lends us money or goods, it is necessary that we repay. Unless, of course, the debt is forgiven. My first wife and I loaned funds to her parents many years ago, but when she died in an auto accident, I forgave them the debt. Other times I've loaned funds knowing they'd probably not be repaid. Such things happen between people we care about.

One thing is certain: we can never repay God for all the things He's given us. The Lord's Prayer says, **"Forgive us our debts, as we also have forgiven our debtors."** (Matthew 6:12 NIV) When we commit sin each day, we are in debt to God. He requires our obedience and when we can not obey, we are in His debt.

Christ's first word from the cross, **"Father, forgive them,"** (Luke 23:34) cancelled that debt. The moment Jesus spoke those words, He cancelled the debts of every man, woman and child who trusts in Him for eternal life.

Because of Jesus, our debt of sin is *"Paid in Full."* It is a wonderful feeling to pay off a large debt, and when someone pays off that debt for us, we are truly "indebted" to Him. Because of Jesus, our debt to God is paid in full. Thus, we praise and thank Him by our words and actions and life.

May you one day hear those words, "Paid in Full."

MAY 6

The Christian faith is given us for the benefit of all people, non-Christians as well as Christians. Nothing illustrates this better than when disaster strikes, such as the tornadoes that hit Grove, Oklahoma, few years ago and many Christians there responded to the catastrophe.

God's people in the area around Grove wanted to help the victims, so they prayed for them and gave them money and other resources. One of my favorite Christian agencies called "Orphan Grain Train" immediately assisted with clothing, fresh water, medicine and mobile kitchens for those who had lost their homes.

Orphan Grain Train began in the 1980s through the efforts of Clayton Andrews of Nebraska who owned a trucking firm. His trucks often came back from their deliveries empty, so he began finding donated things to bring back that would help people, used or new items, things that could be contributed to others in need.

Inspired by Jesus' words to His disciples, **"I will not leave you as orphans, but I will come to you."** (John 14:18), Andrews and other Lutheran Christians founded this highly successful and diverse ministry of procuring and sending used items to people in need.

During the summer I volunteer with others in the sorting and packing of used clothing at Epiphany Lutheran church where Orphan Grain Train is its primary social ministry. Since beginning its branch in 2002, its members have sorted, packed and shipped over a million pounds of used items all over the world, including places in the USA.

As the summer storm season gets underway, we know God will never leave us as orphans. He will bless us and provide the ways and means to help others in their need. As you pray for and help people during a disaster, remember to give thanks for the many ways Christians help each other, including through Orphan Grain Train.

"Whatever you did for one of the least of these brothers and sisters of mine, you did for me." (Matthew 25:40)

MAY 7

The soil and plants of the desert country are far different than in the Midwest. I've planted a cactus garden with two dozen different varieties. Except for one I purchased, all the rest are cuttings from neighbors. At our park in Arizona if a person wants to plant a cactus, he finds one he likes, knocks on the door and asks if he can take a cutting. I've yet to be turned down.

Cactus plants are highly adaptable, living even in cold climates if you cover them in winter. Just stick a cutting into a little soil, water it a bit and it will root down quickly. After that it needs little or no water. The little rain there is enough. The only cactus that will not sprout its own roots is the giant saguaro, which needs a seed to start it from the huge white flowers on top of the "arms." Birds help make this happen.

There are over a thousand varieties of Prickly Pear which grow in most any kind of soil. The saguaro, however, grows wild in only certain kinds of desert soil. They will suddenly appear in the desert as if a line is drawn in the sand, and then they disappear again. These huge plants live for decades and their giant arms can weigh half a ton.

If you get a cactus thorn in your arm, you must remove it right away. Even fine soft cactus thorns must removed or they will go in deeper and cause a rash or infection. Thorns are a protective feature and should not be ignored.

Cactus thorns remind me of sins we commit in life. If we let them remain and don't find a way to stop, they will cause serious problems. Most cactus thorns will implant themselves wherever they can, entrenching themselves into your hand or arm, going deep and not leaving without help.

We must realize our sins and stop them even if they're fun or give pleasure. If we let them continue, they'll injure us and those around us. Jesus will help us stop if we ask Him. He will show us a better way, a life without the sting and infection of sins that shouldn't be there in the first place.

"In all your ways acknowledge Him and He will direct your paths." (Proverbs 3:5)

MAY 8

There is a story of a King in ancient times who wanted to find a worthy man to serve in his court. The King instructed that a huge stone be placed in the middle of a certain well-travelled road. He then ordered a servant to watch and see if anyone would remove the stone.

Many people came by, peasants, merchants and wealthy courtiers, but all walked past the obstacle. Some tried to get others to remove it, and a few complained that the King should keep the roads in better condition. But none did anything to actually remove the stone.

Then a farmer came along carrying a load of vegetables to sell at the market. Upon approaching the boulder, he laid down his burden and tried to move the stone off to the side of the road. After much time and effort, he finally succeeded. As he went to pick up his load of vegetables, he noticed a purse lying in the road where the boulder had been. Opening the purse, he found it contained gold coins and a note saying the gold was a gift for the person who removed the boulder from the roadway.

The King's servant came forward and told the farmer he could have the purse if he came with him to work for the King. From that day on, the man who took time to remove an obstacle served as an official in the King's court.

What do you do when you find an obstacle in the road? Complain? Expect someone else to remove it? Take a different road? Or might you be one of those resourceful people who work to remove it?

An obstacle can be a problem, but it can also be an opportunity. When I my first wife died, I made some mistakes, but I also realized I had to fix them. I chose work outside fulltime ministry for a couple of years, and there I learned a great deal that I could not have known had I chosen to blame someone else or run away. I also met my wife who's still at my side. Most importantly I learned that God is with me in the good times as well as in the bad.

Give thanks unto the Lord, for He is good!

MAY 9

Colorado has the beauty and charm of its mountains, but it also its dangers. One of these is the May snowstorm. About every five years we get one. As I write this on a Saturday night, there is heavy snow blanketing our town.

It should make for lovely scenery or needed moisture, or more ski time for a few, but it also makes for dangerous driving, damaged trees, and electrical outages. This one started on May 9 about supper time and came at us through the night. The rifle-like crack of burdened branches falling to earth, the eerie silence of heavy snow, the whiteness of the night reminds of the dangers of snow. Laden tree branches bow to the earth in homage to the Creator while man tries not to fret over what the storm has yet to bring.

It could be water in the basement, but the sump pump is working well or our newly redecorated basement might suffer yet another bath of destruction. With every lovely forest path or majestic mountain vista there can be a price to pay. When the morrow comes with its sun, we will shovel yet again and assess the damage. We will even be grateful for the snowplow if it covers our driveway again.

We need the moisture and the trees will rebound. But we are also reminded of the power of God's nature and what the Creator allows it to do. **"For as the rain and the snow come down from heaven and do not return there but water the earth, making it, bring forth and sprout, giving seed to the sower and bread to the eater, so shall my word be that goes out from my mouth; it shall not return to me empty, but it shall accomplish that which I purpose, and shall succeed in the thing for which I sent it."** (Isaiah 55:10-11)

In a few hours daylight will come and churches all over the city will decide whether to open their doors or not. We pray for God's mercy on travelers and hope that His Word will accomplish its divine purpose with slightly less disruption then this May snowstorm is giving us.

What blessings can God give in a May snowstorm?

MAY 10
(For Mother's Day from a mother)

Dear Child,

Mother's Day is coming up, and I thought I should tell you what gift I want. This way there's no guilty panic or last minute purchasing of flowers at the closest gas station. So this is what I want, this year and every year after.

I want you to be a decent human being. I want you to be who you are, but don't be an idiot. I want you to work hard at everything you do, because life is too short not to give it everything you've got. I want you to know that you can choose the right thing when the devil offers you his cookies.

I want you to ask for help when you need it, and I want you to help others when they need it. I want you to learn how to cook, do your own laundry, pay your bills and know how to clean a bathroom. When you mess up, and you will more than once, I want you to own it and do your best to fix it. It's the mess-ups that make the victories sweeter.

I want you to travel, because the world is huge and you are an important part of it. I want you to know that even if I may hate what you do, I will never stop loving you. I want you to play nicely with others. I want you to feed your curiosity. I want you to find a way to do what you enjoy, and realize that it might turn out differently than you originally thought.

I want you to respect every human being's right to be who they are. At times I want you to be more interested in someone else than in yourself and help others like you help yourself. I want you to know that you are flawed and yet you are extraordinary. There is no one else like you.

I want you to know that I would lay down my life for you any day of the week. I want you to know you're blessed by our great God who has created you and forgiven you. I want you to know love, even if it means getting hurt. I want you to be good to others and to yourself. You will learn life can be hard, but with God's help you can handle it. Always know that I will love you, no matter what.

    Love, Mom

P.S. And I wouldn't mind getting a card now and then.

MAY 11

One year it was 6:45 AM on the day after Mother's Day, and I was shoveling snow off my driveway. I got to work with the "Colorado Supershovel" I made years ago out of two eighteen inch snow shovels bolted side-by-side. It can push three feet of fluffy snow in one sweep. It's not for the heavy stuff, but it's just right for a morning's fluffy snow on my sloped driveway. I should have patented that thing.

How do they do it, those weather people? They told us this was coming four days ago and their forecast was spot on. It's hard to believe they can be that accurate when the two days leading up to it are sunny and in the seventies.

By 7:45 I had shoveled off the six driveways in our cul de sac. Tire tracks indicate some neighbors have already left for work. We're the oldest folks in the neighborhood now, and it's a way to show them how I get useful exercise. It makes for good neighbors, too.

Late spring snows come to Colorado almost every year. On May 10, 2001, the day after we moved into our home, ten inches of heavy snow split a big cottonwood and dropped half of it onto our roof. Another spring snow knocked the other half onto my neighbor's yard, just missing a window.

This isn't climate change, it's just Colorado. This one probably won't freeze the leaves, as they're just emerging. Some might not make it, but most will.

This snowfall started Sunday morning after Mother's Day church service and lunch with our son. The boys went together on flowers and a huge Mother's Day card for their Mom with pictures and words that brought a lump to her throat. Mine, too. That day I read through the lesson for July 13 when I'll be preaching again. It's from Isaiah 55:10-11:

"As the rain and the snow come down from heaven and do not return but water the earth, making it bring forth and sprout, giving seed to the sower and bread to the eater, so shall my word be that goes out from my mouth."

Great words, but I sure hope the snow is done for today.

MAY 12

(While this story did not happen to me, it could have. It shows the kind of family relationship and attitude on life I admire.)

When I was a kid, every now and then Mom would make breakfast food for dinner. *(note - On the farm, "dinner" was eaten at noon, and "supper" was in the evening. "Lunch" was what we had midway through the afternoon.)* I remember one noon in particular when she made breakfast for Dad when he and I had come in to eat. She placed a plate of eggs, Dad's homemade sausage and some burned toast in front of my Dad. I could smell the toast was burned and wondered if Dad would notice.

Without hesitating, my Dad reached for a couple of slices of burned toast, and asked Mom how her morning was going. I don't remember what she said, but I do remember watching him smear butter and jelly on the black burned homemade bread. He ate every bite on his plate and never made a face nor said a thing about it. Then he took his usual half-hour nap on the sofa while I read.

When we were going back outside, I heard Mom apologize to Dad for burning the toast and he said: *"Burned toast is good for us every now and then. Thanks for dinner."* Later that afternoon I asked Dad if he really liked his toast burned. He stopped working and said, *"Your Mom made that bread herself. She'd already had a hard morning weeding in the garden and was tired. Burned or not, toast is still food. We aren't hungry any more, are we?"*

Life is full of imperfect things and imperfect people. I'm not the best at doing some things. I forget birthdays and anniversaries and am terrible at picking out gifts for people. But I've learned over the years we all have to accept each other's faults and make the best of it.

That's my prayer for you today, to learn to take the good with the bad, the burned with the fresh, and lay them all at the feet of our Lord. He's the One who will help us and make sure burned toast isn't a deal-breaker!

When do you have lunch?

MAY 13

Spring brings new leaves and flowers, and summer feels like it's already begun here in Colorado. I saw a few bees around the flowers and remembered saying back in March that I'd tell you some of the wonders of honey.

Honey is made naturally by bees for their nourishment. The bees collect flower nectar in their mouths where it is mixed with enzymes in their saliva and turned into honey. The bees carry the honey back to the hive, and deposit it into the cells of the hive's walls. It takes 600 bees on two million trips flying 50,000 miles to make one pound of honey. Wow!

Honey has been used since ancient times both as food and medicine, and in some societies it was regarded as sacred. Honey was even used for cosmetic purposes. For a long time its use in cooking was reserved only for the wealthy since it was so expensive.

Honey, properly stored, will last indefinitely. It is still considered an anti-bacterial, anti-viral, anti-fungal substance which helps boost immunity. Research in Israel found honey effective in reducing fever in patients who had a high white blood cell count.

Honey has been used topically as an antiseptic agent for the treatment of ulcers, burns and wounds for centuries. One study in India compared the wound healing effects of honey to a conventional drug treatment among two groups of first-degree burn patients. After one week of treatment with honey, 93% of burns were infection free compared with only 7% receiving the conventional treatment.

The Bible mentions honey sixty times, one of the most recognized times being when God told His people He would give them a Promised Land, a land flowing with milk and honey. Some people compare the United States to the Promised Land today, and it does have some similarities. Our leaders may seem intent on getting rid of God, but they will always have uses for His sweet gift of honey.

Do you have some honey at home?

MAY 14

Do you have a dog? I had one for awhile when the boys were small, but we didn't have time to train him right, and he had some bad habits, so we gave him to a better home. Dogs are often considered man's best friend, but man has to be ready to take care of the dog.

Catherine Moore tells a story about her father that involved the change that came over him when he was old and dementia set in. Her normally kind father began yelling at her, criticizing her every action and even her comments.

He had been a lumberjack in Northwest and had enjoyed being outdoors and pitting his strength against the forces of nature. But the years marched on relentlessly and soon he lost his strength, straining to lift even a light log. He became irritable when someone teased him that he couldn't do something he had done as a younger man.

He had a heart attack and an amazing recovery, but his zest for life was gone. Then Moore read an article describing how depressed patients improved dramatically when they were given responsibility for a dog. She went to a shelter and picked out a lop-eared pointer that was going to die the next day. *"His time is up tomorrow,"* she was told.

Her Dad didn't like the dog at first, but it soon won his affection and feelings he could no longer give to the people in his life. The old man and the old dog became inseparable, walking together, napping together, even watching television together. Their three years of companionship was far better than if either of them had been alone. When her Dad died in his sleep one night, the dog lay down next to the old man's bed and died two days later.

They were both buried the same day. At the service the Pastor spoke on Hebrews 13:2. **"Do not neglect to show hospitality to strangers, for by this some have entertained angels without knowing it."** He concluded, *"We can thank God He sent them both an angel when they needed one."*

Who is your angel?

MAY 15

A young man was on his way to the ship that was to carry him across the English Channel from France to England. From childhood his parents had taught him to submit to God's holy will, and to see God's hand in everything that happened. To remind himself of this, he had the custom of saying in any event, whether good or evil, *"Thanks be to God that this is for my greater good."*

The ship was soon to leave port, so the young man began running to reach it in time. But as he kept his eyes fixed on the ship, he did not see an obstacle on the street. In his haste he stumbled over it and fell to the ground.

The large box he was carrying on his shoulder fell on his leg and broke it badly. His first words were, *"Thanks be to God that this is for my greater good."* Some people who saw the accident and ran to help were astonished at his words.

One said to him, *"How can this accident which has broken your leg be for your greater good?" "God knows,"* the young man said, *"and while I may never know why, He certainly willed it, and that is enough for me. May His blessed will be done."* A few chuckled at this and said he was foolish, but others were amazed and encouraged. Meanwhile, the ship had left port without him, so he was carried back home.

During that night a terrible storm sprang up, common to the English Channel at that time of year. The next day shipwrecks were reported, and among the vessels lost was the one on which the young man was to have sailed. *"Was I not right?"* he said, when he heard of the disaster. *"If I had been on the ship, I would now be at the bottom of the sea. God sent me a broken leg for my greater good."*

It's important to submit our life to God in all things. He knows what is best for each of us and He will never leave us, no matter where or when we live. **"We know that in all things God works for the good of those who love Him, who have been called according to his purpose."** (Romans 8:28 NIV)

Look today for how God will do something good for you.

MAY 16

Dr. Kent Keith focused most of his career on helping people find meaning in Life. In 1968 while a sophomore at Harvard, he wrote "The Paradoxical Commandments." His pithy and positive statements were eventually written into a book of guidelines to help people facing adversity.

His original "Paradoxical Commandments" have circled the globe online in many forms. They have been found on walls and refrigerator doors and quoted in speeches, articles and from pulpits. They have been used by business leaders, military commanders, government officials, university presidents, social workers, teachers, rock stars, parents, coaches, and students.

You can even find them in India. Mother Teresa of Calcutta revised them and had them posted on a wall of her children's home in Calcutta. Here is her version of Kent's "Paradoxical Commandments":

Mother Teresa's "Spiritual Commandments"

1- *People are often unreasonable and self-centered. Forgive them anyway.*
2- *If you are kind, people may accuse you of ulterior motives. Be kind anyway.*
3- *If you are successful, you will win some unfaithful friends and some genuine enemies. Succeed anyway.*
4- *What you spend years creating, others could destroy overnight. Create anyway.*
5- *If you are honest and sincere, people may deceive you. Be honest anyway.*
6- *If you find serenity and happiness, some may be jealous. Be happy anyway.*
7- *The good you do today may be forgotten tomorrow. Do good anyway.*
8- *Give the best you have and it may ever be enough. Give your best anyway.*
9- *In the final analysis, it is between you and God. It was never between you and them anyway.*

St. Paul summarized it best: **"Be kind to one another, tenderhearted, forgiving one another, as God in Christ forgave you."** (Ephesians 4:32)

MAY 17

Some people think the more words you speak, the more important it is and the better they will be understood. Actually the opposite can be true. After Edward Everett delivered his two-hour, 14,000 word oration, Pres. Lincoln spoke the 286 words of his Gettysburg Address in minutes.

It's not how much is said, but what is said, that makes a message important or not. Consider the relative importance of these items:

Einstein's Theory of Relativity	7 words
Pythagorus' Theorem (area of a triangle)	18 words
John 3:16	25 words
The Lord's Prayer	66 words
The Ten Commandments	179 words
The Declaration of Independence	1,300 words
US Constitution with 27 Amendments	7,818 words
US Gov. regulations on the sale of cabbage:	26,911 words

Weddings are interesting events. It is rare that I attend one at which I'm not officiating, but I have attended the weddings of some family or friends. A recent and curious trend has arisen in which couples write their own vows, and the results are often a lot of words but no true vow. Usually they are a long statement of what each hopes their marriage will be. Heartfelt, yes, but not a true vow.

A wedding vow is an *"earnest promise of commitment to live together faithfully in marriage."* Wedding ceremonies may be planned for years, but the marriage often isn't given as much thought. The vows spoken create a new relationship that should give the couple's thoughts and hopes in creation of their new home.

Most first-time marriages have a fairly good chance of success, with two out of three couples remaining married. Communicating honestly and lovingly is essential. Again, it's not how much, but what is promised that counts.

"Submit to each other out of reverence for Christ." (Ephesians 5:21)

MAY 18

It is not easy today to travel to the Democratic Republic of Congo. The DRC is located in south central Africa and has had a stormy history during the past hundred years. Its name has changed, being called Belgian Congo and Zaire before adopting its present name in 1997 when the Congolese civil wars began.

Visitors will be awed by the natural beauty of the Congo River and the Nyungwe Forest, as well as the Ruzizi River which separates Congo from Rwanda. The DRC is rich in natural resources but poor in political stability and providing basic needs for its people. It borders Zambia, Uganda, Tanzania and other African nations. Amazingly, over 80% of its population is Christian. We're grateful God sent us one of our granddaughters from the DRC.

Because of poverty, malnutrition and unemployment, people there often don't know where they will get their next meal. Congolese Christians are moved by their sincere faith that God will provide all their needs. It is said that each time they sit down to eat, they thank God and ask Him to provide their next meal.

This attitude sounds much like the Lord's Prayer in Matthew 6:11, **"Give us this day our daily bread."** The phrase **"this day"** indicates a reliance on God to provide what people will need one day at a time.

Many first century workers were paid one day at a time, so a few days' illness could spell tragedy. **"Daily bread"** could mean bread for the coming day, so the prayer might read, *"Give us today our bread for tomorrow."* It is an urgent prayer for the person who lives from day to day.

What are your needs? Do you worry about having enough for the future, such as retirement? A large majority of people in the world don't have the luxury of thinking about retirement. They just thank God for the needs He provides them from day to day. They don't merely pray the Lord's Prayer, they live it.

Are you grateful that God gives you your daily needs?

MAY 19

In 2006, *USA Today* carried an article that a bundle of 300 "Letters to God" were found floating in the ocean off the coast of New Jersey. The letters were addressed to a pastor who had died in 2004, and how the letters got into the ocean, as well as how they survived being destroyed by the waves, is a mystery only the Lord knows.

An insurance adjuster found the bundle while fishing. The letters were mostly prayer requests from people who had heard that Pastor Brady Cooper of Mt. Calvary Baptist Church would pray for them if they wrote him of their needs. The prayer requests varied from humorous to heartbreaking. Some of them dated back to 1973, so the pastor had been receiving these prayer requests for many years. The bundle also contained personal writings, so it was probably tossed into the sea by an uncaring person.

The journalist who wrote the article gave examples of the requests. One asked God for help with relatives who were abusing drugs or alcohol, another prayed for help with a cheating spouse, and another asked God to send her a husband and father to love her child. The journalist concluded that all of these were *"unanswered prayers."*

But how did he know? God does answer prayer. When we cry out to God, He hears us and supplies our needs. Even if those written prayers were never opened, God knew the desires of their hearts. In Psalm 86:7, David prayed, **"In the day of my trouble, I call upon You, for You answer me."** David was in the middle of a huge crisis when he wrote those words, and he prayed because he knew God would hear and help him. Whether opened or not, God also heard the prayers in those letters the ocean carried along.

It would be interesting and wonderful if we could follow up on some of the prayers to see how God answered them. Only God knows what happened in those cases, but we can be assured that He does listen to us and provide for our many needs.

What are you praying for today?

MAY 20

Several years ago my trusty Mac desktop computer died. I had turned it off the night before, but when I tried starting it up in the morning, I was greeted with what is ominously called, the "blue screen of death." My amazing old computer was broken, but I didn't realize until later just how badly.

I have in the past fixed minor problems on my computer, but this time I was stumped. I finally called my son who told me what was probably wrong, and that I should take it to an Apple Store to hear their verdict. There I got the bad news but also some that was good. The tech said while the computer would no longer work, he was able to retrieve all my files to put on another newer model. I was relieved, since I hadn't backed up my files in several months. I now do that more often.

What bothered me at first was that I couldn't fix the problem. I knew what was wrong, but I had no idea how to make it right. It reminded me of all those newscasters who tell us night after night what is wrong in the world, but few have any solution as to how to make things right.

People face such dilemmas every day. In families, workplaces, schools and churches, things lie there un-fixed because we get fixated on what's wrong, not how to make it right. It doesn't take an expert to know something is wrong. People may quarrel and fight and create problems, but they must spend time fixing the problem.

That's because the real problem is sin, and only God can really fix that. Isaiah the prophet wrote in Isaiah 1:16, **"Cease to do evil, learn to do good."** How easy those words are to say, but how difficult to do! We need God and His mercy. We need Jesus and His wisdom and the power of the Holy Spirit to change ourselves and fix our problems.

Human beings are born with the weakness of sin, and it can only be repaired by the Master of the Universe who desires our welfare in today's world.

Trust in Him and know that you will be okay.

MAY 21

On May 21, 1946, a daring young scientist was carrying out an experiment to learn more about atomic energy. Louis Slotin had done this experiment many times before to determine the "critical mass," the amount of radioactive uranium necessary for a chain reaction to occur and explode. He would push the two portions of enriched Uranium together slowly, then just as the mass became critical, he would push them apart. But always from a safe distance.

But one day something slipped and the two parts of Uranium rolled together. Instantly the room was filled with a dazzling bluish haze. Instead of ducking or running, the young man leaped up into the path of the two portions, keeping them from exploding with his bare hands. He had broken the chain reaction and saved the lives of the other people in the building, but he had also doomed himself. Nine days later, Louis Slotin died in terrible agony from the intense radiation exposure.

Two thousand years ago the Son of the Living God walked directly into the path of sin's deadly forces. He placed Himself between mankind and Satan to save His people, but He was doomed by the deadly power of sin. On the cross of Calvary, Jesus of Nazareth let sin take His life, but He also broke the chain reaction that would destroy mankind. Christ broke the power of sin and set us free. Now we don't have to fear that sin will overpower us. It's been broken for all times by Jesus. Sin separates us from God and each other, but Jesus unites us again with God. In Him, we have eternal life.

Because Christ stepped between us and eternal death and sacrificed Himself, all things are different now. God has given us new definition of normal. It's no longer normal that we should act according to our sinful nature. We can live by the Spirit, not by the flesh. St. Paul said it plainly:

"Those who belong to Jesus Christ have crucified the sinful nature with its passions and desires. If we live by the Spirit, let us keep in step with the Spirit." (Galatians 5:24-25)

MAY 22

Change is something we must learn to live with. We should accept it if it is beyond our control, or else oppose it if its effects are negative. Poet Maya Angelou wisely wrote,

"If you don't like something, change it.
If you can't change it, change your attitude."

In 1997 I began writing regular weekly devotionals I dubbed *WEEKLY MESSAGE*. These e-mails eventually went to over a thousand addresses a week through my internet provider which has been patient and exceptional helpful with my technical questions.

I finally had to make a change, not of internet provider but in how I send out *WEEKLY MESSAGE*. Due to spam laws, I was restricted in how many messages I could send each week. I changed my methods, but then the rules changed again, forcing me to use an E-mail service.

I mentioned to my readers the probability of coming changes and was delighted to receive dozens of requests not to stop writing. Complimentary notes came from all over urging me to continue. I knew I'd been striking a chord with my readers, so I decided to continue *WEEKLY MESSAGE* as long as I could. God willing, it will continue unless there are unavoidable changes to internet laws or to my health.

Our Lord Jesus knew life could not remain the same. After three quite peaceful years with His disciples, He told them it was time for Him to go to Jerusalem. There, He said, **"The Son of Man will be delivered over to the chief priests and scribes, and they will condemn Him to death."** (Matthew 20:18) The disciples urged Him not to do this, but He said change was necessary.

Because Jesus accepted this change, He was able do His Father's will and fulfill the plan of eternal salvation for all who trust in Him. May He also give us the grace to make changes in our lives when it is needed.

"Change and decay in all around I see;
O Thou who changest not, abide with me." (from the hymn)

MAY 23

I enjoy being outside in a light breeze. Not everyone agrees with me on that, especially my wife. I don't like a strong wind, of course, but a breezy day with clean air and a bright sun is nice. This happens often in Colorado and is one of the many reasons we enjoy living there.

The air currents that cause the wind are an element of solar power, a source of renewable energy that is getting a great deal of attention these days. All over America and others parts of the world tall white windmills are sprouting up on the landscape with their blades "whooshing" in the wind and generating electricity for the needs of people. There are thousands of "wind chargers," some even anchored in the ocean off the coast that are churning out energy night and day in the constant ocean breezes.

These turbines are expensive to install and not without problems, but they must produce or governments wouldn't be investing so much in them. They are not the most pleasant things to look at, but they do their task well.

Jesus once compared the Holy Spirit to the wind. He was talking with Nicodemus who had come to Him one night wanting to know more of His teachings. Jesus said, **"The wind blows where it wishes, and you hear its sound, but you do not know where it comes from or where it goes. So it is with everyone who is born of the Spirit."** (John 3:8)

That passage contains a lot of information, some of which we can't fully grasp. It tells us the Holy Spirit is powerful and not always predictable. His power moves through the world and affects people and events as God chooses. The power of the Holy Spirit is greater than we can imagine, and it touches our lives in positive ways.

We state in the Nicene Creed, *"I believe in the Holy Spirit, the Lord and giver of life, who proceeds from the Father and the Son. Who with the Father and the Son is worshipped and glorified, who spoke by the prophets."* The Holy Spirit works to bring us to faith in Jesus. He is the power of God.

The Holy Spirit helps us understand God's Word.

MAY 24

I played my first round of golf when I was 16 years old and joined my high school golf team. I learned a lot that year and actually played fairly well, but I don't think I've really gotten much better. When I tell friends all I ever knew about golf I learned as a teenager, they usually nod and smile. They know my "sub-par" game fairly well.

Golf is good for exercise and relaxation. Walking a couple of hours on nicely kept grass fields can be a pleasure, even if your game isn't "up to par" that day.

But there's something strange about golf terms. "Par" means what you should score for a hole and, but a score under par is better. Yet don't call a golfer's score "sub-par." A "sub-par" performance means he has a score that's over par and he'd rather be under par. But not sub-par. Go figure!

The one score every golfer would like to get is the perfect shot, the hole-in-one. I've never had one but I've come close. I'll be glad to tell you about an eagle I got on a par 4 hole, but I've never gotten a Big One, the elusive hole-in-one. There's something special about attaining the perfect shot. It's like getting a perfect game in bowling, scoring 300, an achievement that helps a person's self-concept. I am fairly sure I will go to my grave with neither.

But there is something far better, infinitely greater than any perfect score in athletics, no matter how well a person may do. That's the prize we receive from Jesus when we trust Him. When He arose from the dead, He scored the biggest prize of all. The resurrection of Jesus is greater than winning the Super Bowl, World Series, Stanley Cup, the Master's, Indy 500, World Cup and any other game of life.

And it's all ours by faith in Him. He's already earned it for us and He gives it to each one of us who trust him as Lord and Savior. When you put it that way, what we win by faith in Jesus is overwhelming and impossible, yet perfectly attainable without doing a thing to earn it. **"In all these things we are more than conquerors."** (Romans 8:37)

Would you run that by me again?

MAY 25

Do you have a "coffee friend?" Many people have such a person they will often meet at home or café, for a time to enjoy a cup of coffee or tea and talk about things. Mark and I usually meet Friday afternoons at a local café in our Colorado town. It's enjoyable to look forward to visiting a friend you enjoy being with.

We talk about our kids or what's happening around town. Or we talk about our work. Mark is an artist who specializes in designing internet websites. He's also an salesman with an array of items he's designed and invented. He and his wife and daughter have been special friends since we moved to Castle Rock in 2001.

God created people to be together. Whether related by blood, marriage, or common interests, people like to be with those of like mind and interest. Proverbs 17:17 says, **"A friend loves at all times and a brother is born for adversity."** God brings friends into our lives who can be as important as family, and for this we are thankful.

Some friends just come to us in church, town or work, but others are sought out. A person who wants a friend may need to work to find one, and once a friendship is there, continue to nourish it. If a person feels lonely, there are churches, clubs, and other groups in which friendships can be found. Internet friendship groups have made this easier as well.

Someone has said a man should consider having three friends: a Paul, a Barnabas and a Timothy. _Paul_ would be someone older who can share his wisdom; _Barnabas_ would be someone our own age with whom we meet on a level field. _Timothy_ is someone younger for us to mentor. This may be different for women, but I think it's similar.

While being Rabbi to His chosen twelve men, Jesus considered them His friends. He told them in John 15:15, **"I have called you friends, for all that I have heard from my Father I have made known to you."**

What a friend we have in Jesus!

MAY 26

When I was a young man, I convinced myself I would not become like so many of the old people I saw, those who didn't take care of themselves, or who complained about their health. I surely would not become as disdainful of change or new things as some elders I knew, especially of changes suggested by those younger.

But I have now changed my tune. I had thought keeping a lean and healthy body was only a matter of habits, but now I also see much of it has to do with one's genetics. How many pills a person takes are more often dictated by aging than of one's body type. And if an aging person can't understand and accept changes, he does not understand life at all. All things change with time - all things except those few that are lasting.

God's plan of salvation has not changed, nor has the importance of His Ten Commandments. They have not, as some believe, become *"Ten Suggestions"* or *"Ten Best Ideas."* God's Ten Commands are eternal and changeless.

Another lesson to be learned is that we all have something wrong with us, so we'd best stop complaining. At first I thought I was the only person with deteriorating hearing or arthritis. Then I began to realize how many my age were having hips or knees replaced. I saw relatively young people have difficulty climbing steps, and realized weakness and disease come at any age. I'm glad now that all I have is poor hearing or a few joint pains. Could be worse!

We all have something wrong with us. No one is without some kind of shortcoming or problem. A neighbor in her mid-eighties still works, walks spryly and looks like she's sixty. But she knows pain and loss of a different kind, for she has lost a son to crime and drugs.

Our Creator and Redeemer God cares for us, and has prepared a better place where there will be no more pain or sorrow. St. Paul wrote, **"My desire is to depart and be with Christ, for that is far better."** (Philippians 1:23)

Life is good here, but it will be far better there.

MAY 27

William Adams was a navigator who lived during the sixteen century (1564-1620) and is believed to be the first Englishman to reach Japan. Soon after his arrival he became a key advisor to Shogun Tokugawa and built western-style ships for him. He assisted the warlord in opening trade with Southeast Asia, Netherlands and England. He died in Japan at age 55 and has been recognized as one of the most influential foreigners in Japan during this period. His life is the subject of James Clavell's novel, <u>Shogun</u>.

During his life in Japan, Adams was presented with two swords and given the honorary rank of Samurai, gifts which showed how much the Japanese revered him. Because he served his foreign king well, he was also accorded greater opportunities for influence among his own people.

Many centuries earlier, another man in a foreign country also had great influence over the king there. Nehemiah was the trusted cupbearer to the Persian King Artaxerxes and a member of his royal court (Nehemiah 1:11). The cupbearer would test wine given the king to protect him from poisoning. This position also made him advisor to the king. Nehemiah's integrity and wisdom made him the king's trusted confidant, paving the way for the reconstruction of the walls of Jerusalem.

Each of us is also given a unique area of influence. Whether among our fellow workers, in our home raising children, or in a church or community organization, we can have a beneficial influence on the lives of others. Like Nehemiah, we are placed there by God for the good of all.

Another influential believer in God was Esther who saved her Jewish people from destruction. Her uncle urged her to use her position to help her people. Her uncle Mordecai once told her, **"Who knows whether you have come to this kingdom for such a time as this?"** (Esther 4:14)

Has the Lord placed someone in your life in a special relationship? How can you influence them positively?

Lord, help me to bless those you've placed in my life.

MAY 28

Pianist Leon Fleischer was the child of poor Jewish immigrants from Eastern Europe. He began playing piano at age four and became a prodigy, learning under a man who traced his piano heritage through noted instructors back to Beethoven. At the age of eight Fleisher made his formal debut in concert and at sixteen performed at Carnegie Hall with the New York Philharmonic. He recorded several acclaimed albums and went on to win prestigious international competitions, playing in the world's finest concert halls.

In 1964 at the age of thirty-seven, Fleisher lost the use of his right hand due to medical condition called *focal dystonia,* but this did not end his career as a pianist. He began performing concerts with pieces composed for the left hand, all the while seeking help to restore the use of his right. Finally, forty years later in 2004, Fleischer was able to play well enough to perform with two hands again.

During the interim, Fleischer did some amazing things. He composed a Concerto for two pianos, one for the left hand and the other for the right, played by Gary Graffman who'd lost the use of his left hand. He also conducted many orchestras around the world with great acclaim. He often said he loved music more than he loved the piano.

What would we do if our dreams were shattered? How would we react? After Joseph was sold into slavery by his brothers, he could have succumbed to self-pity or hatred. Instead, he remained faithful to God. The Bible several times says, **"The Lord was with Joseph"** (Genesis 39:23) and shows his exemplary life of trusting and obeying God.

Fleischer said he loved music more than the piano. Do we love God more than we love our dreams or plans? Joseph could have pitied himself or turned against his family. Instead, he accepted his life and found ways to honor God and serve people, eventually saving his family and the whole Egyptian nation during a famine.

Are you willing to trust God let him direct your life?

MAY 29

Several times I have struggled with my computer, especially the printer. Several times when I needed it most, it sent me an error message and refused to print. More than once I have called a friend for advice and was told to do one of two things: 1) check my cables, and 2) turn the printer off a minute or two and then re-start it.

Sometimes I've tried my own remedy of re-installing the printer driver which is a waste of time. When I finally call my tech friend, she always says the same – check my cables and re-start it. Invariably, it was a loose cable, or it needed to rest and re-set its electronics. Like Occam's Razor says, *"When confronted with several solutions to a problem, the simplest is usually the correct one."*

I have had computers since 1987, and they've always been Apple products. Once I bought a used PC laptop and tried learning to operate it. After four or five frustrating months, I sold it at a garage sale. Years ago I began keeping a file of computer solutions. Whenever I fixed a certain problem, I wrote the problem and solution in a file and stored it. That file has often come in handy, because I easily forget and problems re-occur.

In some ways that file is like the Ten Commandments. When I was young I knew the general ideas but often I forgot the specifics, so I would read them and Luther's explanations once again. I also memorized them for easier remembering. It is always wise and good to read the Bible, so I can recall how God helps us in our needs. **"God Word is a lamp for my feet and light to guide me."** (Psalm 119:105)

Our world today is getting more and more complex. People create odd and questionable behaviors that make us shake our heads and wonder how to deal with them. Gay marriage, elective abortion and recreational drug use are only a few. For these we should pray and seek God's help. William of Occam would agree!

Lord, show me how I should deal with these problems.

MAY 30

Aren't you always amazed at what people consider important? November 11, 2011, was important for some because, *"11-11-11 will not come again for a thousand years."* Or, August 9, 2010 was considered very important. People said, *"08-09-10 will be the last time you'll see what date."*

But every day is the last time we'll see that date. There will never be another date with the month, day and year that it is today. Every day is unique in that regard.

But I still think you should mark your calendar for November 18, 2052. That is the next time you will be able to see the celestial convergence of Venus, Jupiter and our moon. Or will you be able to see it? Maybe it will be cloudy, or maybe you will forget about it until the next morning. Or maybe you won't see it because you won't live that long!

If the sky is clear on that date, you will be able to see these solar neighbors gather together in a tiny area of the sky and sparkle more brightly than any single star you've ever seen. And if you are alive on that date, try to remember that I reminded you about it.

The predictability of celestial events is amazing. They say Halley's Comet will return on July 28, 2061. How do "they" know this? Because God has given the universe a set of laws that make predictions accurate. Astronomers also say that the universe is not static, and that some of its movements are erratic. Even the earth and moon don't move evenly. Both "wobble" a little in their celestial orbits.

God's laws have governed our universe since its creation, and they continue to do so with amazing predictability. God loves order, both in His universe and also among His people. He gives us life in moments and days and He has ordered the earth's seasons to give us food. Most importantly, He has given us the promise of salvation through Jesus, a plan that will not wobble or change. **"Jesus Christ is the same yesterday, today and forever."** (Hebrews 13:8)

Wouldn't it be nice sometimes if life was that orderly?

MAY 31

(Good oratory is hard to find these days, but during my life one president was probably the best, Pres. Ronald Reagan. A trained speaker from his acting days, Reagan became a wordsmith of phrases. This speech was given on Memorial Day, 1982, at Arlington National Cemetery. Regardless of your political affiliation, I am sure you will find it an example of thoughts well spoken.)

+ + +

"Once each May, amid the quiet hills and rolling lanes and breeze-brushed trees of Arlington National Cemetery, far above the majestic Potomac and the monuments and memorials of our Nation's Capital just beyond, the graves of America's military dead are decorated with the beautiful flag that in life these brave souls followed and loved. This scene is repeated across our land and around the world, wherever our defenders rest. Let us hold it our sacred duty and our inestimable privilege on this day to decorate these graves ourselves -- with a fervent prayer and a pledge of true allegiance to the cause of liberty, peace, and country for which America's own have ever served and sacrificed.

"Our pledge and our prayer this day are those of free men and free women who know that all we hold dear must constantly be built up, fostered, revered and guarded vigilantly from those in every age who seek its destruction. We know, as have our Nation's defenders down through the years, that there can never be peace without its essential elements of liberty, justice and independence. Those true and only building blocks of peace were the lone and lasting cause and hope and prayer that lighted the way of those whom we honor and remember this Memorial Day. To keep faith with our hallowed dead, let us be sure, and very sure, today and every day of our lives, that we keep their cause, their hope, their prayer, forever our country's own."

+ + +

America was founded in 1776 on Christian principles of law and justice. All who seek to change this fact are denying the basis for the gifts God has given us in this nation. They may even be imperiling these freedoms so long fought for. May we ever be vigilant to protect those Godly principles, and may we always be led by those who would never deny our God of the Holy Scriptures.

May God always give America leaders who honor Him!

MEMORIAL DAY

Sgt. Bill Mauldin was a cartoonist for the military newspaper, "Stars and Stripes." Mauldin's drawings of the two muddy, exhausted, whisker-stubble infantrymen, Willie and Joe, were the voice of truth about what it was like as an infantryman on the front lines. Sgt. Mauldin was an enlisted man just like the soldiers for whom he drew. His gripes were their gripes, his laughs their laughs, hand is heartaches their heartaches. He was one of them and they loved him.

Sometimes, when his cartoons got too close for comfort, superior officers tried to tone him down especially if he lampooned one of them. But Bill Mauldin had a big fan. Gen. Dwight D. Eisenhower, Supreme Allied Commander, who more said, *"Mauldin draws what Mauldin wants."* Not a bad recommendation for a 23 year old Sergeant.

He won the Pulitzer Prize and was on the cover of Time magazine. His book <u>Up Front</u> was the No. 1 best-seller in the United States for a time. And all of that he did at age 23. Yet when he returned to civilian life and grew older, he never lost that boyish Mauldin attitude. He never outgrew his excitement about his job and never acted important. He was still Sgt. Bill Mauldin, the enlisted man.

During the late summer of 2002, as he lay in a California nursing home, some old World War II guys caught wind of his condition. They didn't want Mauldin to go out alone so a columnist for the Orange County Register put out the call for people in the area to send him their best wishes. More than 10,000 cards and letters arrived at Mauldin's bedside. A few old soldiers showed up just to sit with him, to let him know that they were there for him, as he so long ago had been there for them. Some wore uniforms, medals or caps. One veteran said, *"You'd have to be part of a combat infantry unit to appreciate what moments of relief Bill gave us."*

Mauldin is buried in Arlington National Cemetery and even made it onto a first-class postage stamp. Few generals or admirals ever got there.

Give thanks to God for all those who have fought for our country.

DAY BY DAY WITH JESUS
in
June

+ + +

JUNE 1

Keith Green was a rock musician who became a Christian and wrote and sang some of the most challenging Christian songs of the 1970's. His career was sadly cut short by an airplane crash in 1982.

His songs were filled with such excitement and power and faith that after hearing them, their melodies and words would remain with you for days. But one of his songs was in the form of a prayer that reflected his weariness at life.

> *My eyes are dry, my faith is old, my heart is hard, my prayers are cold.*
> *But I know how I ought to be, alive to You and dead to me.*
> *So what can be done to old heart like mine?*
> *Soften it up with oil and wine. The oil is You, Your spirit of love.*
> *Please wash me anew in the wine of Your love.* (© Sparrow Records)

The sentiment of that song reminds me of Matthew 13:15 where Jesus said, **"For this people's heart has grown dull, and with their ears they can barely hear, and their eyes they have closed, lest they should see with their eyes and hear with their ears and understand with their heart and turn, and I would heal them'."**

The cares of life can wear us down. Making a living, raising a family or trying to achieve our goals can leave us exhausted. At all such times in life, we need the renewal of God's Word, as well as Christian fellowship and prayer. We need to be washed anew in the blessing of God's love.

That's why it's important to seek the grace of the Holy Spirit to soften our hardened hearts. God's Word and Holy Communion are His means of giving us His grace. May God give warmth to our prayers and new life to our dry faith.

Thank You, Lord, for Your Word of grace in my life. Amen

JUNE 2

People work hard trying to win. Whether it's with a favorite sports team, trying to make a winning financial deal, or just trying to getting ahead in life, people work hard to win. Sometimes winning is a matter of life and death.

This past weekend the mailman brought a new copy of our denomination's magazine that's been in print 135 years. The edition was all about persecution of Christians around the world. One of its articles quoted the "World Watch List" stating that of the 196 world nations, Christians are persecuted moderately to extremely in 39 of them. The list is growing, including in some supposedly Christian nations.

Persecution of Christians takes many forms, but all push us to deny our identity as a Christian or to discredit the Lordship of Jesus Christ. Despite the fact that there are over two billion Christians in the world today, tens of millions have targets on their backs from the enemies of Jesus Christ. At times it seems as if Christians are losing ground.

But our Lord Jesus and His Holy Christian Church will not be defeated or overcome. We have God's promise on this. St. Paul tells us in Romans 8:31, 37, **"If God is for us, who can be against us? ... In all these things we are more than conquerors through Him who loved us."**

Since all persecution of Christians is against Jesus, His followers should expect it will come to them also. Jesus said in Matthew 10:24, **"A servant is not above his Master."** He was persecuted for us first, and we will be, too. Because He was persecuted unto death, we are given eternal life when we trust that His suffering was to forgive us.

Hatred for Jesus must be countered, not with anger and bitterness, but with love and forgiveness, no matter how difficult that may seem. Only Christ Himself can give us strength to forgive our enemies. We take courage knowing that Jesus is faithful and will keep us as His own, and help us when we are also persecuted.

With faith in Jesus, we are more than winners.

JUNE 3

When trouble comes, where do you turn for help? Police? Family? Weapons? Government? In Psalm 121:1-2 the writer tells us, **"I lift my eyes to the hills. From where does my help come? My help comes from the Lord, who made heaven and earth."**

The central part of Israel is a range of hills. At this time the Jews had been held captive fifty years in the flat land of Persia, trusting the God of Abraham to help them return. He who had given His people the Promised Land would surely help His people return. They needed to look to the hills, because that's where God's help would come.

When we are in need of major or minor help, we need to know where to find it. It's tempting to think the only help we can get is from people. We're told today to look to educational institutions for our help, because with enough information we'll learn how to help ourselves. Or we should turn to the government for help, and they will give us our needs together with regulations on how to accept their help. Some are taught to look to themselves alone for help. *"If it's to be, it's up to me"* they say, and they believe it.

The Psalmist knows his problems will not be solved by more learning, government, or self-determination. His help will come from God who made heaven and earth, the God who commands the planets and stars to move in the heavens and gives life to the earth. He is not asleep or imaginary, but awake and ready to help. He who keeps us from evil will keep our whole life if we will but let Him do so.

Christian life means surrendering, not conquering. It is surrendering our hours, days and lives to our loving God for the help we need. He who can care for whole nations can take care of us, too. He is our keeper and our shade from the heat of life's troubles. With His wise counsel and help, we can conquer whatever troubles will come.

Help me, O God of the Universe, to surrender my life to You. Amen

JUNE 4

Do you like jigsaw puzzles? Being willing to concentrate to assemble a 1,000 or 1,500 piece puzzle takes patience I don't have. How about solving a 19,000 piece puzzle with pieces in four languages? I once led a video and discussion called, *"How We Got the Bible,"* offered by the Lutheran Hour Ministries which features Dr. Paul Maier.

In one segment Dr. Joel Lampe, of *The Bible Museum* in Goodyear, Arizona, gave fascinating information about the Dead Sea Scrolls. He said that in the caves along the Dead Sea they found 19,000 fragments of the Old Testament writings in Greek, Hebrew, Aramaic and Nabataean. It took experts 60 years to assemble pieces into 961 Old Testament writings. They used DNA tests to match some of the pieces.

The scribes of Qumran were the ancient printing press. They faithfully and carefully copied worn out Old Testament books onto new scrolls and papyrus pages. Out of respect they buried the old texts in jars in the Qumran caves.

Most amazing was not their condition but their content. When compared to oldest Greek and Hebrew texts we have today, they are virtually the same. The few tiny differences did not change the meaning of the text. God's people did their best to make no changes while copying. As a professor said, *"The Word of God survives translation!"*

It's estimated that since Gutenberg's first Bible was printed in 1455, there have been six billion copies of the Bible printed in hundreds of languages. Thirty million Bibles are still sold each year. No other book in history has even printed one billion. God's Word is the best seller of all times.

And it should be. The Bible contains the most important information of all time. The Old Testament points forward to the coming Savior of the world, and the New Testament points backward to Jesus of Nazareth as being that promised Savior. The message of the Bible is not history or behavior, but Jesus as our Savior. God made sure His Book would survive with the precious Gospel of forgiveness.

Thank You, Lord, for giving us the Bible.

JUNE 5

I always find lessons in summer yard work. One came when I planned to mow my lawn but my mower refused to start. The trusty old Craftsman had been fickle before, but always its motor worked. But not that day. It would start, then stop. Start, stop. Finally, not even start. I pushed it to the garage and got out the tools. The gas tank was nearly empty, but after more gas was added, it still refused to start.

I figured it was a fuel problem, so I took the carburetor off, cleaned things and put it together. Still wouldn't start. Took it apart again, cleaned it more, put it together. Still wouldn't start. Finally, I took it apart a third time. This time I blew out all lines and openings with compressed air. Put it together and, YES! It started - on the first pull!

What did I learn? 1) I can't always fix a problem on a first try, 2) A small bit of dirt can create a big problem, and, 3) Problems don't fix themselves - I have to get involved.

I usually try to follow *"Occam's Razor."* William of Occam (d. 1347) said when there are several solutions to a problem, the simplest is usually the right one. Example: when your printer won't print, check your cables before buying a new one. In this case: blow out the fuel line before putting the carburetor back together.

Bits of dirt can clog our life. We know dirt is there, but we don't believe it's a problem. Something else or someone else is the problem, not us. Rather than cleaning our own dirt, we blame other people's dirt, or we claim dirt is good for us, or we ignore dirt and hope it will disappear. But dirt stays, and life will not run well again until it's gone.

That's why Jesus is so important. He died on Calvary to get rid of our dirt. But first we must admit we're dirty, and then believe He's the only one who can cleanse us. Trusting Jesus is the simplest solution and He works best. William of Occam (priest, philosopher and theologian) would agree.

"If we confess our sins, He is faithful and just and will forgive our sins, and cleanse us from all unrighteousness." (1 John 1:9)

JUNE 6

On June 6, 1944, Gen. Dwight D. Eisenhower, Supreme Allied Commander, was the most powerful man on earth. Under his authority was the largest amphibious army ever assembled, and they were crossing the English Channel to invade Europe and liberate it from the Nazis. Adolph Hitler wanted to be the most powerful man on earth, but he failed, taking a backseat to man unknown before World War Two.

How was Gen. Eisenhower able to lead such a vast army of several nations? Part of the answer lay in his amazing skill at working with many different kinds of people. Another part of the answer centered in one of his character traits few still know about.

"Ike" was a fighter from his youth and often got into fistfights as a boy in his Kansas High School. He was blessed, though, to have a mother who cared about him and instructed him in God's Word. Once while she was bandaging his hands after an angry outburst, she quoted Proverbs 16:32 to him, **"Better a patient person than a warrior, one with self-control than one who takes a city."**

Years later Ike would write, *"I have always looked back on that conversation as one of the most valuable moments of my life."* He took to heart her words and learned to control his anger. Surely this affected his leadership in the war that helped the Allies win a victory over the Axis Powers who sought to impose dictatorships all over the world.

All of us at times will be tempted to settle a problem with angry words or even our fists. But let's remember that God's Word says a person with self-control is even greater than a conqueror. Patience and self-control are fruits of the Holy Spirit that show themselves in our lives when we honor Jesus as Lord.

Jesus' patience and self-control while being innocently convicted and sentenced to death are part of the reason we have hope for forgiveness and salvation. His resurrection gives us hope for our own resurrection.

Have you learned patience and self-control? How did you do it?

JUNE 7

Our neighbors of twelve years just moved. After days of packing, moving and house touch-up, their house was empty. The garbage man hauled away the leftovers, the realtor placed a "For Sale" sign on the lawn, and their former home was ready for a new resident. Their home is a ranch style with a finished basement, and like ours, smaller than other big ones around. They raised five children in it during their twenty-five years there.

I've often thought of what it takes to make a home. It's surely more than size, shape and usefulness of the building. Many homes today are huge for the number of people in them. Carol and I have lived in our home the longest either of us have lived in any one place. That means we've moved a lot, and also that we like being here.

Losing a home can be devastating. One summer 480 homes burned in the Black Forest fire south of us, and it made us contemplate the value of our own home. To lose a home through divorce or finances is also devastating.

How many rooms do you have in your house? Jesus once said, **"In my Father's house are many rooms, and I am going there to prepare a place for you."** (John 14:2) How many of those rooms do you live in? It's estimated that regardless of a house's size, people usually live in about one thousand square feet of space. I have an idea our neighbor's family of seven lived in every square inch of their home.

I was born and grew up in a house that was built from a kit. It was an exact replica of one we saw in a 1909 Sears Roebuck catalog for $2,999. Mom and Dad lived there forty years, and it is still standing today, but just barely.

More important than how many rooms our home has is whether or not we will be in our Father's House when we depart this life. Believers will be there, not because of the goodness of their lives, but because of Christ's perfect life and death and His promise that all who trust and have faith in Him will have eternal life.

What a houseful of children our Father will have then!

JUNE 8

It started one night and it was spooky. The lamp on Carol's night stand turned on and off by itself. She had noticed it flicker one day, but in the middle of the night, it startled us. The lamp went on, got brighter, then went off. It went on and off several times so she nudged me and asked, *"What's going on?"*

As the lamp went on and off, I walked around to her side of the bed. Two o'clock in the morning made this quite fascinating. We both knew it was one of those lamps with a touch-sensory switch that worked through the lamp's metal, so I touched the shade, and it went on and off again but sporadically. Why?

"Ah," I thought, and reached over to the lampshade knob. It was loose! I tightened it and the flickering stopped. I tested it and it worked as it should. Amazing! A tiny turn on the knob and the problem was solved. How simple! The loose knob allowed the lamp to wobble as if someone was touching it. It was not spiritual phenomenon but a physical one. It was a loose connection, not a message from God.

Or was it? When small or large things work loose in our lives, when we are no longer conducting our lives as we should be, or if we are farther away from God than we once were, our lives also may start to flicker. If we don't do something about it, we'll soon find our lives out of control. But if we seek the reasons, perhaps seeing that we are no longer as "tight" with God as we should be, then we can change things.

When we turn to God in repentance and faith, the flickering of life will change and hopefully stop. Our spiritual bulb may be dim, or it may need to be changed or our spiritual lamp may need to be plugged in. We may need to check whether or not we have moved away from God.

Only when we realize that we are part of the problem, will the flickering of life be dealt with in a positive way. Only then can we realize Jesus is the solution to our problems. Remember, He once said, **"You are the light of the world."** (Matthew 5:14)

How steadily will you shine today?

JUNE 9

A 2008 article in the *Sacramento Bee* newspaper by journalist Carlos Alacala told about a father and son who lived by the ocean and decided that for one year they would spend at least fifteen minutes every day searching the beach together for treasure. The article said they went out each day in every kind of weather to see what they could find.

One result of their year of adventure was a collection of coins, golf balls, bottles and cans and various items that they sold for over $1,000. An even more precious result was their improved relationship from their hours of companionship and fun spent together.

Joint adventure can be a good thing for many fathers and sons. Regular visits or activities can strengthen their relationship as they walk, talk about things and discover not only physical treasures, but also the treasures of love and trust. While it is rare that fathers and sons are best friends, they can be good friends.

God would like to be good friends with us, and one way this can occur is if we decide to spend some time each day reading His Word. Luther once said prayer was like a conversation with God: God speaks to us as we read His Word, and we speak to God in our prayers and thoughts as we hear and react to His Word.

We are guaranteed that those times will bring us closer to God. Wise King Solomon wrote, **"If you seek insight like silver and search for it as for hidden treasures, then you will understand the fear of the Lord and find the knowledge of God."** (Proverbs 2:4-5)

Growing closer to God in faith and love will not happen quickly. Gradually, day by day, we will find our self changed as we read what God has recorded for us through His prophets and apostles, and then learn to obey it.

Think of the enjoyment we can have, knowing we will be drawn closer to God as we search for the treasure of wisdom and insight about God's Word and our own life.

God's Word is a lamp to guide us in life.

JUNE 10

In Mere Christianity, C. S. Lewis devotes his chapter "Counting the Cost" to explaining the troubles a Christian experiences. Among his many thoughts, he wrote, *"We must not be surprised if we are in for a rough time."* He goes on to explain that when a person is following Christ, (s)he feels that now things should go fairly smoothly in life. When trouble comes along, the person becomes disappointed and wonders why it is happening now.

But, Lewis tells us, God is helping us become better. He is moving us up to a higher level, putting us in situations where we will have to be braver, more patient and more loving than we ever thought possible. It may seem unnecessary to us, but that's because we don't realize the tremendous thing God wants to make of our lives.

He uses an example: Imagine we are a living house that needs some fixing. We can understand this, and we can accept that God needs to come and rebuild us. At first we can understand why He is fixing our leaky plumbing or repairing the roof or making our drafty windows tighter.

But then God goes too far. He starts knocking walls out in a way that hurts and makes no sense. Why is God doing this? He doesn't need to knock us around like this!

We don't realize this is happening because He is building a different house from the one we thought we'd like. He is adding another room, building a tower or making a courtyard. We were satisfied being a decent cottage, but God is building us into a palace, and He intends to come and live in it Himself.

Now, we surely can prevent God from doing this. But If we choose to let Him, He will take the weakest and dirtiest of us and form us into strong, attractive and even energetic beings that will bless Him and others around us. The process may be long and painful at times, but this is what God wants for us – the best and nothing less.

"You are living stones, being built up as a spiritual house."
(2 Peter 2:5)

JUNE 11

Here are some really good Christian one-liners:

1. *Many folks want to serve God, but only as advisers.*
2. *When you're at your wit's end, you'll find God lives there.*
3. *Opportunity may knock once, but temptation bangs on the door forever.*
4. *If a church wants a better pastor, it only needs to pray for the one it has.*
5. *We're called to be witnesses, not lawyers or judges.*
6. *Some minds are like concrete: thoroughly mixed up and permanently set.*
7. *The good Lord didn't create anything without a purpose, but mosquitoes come close.*
8. *Be ye fishers of men. You catch 'em – He'll clean 'em.*
9. *Don't put a question mark where God put a period.*
10. *Don't wait for six strong men to take you to church.*
11. *God doesn't call the qualified, He qualifies the called.*
12. *God grades on the cross, not on the curve.*
13. *God promises a safe landing, not a calm trip.*
14. *If God is your co-pilot, you'd better swap seats!*
15. *The task ahead is never as great as the Power behind.*
16. *We don't change the Message, the Message changes us.*
17. *Best mathematical equation: 1 cross + 3 nails = 4 given.*

Which one struck a chord with you? I think #13 has quite a message, and so does #16. Some of them are a bit humorous, and all give us food for thought.

There is a lot of wisdom in learning from the wise sayings of others. Wise King Solomon tells us, **"Listen, my son, to your father's instruction, and do not forsake your mother's teaching."** (Proverbs 1:8 NIV)

As we grow older, it is a natural thing to rely more on one's own wisdom, but we are never so old so that we should ignore the wisdom of our parents and those who love us, especially our Heavenly Father.

What special saying do you recall from your parents?

JUNE 12

People all over the world are constantly looking for something better. Whether it is better fruit at the store or a better place to live, a better car or a better relationship, Most people are constantly on the lookout for what they can get that is better. I am not sure what the cure of this can be for others, but I have found out what works for me. With some things, I just stop looking.

I have always been fascinated with cars and ever since buying my first one in 1966, I have been on the lookout for the next one, hoping it will be better. A few years ago I got a used luxury car, one of those big ones that drive quietly and made with lasting quality. I liked it so much that I bought another one and now I have two, one in Arizona and one in Colorado. Neither cost much since they were used, so I have decided to keep them in good condition and not get any more. They will be my last cars, God willing.

The book of Proverbs is filled with comparisons that point us to the right things in life, right decisions and words, right deeds and thoughts. The purpose of the book is to give the reader the knowledge and wisdom based on faith in God. It is not surprising to find many statements that say, *"This is better than that."*

For example, Proverbs 16 tells us it is **better to seek wisdom than to seek riches** (v. 16). It also says it is **better to be poor and humble than rich and proud** (v. 19). It is **better to keep our temper under control than to be a ruler** (v. 32). Some people are fortunate to have the ability to be both wise and wealthy, but when faced with a choice Proverbs says wisdom is better of the two.

When Jesus spoke to His men in parables, He would often begin by saying, **"What do you think?"** (Matthew 18:12) He was teaching them to make good choices, and His stories showed them a better way. When we allow the Word of God to help us make decisions and guide our choices, we will find God's way is always better.

Show me the best way in what I do today, Lord Jesus!

JUNE 13

The Lord has given me the privilege of being pastor of several churches, one very large and the others small. I found that being a pastor in a smaller congregation was more to my liking, the way I envisioned a pastor should be. "Pastor" means shepherd, and the Bible tells us a shepherd knows his sheep. The way to do that is to have a smaller group. A shepherd of thousands can't get to know his sheep.

A ministry book I once read compared the ministry of a shepherd with the ministry of a rancher. A shepherd has a flock he can identify, and whose sheep will know him. He knows how many sheep he has, where they live and what they do. He also knows their struggles and preaches God's Word to help them face life.

A rancher has a lot of cattle. He knows what it takes to keep the cattle well-fed and healthy. He has a good idea how many cattle he has, but he does not recognize them easily. He just knows when he looks over the range, that most of the cattle he sees are his. He knows their general needs and problems, but he does not know his cattle by name.

When people are part of a huge congregation, they can learn new things, hear fine worship music and perhaps be part of a small group. But they will not have a personal relationship with their pastor. Because of the hundreds or thousands of people there, the pastor will not know them.

I am not advocating that large churches are not good, nor are all of them impersonal. God needs large congregations to carry on large ministries. He also needs small congregations to nurture the community and special needs of the members who want a more intimate relationship with other members.

Jesus knows our names, our needs and where we are. He even knows our thoughts and tears, and He hears us when we call on Him, no matter where we are. He said, **"I am the good shepherd, and I know my sheep."** (John 10:3) God in His greatness will always keep track of us.

God knows you and loves you, wherever you are.

JUNE 14

Colorado winters can make driving an adventure. Snow can come early in October or visit us in May. Whenever it comes, a driver must be ready to handle the road conditions. One snowy night, a man and his wife were driving home from visiting friends. It had been a warm day, but a sudden, huge temperature drop followed by snow flurries made the roads a slippery mess.

On the way home the couple saw numerous cars in the ditch and even an accident occur right in front of them. Fortunately, they made their trip home safely. As they left the freeway on the final road home, the husband said, *"Thanks Lord, I think I can take it from here."* Just then his car began a slow spin, doing a complete 360 degree turn before stopping on the side of the road. The car wasn't damaged and it didn't come close to other drivers, but the man's heart was pounding. He thought he could drive the rest of the way alone, but God was saying, *"Are you sure?"*

Our weak human natures make us think we can make it okay in life without God, but God has to remind us now and then that we need Him every moment of life. There is never a time in our life when we do not need God, His provision or His caring for us. He once told Abraham, **"I am with you and will keep you wherever you go."** (Genesis 28:15) Those are His words to us, also.

Christian hymn writers often pick up on this promise from God. In 1905 poet Civilla Martin wrote:

> *Why should I feel discouraged, why should the shadows come,*
> *Why should my heart be lonely, and long for heaven and home,*
> *When Jesus is my portion? My constant friend is He:*
> *His eye is on the sparrow, and I know He watches me.*

Each of us needs a reminder like this. Whether we have narrowly missed an accident or we are confident of our abilities and grateful for them, God watches over us.

See today how God watches over you, at home or at work.

JUNE 15

What is your credit score? Have you ever answered one of the ads that say you can get a free credit report, but only if you give them your credit card number, even though your credit score is "free"? I am always suspicious when advertisements ask for our credit information and then offer us something free. It seems to me they are the ones getting something free – our personal information.

The 2008 global financial crisis caused people to pay close attention to their credit report. When credit was easy to obtain, people used it carelessly and didn't save money for what they wanted. They followed the credit slogan, *"Buy now; Pay later."* But they found repayment much harder to do than they thought. When borrowed money is easy to get, debt seems like no big deal. But when a financial crisis comes, debt really is a big deal.

When one's credit goes bad, it takes work to make it good again. An advertisement once said, *"Credit isn't something you can buy, it's something you have to work for."*

When I received my first assignment in ministry to a small town, I had little money and no local credit. I needed to pay a bill, so I went to the local bank and asked to borrow $47.50 for one month. Since I was using my car as collateral, the loan officer offered to give me $50 or more, if I needed it. I said, no, all I needed was $47.50, so that's all I wanted to borrow. When I said I also needed to establish credit there, he smiled and handed me a bank check for $47.50. Although my request must have seemed odd, I accomplished two things – paid what I owed and established my credit.

There's a similarity with credibility in our lives. We can't buy credibility, but we can earn it. We may be able to "borrow" credibility due to our position or associations, but sooner or later we will need to prove ourselves.

This is also true of Christians. Our lives affect God's reputation among those who don't believe in Him. If we call ourselves Christian, we must honor the name of Christ.

How will I honor the name of Christ today?

JUNE 16

"You need to trust your mirrors." That the advice I got from an old fellow when I was learning to back up our travel trailer. *"Good mirrors don't lie,"* he said. *"They tell you what's really back there."*

For 22 years Carol and I owned a vintage Airstream travel trailer. It was given to us by Carol's parents and we enjoyed using it those years, either parked in the mountains, or pulled on a trip behind our Chevy Blazer.

The first time we used it we were not well prepared. I forgot some essential items for the inside and discovered the furnace didn't work well. The hardest part, besides pulling it up a steep mountain road, was backing it into the narrow space we'd rented for the night. After several attempts, the old fellow came over and helped me. Seeing me turn my head around, he said, *"You need to trust your mirrors."* It was good advice for seeing, and it saves some neck pain as well.

People often tell us not to look back on our lives, to leave the past and just keep moving forward. But there are times when looking back is helpful and even necessary. The mirror of our memory can help us recall where we've come from as well as how far we've come. The mirror of another life well-lived, that of a parent or valued friend, can also help us in the choices we make.

The mirror of God's love is most evident in Jesus. When we look at Him, we see God's love in action. Jesus urges us to live so that when others see us, they can also see God. That's why He said, **"Let your light shine before people, that they may see your good deeds and glorify your Father in heaven."** (Matthew 5:16)

Not trusting our mirrors can force us to twist our head so far around that we can't drive properly. It's always best to trust the mirror God gives us in His Word. That means trusting Him when we're moving forward. Good mirrors don't lie, and God's Word doesn't either.

How can you trust your mirrors today?

JUNE 17

I am a fairly well educated person, but I am not sure education has made me smart. One of my older brothers often noted this. When I came home from college he'd usually say, *"You don't look any smarter than the last time I saw you."* I didn't mind the sarcasm, because he was right. Learning may show itself in a person's life, but it's usually not evident right away.

But some things are hard for me to learn. For example, every time I use the remote to change a TV channel or increase the volume, I marvel how it can work. Somehow an electrical wave is emitted from the small "channel changer" (my term) and the TV does what it tells it.

The same is true when I turn on a light switch. I have done some electrical wiring so I know the principles behind electrical impulses going through copper wiring. I also have learned (the hard way) that one should not cross a positive and negative wire when they are connected to an electrical source. The sparks can be quite spectacular and the fuse hard to locate. I give thanks someone invented the "breaker" which eliminated the need for fuse replacement.

While I'm on this subject, I also give thanks for the invention of the fuse. In 1957, our farm house caught fire due to lack of a fuse in an electrical line. It didn't burn completely, just needed a lot of repair. That's another story.

But electricity is amazing. Just walk into a room, flick on a switch and you can see in the dark! Do you ever stop and think how it happened? No, we just expect it to happen. We've become accustomed to modern miracles.

It's the same for us each day. We expect miracles every time we open our eyes, such as the miracles of sight (it's morning!), memory (time to get up!), mobility (get out of bed!), and knowledge (turn on the coffee!) God gave us ability to do all these things that require the miracle of a billion brain cells to help us do this every day. I have a friend who's had a stroke. He misses all these miracles.

What miracles from God will you look for today?

JUNE 18

Now that I've brought up the subject of our house fire, I should explain it further. It was the fall of 1957, and I was a seventh grader in Junior High School. I'd completed six grades of Country School and was trying to fit in with the "townies" but not doing so well.

One Sunday night in October we were awakened by my mother's shout, *"Fire! The house is on fire!"* Someone found a light switch, but there was so much smoke that we couldn't see to walk, just dense, choking, white smoke. We were all upstairs so Dad yelled for my brother and me to go through the windows and jump down to the lawn. He covered Mom's head and they made their way down the stairway. We were all safe and the house was saved, due to the rapid response of the local fire department.

An event like that sears itself into your memory. Interestingly, what I recalled later was not how fortunate we were to be alive, but how badly I smelled in school the next day. My clothing smelled smoky for days as we tried to wash the smell out. It was just one more reason that I'd always be just another "country kid." Leave it to a teenager to think of himself rather than be grateful for being alive!

Especially in a disaster it is difficult to see the larger, more important picture. All four of us could have passed out and been burned in that fire, but that wasn't important to me. It was what other kids thought of a country kid. It wasn't until several years later that it dawned on me how blessed we were that coughing in the smoke woke my mother and saved us all.

Have you ever had a house fire? I hope not because it is terrifying. But rest assured, God watches over us even while we sleep. He keeps us in His care and hides us in the day of trouble. When we die in faith, we are promised a better life, but it's only when you realize how close you've come to dying that this life becomes precious. An auto accident would re-enforce that lesson to me, but that's another story.

"Save us, Lord, or we will perish!" (Matthew 8:25)

JUNE 19

Do you believe in miracles? On several occasions the Bible tells us Jesus told people a miracle was coming, but they doubted Him. I wonder how many times God has spoken to us but we weren't listening. How many times have we doubted God could do something and explained it away? Many times the Bible records Jesus saying, **"O you of little faith!"** (Luke 12:28) After seeing so many miracles today, one would think we would believe He could still do them instead of looking for some other explanation.

It is part of our human nature to fear what we do not understand. It is natural for us to be surprised, even after seeing something happen again and again.

Nick Wallenda is a circus performer and grandson of the great Karl Wallenda. Both men could walk a cable or other tightrope hundreds of feet above the ground with no safety net. In 2012, Nick Wallenda walked over Niagara Falls from the American to the Canadian side, a quarter mile through slippery mists and windy gales, four hundred feet above the raging water falls. I watched a film of him doing that feat and was totally amazed. It was not just a lucky trick, it was a real miracle.

People in our sophisticated world today generally don't believe in miracles. Even if something totally unexplainable happens, it is called a coincidence or "unexplained event." Yet Christians in Africa believe in miracles, as do Christians in other lesser developed countries. God shows them He is alive and can help them, especially through His Son Jesus.

It isn't presumptive to expect God to do amazing things, but it takes faith. God wants us to pray expectantly, because He wants us to understand His power and presence on earth. He shows us miracles every day in medicine, science and daily events, but it takes faith to see them.

Most people do not know Nick Wallenda is a Christian. When he takes his dangerous wire-walks, he is praying constantly. He'll tell you it isn't a trick. God walks with him.

Have you done a "wire-walk" lately?

JUNE 20

In the summer I fertilize my lawn to make it green and thick. Every two months or so I buy a bag of tiny beads of appropriate chemicals and spread it with my hand spreader all over the lawn. I take care not to spread it too thick or too thin. If it's too thin, it does little good, and if it's too thick, it will burn the living grass and maybe even kill it.

I try to spread the little beads to four to six inches apart. Although they are tiny, those amazing chemicals spread nutrients around as they dissolve, bringing richness to the worn and weary soil and helping the grass to grow. Sometimes I also need to get rid of weeds, so I apply "Weed and Feed" then as well.

Applying too much always hurts more than it helps, which is true in our lives as well. People need love, but they don't need to be suffocated by it. They need caring loved ones nearby, but they don't need people to live their lives for them. They need to hear of Jesus, but they don't need it from demanding Christians. A little goes a long ways and a smothering love can be hurtful. We benefit most when the right amount is given at the right time.

Christians often speak of love but may not always know what they mean. Of the three kinds of love – physical love (eros), friendship love (philos) and self-sacrificing love (agape) – we must show the right kind when it's needed.

After the resurrection, Jesus took Peter aside and asked him three times if he loved Him, since Peter had denied Him three times. It's not often known that Jesus used two different words for love. The first two times He asked, *"Peter, are you willing to die for me?"* Peter said, *"Yes, Lord."* It's easy to say that when you're safe and not in danger.

But the third time He used another word for love and asked, *"Peter, are you my friend?"* Peter was hurt when asked this. *"Of course I am your friend,"* he said. Are we willing to die for Jesus? Are we willing to be more than His friend?

If so, are we willing to feed His lambs and sheep! (see John 21:15-17)

JUNE 21

I never thought I would depend on a cell phone the way I do now. My lumpy little flip-phone was useful, but my slick iPhone has become a near-necessity. And not just for phone calls. I use it to check e-mail messages, look up subjects, check how to spell words and even entertain myself. My wife and I only have one and that's enough.

The smart phone craze has been enhanced by the emergence of cell-phone applications (Apps) that are really mini-computer programs. These Apps allow a person to read the news and weather, get the latest sports updates, and even set our home alarm system and pay our bills. There is an App out there for just about anything, and more are being invented every day. A 2015 internet article told of there being over 306,000 phone Apps. That's staggering!

But phone apps are nothing compared to the what the Bible can give us. "Applications" of the Holy Bible are direct notes from God. They come absolutely free and require no battery power. God's Apps from the Bible *APPly* His Word to our life and show us His will for how to live.

There are dozens of "Bible Apps" that Christians can tap into. The Psalms App contains hundreds of good words to stay close to God. Proverbs App is teeming with practical life applications, and the Prophets App gives us God's warnings and aid to keep us on the right path.

In the New Testament, consider Philippians chapter 2: There's a Unity App (2:2), Humility App (2:3), Contentment App (2:14) and an Example App (2:15). Ephesians 5 has an Imitate God App (5:1), Showing Love App (5:2), Purity App (5:3) and a Speech App (5:4).

Thousands of people make their living these days by writing new Apps. Some of them are questionable in content and morality, but God's Word has all the Holy Apps we'll ever need. His Apps are all good, and we will find nothing "fishy" or useless about them.

"Apply your heart to instruction and your ears to knowledge." (Proverbs 23:12)

JUNE 22

Have you ever been to see Mount Rushmore? Located west of Rapid City, South Dakota, this National Memorial has the heads of four American presidents carved on its granite mountain top. Sculpted by Gutzon Borglum and his son Lincoln, the colossal work covers 1,200 acres and stands 5,700 feet above sea level. On it are the heads of presidents Washington, Lincoln, Jefferson and Theodore Roosevelt. Hundreds of thousands of people visit there every year.

Millions of people know about the mountain and the Danish artists who carved it, but fewer know about Doane Robinson, the South Dakota state historian who came up with the idea. It was Robinson who managed the project and made it a reality. While this masterpiece is admired by millions, Doane Robinson is the unrecognized worker, the forgotten man behind the work.

There are millions of persons in God's kingdom who work behind the scenes to serve others, and none of them are forgotten by God. They may not be recognized, but they are remembered by their Heavenly Father. Whether they are workers in churches or schools, hospitals, rest homes or homeless shelters, whether they are Americans or Africans, Indians or Swedes, Coptics or Catholics, they are all known and recognized by God.

There may be times when we feel our service has been forgotten or unappreciated, but it is not. Even if the people we serve fail to thank us or even reject our efforts, we must remember the Holy One who loves us, died for our sins, and grants eternal salvation to all who trust Him as Lord.

The Bible says, **"God will not forget your work and the love you have shown him as you have helped his people and continue to help them."** (Hebrews 6:10) That's good to know when we feel tired from serving unappreciative people. It is a wonderful promise of God never to forget our service. God's appreciation is far better than the applause of the crowds.

Serve God and know He is glad you are doing so.

JUNE 23

I recently removed my old portable GPS directional system from my car. It had quit working due to a weak battery and outdated maps, but I also didn't need it any longer anyway. I have considered getting one of those new in-dash radios that include GPS navigation, but the cost is high, and my old car radio is a very good one.

But let's be clear - this was not done because I returned to using only paper maps, or that I have finally decided to stop and ask for directions. It's because I have a new GPS App on my iPhone. Just type in the address and let it guide you there. Everyone can have a fine GPS system so long as you remember to bring your iPhone along!

Ever wonder what airplane pilots use in their navigation? Most use a VHF Omni-directional Radio Range, usually called a VOR or "Omni." It is a navigational system invented in the 1950s that is still used to guide many aircraft today. The pilot sets coordinates on the instrument panel at the beginning of the flight. If the aircraft drifts from the set course, certain instruments indicate that the plane is going away from its pre-determined course. The pilot then corrects the aircraft to where it should be going. One of my nieces is an Air Force pilot in those huge refueling planes, and her course coordinates are essential.

In the Old Testament, God's people often needed a reliable system to know where they were going in relation to God. Their "spiritual VOR" came via the prophets. Sadly, the people rarely heeded what God's prophets told them. Perhaps it was because they had a prosperous life, or they felt secure from their enemies, or they had aligned themselves with a pagan nation. When the prophets spoke God's Word, the people rarely paid attention.

Christians today also have a divine navigational system. The Holy Spirit prompts us to follow God's will and leads us to live according to God's truths, if we let Him. Following God's leading will take us in the right direction.

Where are you going in life today?

JUNE 24

I recently watched a 2003 History Channel series which explained how mankind has been able to flourish in the world as we know it. Each program began with these words:

> *"Amidst the chaos of an unforgiving planet, most species will fail. But for one, all the pieces will fall into place, and a set of keys will unfold a path for mankind to triumph. This is our story, the story of All of Us."*

"Mankind: The Story of All of Us" was an informative series, and although it could not go into much depth, the episodes I watched taught me many things. As each show began with this introduction, those words stayed with me, but in an unsettling way.

They were obviously written from the viewpoint that human beings on our planet have flourished only because of chance. While the programs spoke of mankind's triumph, one is left with the feeling there was nothing behind the success of humanity's survival except good fortune. Of a gazillion chances and possibilities, things just fell into place for us. People lucked out! How unsettling that intelligent members of mankind can look at all the facts and come to only one conclusion - we just got lucky.

Yes, I believe, *"all the pieces DID fall into place,"* through the power of the Divine Creator. And I believe *"a set of keys DID unfold a path for mankind to triumph,"* keys designed and revealed to us by our Creator God. But to make the assumption that chance was the only way it could have happened is to wear blinders. It is making a scientific decision based on assumptions, but not facts.

Our earth is a creation of God, and I say this not to convince myself, but to give witness to what I see and also believe. Today, some believe it necessary to abandon the notion of a Divine Being. Despite an assault on Christianity, a vast majority of Mankind does acknowledge in creation by God. *"The Story of All of Us"* must always include God.

What do you see today that shows God's hand in the world?

JUNE 25

Carol and I attended the funeral of a retired Lutheran School Teacher. During the sermon, my pastor said, *"Never underestimate what God has done through your life."* When he repeated it again, I realized how important his thought was. Never think God can't do something wonderful through your acts, your teaching or witness. He does so every day.

Sometimes we think that wonderful things are only done by others, especially the talented, the trained, or the clever. But God speaks wonderful words, does fine deeds, and instills lasting values in people through the lives of His men, women and children, and especially those who live their Christian Faith.

I attended Country School during Grades One to Six. Our school building was six miles from the nearest town with one main room that often held 12-24 students. It had a big basement where we played when it was too cold outside. Bathrooms were outside and drinking water was carried from the farm across the road. Their telephone was our only connection with the world during the school day.

But charm didn't make that school important; it was our teachers. They imparted the knowledge we needed and opened young minds to the wonders of history, arithmetic, reading, writing, spelling and science.

Sometimes our teachers taught us several years. I had one teacher nearly five years.

The teachers I've had helped nurture a lifetime of learning. I wonder if anyone reading this book also spent time teaching or learning in a one-room school. I wonder if our teachers realize how much they influence the lives of their students.

At the funeral, the pastor said of that faithful teacher, *"Never underestimate what God has done through your life."* Teachers are how God gets much of His work done. **"Show me Your ways, O Lord, and teach me Your paths."** (Psalm 25:4)

If you can read and understand this, thank a teacher!

JUNE 26

Allen Swift (1908 – 2010) of Springfield, Massachusetts, received a remarkable gift from his father for college graduation. It was a brand new 1928 Rolls Royce. Many a man wishes he would have gotten such a gift for graduation, but none would have considered keeping and driving that car for the rest of his life.

But that's just what Allen Swift did. Swift received his Rolls Royce Piccadilly-P1 Roadster in 1928, and he achieved the remarkable feat of continuing to drive it right up until his death in 2010 at the age of 102. He was the oldest, living owner of a car that had been purchased new. His 1928 auto is a marvel of craftsmanship.

When it was donated by his family to a Springfield museum after his death, the odometer showed 1,070,000 miles on it. That's approximately 13,000 miles per year, or 1,100 miles per month. It still ran very well, almost like a Swiss watch, engine quiet at most speeds and its body in near-perfect condition even though it had been built 82 years before. I don't think they make them like this anymore – neither car nor driver.

How many miles does your odometer show? I am not asking about the one on your car, but the odometer on your life. How old are you and how have you held up over the years? God wants us to take care of our bodies, but He doesn't give us all the same one. All men or women have body types that vary. I see men at 85 who are in better condition than some at 65, and I have noticed that no matter how carefully some have properly eaten and exercised, their body deteriorates like the one who didn't care as much.

A car body isn't like a human body. God has given us the miracle of human life for a determined time. When our time comes to leave this earth, we then will all know what it will be like on the "other side." He promises an eternal glory in His presence to all who believe in His Son Jesus Christ.

Give God thanks for all the miles on your life odometer!

JUNE 27

Of all the things I am called upon as a minister to do, I like teaching the best. Whether it's teaching the Bible, or history, or archaeology, or even a topic of modern times, I enjoy teaching, especially in a room full of eager people who have questions and are not afraid to ask them.

I often am asked why the Bible seems to contradict itself, or why there are four Gospels, stories that have essentially the same purpose in telling of Jesus Christ, His life and teachings. This was brought to mind through a cartoon that showed Jesus speaking to His disciples on a hillside. In the artist's panel He says, *"Okay everyone, listen carefully. I don't want to end with four different versions of this."*

I think that's a clever thought. It brings to mind another question I heard asked in a seminary class a long time ago. A brash young seminarian asked, *"Does God have a sense of humor?"* The professor responded, *"He must - He created you, Mr. Tasler."* He was right! All our differences are proof of God's sense of humor.

They say no two snowflakes are shaped the same, but that really can't be proven. The simple elements in a snowflake, hydrogen and oxygen, would surely lead to duplicates. But it is a fact that no two people are the same. Science tells us even identical twins who share the same genes have different DNA and fingerprints. They may look identical, but they have separate feelings, preferences and traits, all of which become more obvious with time.

God's humor shows itself in some of His animals. Consider the platypus with its "duck bill," or that it finds food using electricity, or walks on its knuckles, lives in water by day and a dirt burrow at night. It has no stomach, yet has precious fur, lays eggs to procreate and has a venomous claw to protect itself. What was God thinking?

The Bible says, **"He who sits in the heavens laughs!"** (Psalm 2:4) and, **"The Lord laughs at the wicked."** (Psalm 37:13) He may laugh at what we do, but He never stops loving us.

Have you ever felt His laughter?

JUNE 28

I have always admired accomplished musicians who have learned to master their instruments and make wonderful music. Whether it's the violin, trumpet or even bagpipe, hearing a professional musician perform is a thrilling thing. I once heard a husband-wife tuba duet during a concert of the Denver Brass. I have a CD of that performance and enjoy the tuba duet each time I hear it. I am told most professional musicians still rehearse daily.

Midori is a Japanese violinist with a fine international reputation, but she still practices. Because of her rigorous schedule of 100 or more performances each year all over the world, Midori must practice, usually an average of five hours a day. *"I have to practice for my job. It's not really the hours but the quality of the work that needs to be done. Students may play and say it's practicing. But if you have your textbook open, it doesn't mean that you are studying,"* she said.

In college I was required to take piano lessons for two quarters, and was trained by a petite woman with very small hands. One day I heard her playing in a practice studio and marveled at how well her tiny hands made such fine music on the keyboard. She later told me practice was required because her hands were so small. She said, *"If I don't keep them working, they won't do what I need them to do."*

The same principle could be applied to our faith in Jesus. Paul once wrote young Timothy, **"Do your best to present yourself to God as one approved, a worker who does not need to be ashamed and who correctly handles the word of truth."** (2 Timothy 2:15)

Paul was telling Timothy the importance of working hard at being a new pastor. **"Do your best,"** he told him, as one **"who correctly handles the word of truth."** Working to improve requires continual effort and leaves no room for carelessness and inattention. Doing our best should also relate to our relationship with God. He has given us His best through His Son Jesus. We can give Him our best, also.

To what are you giving your best efforts?

JUNE 29

In the winter I live next to a golf course. Although I am not an avid golfer, I like the "green lawn" in my backyard as well as the evening sunsets. I can hear some golfers as they walk by and once heard of a "hole in one" achieved on the previous hole. That's a goal I have yet to attain.

In 1945, professional golfer Byron Nelson had an unforgettable season. Of the 30 tournaments he entered, he won 18 times, including 11 in a row - incredible! If he had chosen to do so, he could have continued his career and may have become the greatest player of the game.

But that was not Nelson's goal. He wanted to earn enough money to spend his life doing what he loved to do. At the age of only 34, Byron Nelson retired from the PGA to become a rancher, his real goal in life.

Our world may find that kind of thinking to be foolish. We assume if a person excels in a field, (s)he must remain in it as long as possible. Yet there have been numerous great athletes who have walked away, often at the top of their game, in order to achieve other, more important goals.

Winning may be wonderful, but it can't supply all our needs. However, the world doesn't always like that attitude. It believes wealth and fame produce real satisfaction, but most people know that's not true. Contentment comes from a good relationship with those we love, our family and God.

The goals of a Christian man or woman may include some winning or high achievement, but they realize God's eternal goals are more important. Paul once wrote, **"God chose the foolish things of the world to shame the wise; God chose the weak things of the world to shame the strong."** (1 Corinthians 1:27)

The Christian choice to live according to God's Word may make us look foolish to the world, but it is wisest in the long run. When we follow Christ and His Holy Word of life, we bring honor to God and His kingdom, and we have satisfaction only He can give.

What "foolish" thing can you do for God today?

JUNE 30

You can tell a lot about a person by the pictures he displays. If you enter either of our homes, you will immediately see our walls filled with family pictures, especially our grandchildren. If you look at our refrigerator doors, you will see other family members and friends.

When you turn on your computer, what "desktop" image does it show? One of my sons has a photo of his family on his laptop. Our laptop shows majestic vistas and views of nature from countries around the world. I've gleaned many sets of screensavers from sources and I change them about once a month.

What we view will affect our thoughts, words and deeds. Watching wholesome video programs brings us an entirely different mindset than a constant diet of murder mysteries or programs with vile language and activities. When my wife and I spend an evening watching TV, we try to choose programs that have beneficial subject matter. It may be an old comedy, a family movie or a documentary from which we can learn something useful. Neither of us have much interest in most network programs.

A father was once surprised when a string of foul words poured out of his young son's mouth. *"What did you say? Where in the world did you learn that language?"* he demanded. His boy said with a frightened voice, *"From the movies you watch. I may be in my room, but I'm not always asleep, and I hear those words. What do they mean, Daddy?"*

What we see and hear does make its way into our hearts, and when bad things enter, good things are often pushed out. Keep that in mind when you buy a movie ticket or choose a program to watch. Even hearing a constant stream of critical commentary or foolish advertisements can affect our attitude and actions.

We can rest assured that if we read and watch good things, **"Wisdom will enter your heart, and knowledge will be pleasant to your soul."** (Proverbs 2:10)

What wisdom have you seen so far today?

DAY BY DAY WITH JESUS
in
July

+ + +

JULY 1

Despite the casualness of the age in which we live, many feel they must say the right thing or suffer consequences. So they often choose not to say anything. This can be true when someone dies.

I conducted a funeral for a popular church member and only half as many people attended as expected. When I asked one member why he hadn't come, he said he didn't attend funerals often because he wasn't sure what to say. Rather than saying the wrong thing and possibly making the family feel worse, he avoided funerals all together.

That's unfortunate. In times of loss, mourners rarely remember what you say, but they will remember that you were there. Attendance at funerals seems to be declining, and I wish that were not the case. Just being present is more important than whether or not you say the right thing. Family, friends and even strangers can offer strength and comfort in our loss and loneliness whether their words are appropriate or not.

Jesus didn't preach a sermon or raise the dead every time He attended a funeral. He helped people by His presence and even wept with them. John 11:36 says of Jesus at Lazarus' grave, **"See how He loved him."** Just as Jesus was, so we can be there with our comforting presence.

The next time you hear of a friend who has passed from this life, don't worry about whether your words will be exactly what others think they should be. Just express them. Call them, write them a card or speak your words of comfort in person. By doing so, you are an ambassador for Christ.

Even if you say nothing, your presence says a lot!

JULY 2

Freedom is one of the basic tenets of being alive. Freedom is a basic human right and privilege. Our Declaration of Independence speaks of *"Life, Liberty and the Pursuit of Happiness."* But what exactly is *"Freedom?"* Is *"Liberty"* the same thing? Driving back recently from Minnesota through Nebraska, I saw a large billboard beside a farmyard that gave me a chuckle. It said,

> EAT STEAK
> WEAR FURS
> KEEP YOUR GUN
> SALUTE THE FLAG

In ten words the owner of that sign told people what he believes a free person should be able to do. Instead of bowing to political correctness, he wanted to make it clear that freedom means being able to do those things.

"Freedom" and *"Liberty"* are not quite the same. Liberty is what a government grants its people for their personal pursuits. Freedom is one's individual ability to believe or think whatever one chooses. Freedom is our right to make choices given to us by birth. It is a basic human right that cannot be taken away even by a totalitarian government, though they may try. Liberty is a governmental structure that allows us expression of freedom.

A serf toiling a thousand years ago in Europe had very little liberty. He was a vassal of his overlord. But he did have freedom to think his own thoughts and make his choices, whether others agreed with him or not. That freedom couldn't be taken away.

While we do have freedom to eat steak, wear furs or keep our guns, we must always make sure we exercise our freedom for a good purpose and avoid bringing harm to others. Saluting the flag is a sign of respect and is always good. Jesus said **"You will know the truth and the truth will set you free."** (John 8:32)

Would you agree with the farmer's sentiment?

JULY 3

Someone once said to me, *"People don't respect important things like they should."* I agree. Even in our modern culture with all its odd twists and changes, there are still foundational principles we must respect and maintain, despite what polls might show.

Respect for Law: Abraham Lincoln said in 1838, *"Let reverence for the laws be breathed by every American mother to the lisping babe that prattles on her lap; let it be taught in schools, in seminaries, and in colleges; let it be preached from the pulpit, proclaimed in legislative halls, and enforced in courts of justice."* Great words from a great man.

Respect for God: There was hardly a man or woman among our nation's founders who did not respect God, even if they didn't agree who He was or what to believe about Him. They believed God must not be ignored or denied, and certainly not mocked. Today this is routinely done in Universities, politics and special interest groups, and we are paying dearly for it.

Respect for Marriage: Marriage of a man and a woman has been the foundation of civilization and the primary building block in the walls of human culture for millennia. God has given it to us to make humanity strong. Let's hold fast to God's will in this.

Respect for Human Life: Life is a fragile gift. Modern laws allow elective abortion of unborn infants for a variety of reasons, most of which are invalid. Most abortions are done for convenience, including even its most grizzly procedures. A flippant attitude towards abortion disrespects human life, no matter how one tries to justify it.

Respect for our Nation: Despite what some of its citizens may do to prove otherwise, our nation is still the best on earth. Tomorrow is July Fourth, the birthday of America. Fly your flag proudly. **"Give to Caesar what is Caesar's and to God what is God's."** (Matthew 22:21)

Let's always respect the important things even if others don't.

JULY 4

Have you ever left an event too early? Maybe a ball game seemed lost, so you left and later heard your team won. One Fourth of July my wife and I had sat in our car over a half an hour waiting for the fireworks to start. We did see a few small rockets here and there and had heard there would be fireworks. But it seemed they were over, so we went home. We were sure there'd be no more, so we went home to watch fireworks on TV.

Within minutes of closing the garage door the largest fireworks display our town has seen in years started going off only a mile or two from our house. We went outside, but trees hid most of it. We should have waited longer, but we missed it. Oh well, there's always next year.

However, there might not be a next time or a next year with something really important, like missing out on heaven and landing in hell. People don't talk much about hell these days. The idea of a loving God casting people into a pit of flames or a lake of fire seems far-fetched. Hell would be bad enough just knowing you missed being with God! If we don't take God seriously or turn our backs on Him for any reason, we'll miss being with God – that would be hell!

The Bible says in hell unbelievers can see believers rejoicing in God's presence, but they missed it! That kind of regret would be hell of the worst kind.

Perhaps the small regrets we have in life today are given to remind us of the greatest regret of missing out on being with God. Maybe we'd better not say no to Him again. We'd better not turn our back on God, not ever.

But we can be sure of this: He'll be there waiting if we turn back to Him now. Isaiah 55:7 says, **"Let them turn to the Lord, and He will have mercy on them, and to our God, for He will freely pardon."** That's Good News. Knowing God will take us back if we repent is excellent news!

Is any reason for turning from God worth what we will miss?

JULY 5

When my wife and I take our annual trip to visit family in the Midwest, we travel the same route. After crossing Colorado, Nebraska and Iowa, we take Highway 60 northeast into Minnesota. Over the years they've made improvements to Highway 60, and although we no longer pass through many Iowa towns, we enjoy the new road.

The first ten miles into Minnesota is a different story. For years that stretch lay unfinished, delayed by an ongoing haggle between state and city governments. The first year we nearly got stuck driving onto the unfinished roadbed not identified by signs. The finished road abruptly ended, and we sailed out into the mud. In the ensuing years, detour signs took us far out of the way before returning us to Highway 60. For 10 years that road lay unfinished.

We are all traveling roads through life. Some roads are right and lead us to good things. Others roads are bad, but we keep taking them anyway. A bad road will not make itself better. We need to travel a different road.

There are times we need to get stuck to realize we can't go that way again. Maybe it will take getting ourselves so clogged with the mud of foolish choices that we will finally see our need for help. We won't find a better road unless we have a roadmap to show us where best to travel.

That roadmap is the Holy Bible. It tells us Jesus walked the way of sorrows on earth to forgive us our sins. He was mired in the mud and blood of Calvary so we could be rescued. He got stuck for us, but not for long. He got out!

Today Jesus wants to travel with us and show us a better way. Traveling with Him is an adventure. He's there if we have an accident, and He will show us a better way if we get lost. With Jesus by our side, we may still take a wrong turn, but we won't stay lost. He knows the right way and will lead us there if we will let Him. **"He leads me in the paths of righteousness for His name's sake."** (Psalm 23:3)

Which road will you travel today?

JULY 6

An old man was camping in a field by a country road when he discovered a teenage girl hiding in some bushes nearby. She was cold and hungry, so he invited her to his campfire. She'd run away from home because she felt no one cared for her. She thought she was better off being alone.

The old man told her of a game he played with his sons when they were little. He'd give them each a stick and told them to break it. Each of them quickly snapped the stick in half. Then he gave them handful of sticks and asked if they could break them all at once. They'd try but were unable to break the bundle of sticks all together.

"That single stick is you," he told the girl, *"and the bundle of sticks is family. Alone you can break, but with family you are much stronger."* In the morning the girl was gone, but where she had slept lay the small bundle of sticks. She realized being with family was better than being alone.

Carol and I have attended many weddings and enjoy the sisters and brothers, nephews and nieces and children who come. The experience of being with family is always a strengthening event.

It is family, the bundle, that holds us together and gives us strength. As Psalm 68:6 tells us, **"God brings the lonely into families."** Sometimes weddings can help you make new friends, and they can also bring the surprise renewal of old friendships. At several weddings over the years I've met old friends and enjoyed seeing them once again.

Family is made strong when it is knit together of many different strands. Wise King Solomon knew this as he wrote, **"A cord of three strands is not easily broken."** (Ecclesiastes 3:13)

Recently I officiated at the wedding of our youngest son. It was such a joyful occasion as we saw our son and his wife beginning a new family. Her children and his family have given them both a strong bond for life.

Have you thanked God for your family recently?

JULY 7

Christians believe God is all-powerful. We confess in the Apostle's Creed, *"I believe in God the Father ALMIGHTY."* We learn in the Bible that our God is OMNIPOTENT, meaning He is more powerful than all other gods and is the most potent force in the universe. But how does God use His power? And what does it mean for Him to have power? Does power mean only that He rules us or has the power to give or to take life?

If a person has done something deserving of death, the person that takes his life is not really exercising power. Punishing someone who has broken a rule or committed a crime is exercising justice, not power. Power is exercised when the one in authority chooses to pardon the wrongdoer rather than punish him. Having ultimate power and not using it is true power, and God is truly all-powerful.

God chose to use His power to pardon sinners rather than punish them. Yet because He is also a God of justice, He must still punish the sins. This He achieved by punishing His only Son Jesus on the cross.

When Christ was crucified, He took on Himself the punishment of the sins of the world. The almighty Father placed the sins of the entire world on His only Son. We should have died the cross, but Jesus took our place instead. God's justice was satisfied by Christ's death, not ours.

God created the world and all life, including human life. That shows His omnipotence, His all-powerful nature. But the greatest example of God's power is shown when He chose to pardon sinners rather than punish them.

How do you exercise power in your life? With money? By giving or withholding love? By enforcing rules? Or do you feel you are powerless? Whatever the case, we have a Savior who has earned our pardon on the cross. And for that we praise and thank Him. **"For our sake God made Jesus to be sin who knew no sin, so that in Him we might become the righteousness of God."** (2 Corinthians 5:21)

How can you exercise power in your life now?

JULY 8

My son received some good news one day: his car transmission did not need to be overhauled. His twelve year-old Ford truck had lots of miles on it and he noticed it was shifting hard, so he took it to High Country Transmission, a very good repair shop near his home for a check-up. I'd had transmission repair done there and was very satisfied.

A few days later my son called to tell me the diagnostics showed the transmission's okay. It just needed a thorough servicing, new filter and fluid. That's good news since a transmission rebuild is a big ticket item these days.

Power train items don't usually fall apart over night. They wear out over time. Little by little with constant shifting, heating and cooling, dirt and sludge can build up and damage internal parts. Without periodic fluid and filter changes, it can break down.

It's just like people. We ignore our relationship with God and let all kinds of "gunk" in our lives come between us and others, as well as between us and God. Without the regular spiritual cleanups of confession, prayer and Holy Communion, we will "shift" harder until we come to a spiritual stop. We need regular spiritual repair to stay close to God.

King David got himself into big trouble with another man's wife and knew he had dirt in his life. In Psalm 51 he said, **"Cleanse me, O Lord, with hyssop and I will be clean; wash me and I will be whiter than snow."** Those are good words to remember when you feel spiritually sluggish and run-down.

Today give thanks to your Lord that He gave His life for you on Calvary. When we believe Jesus is God's Son and trust Him to forgive us, we can be confident God will not toss us into that eternal Junk Yard. The best way to keep from losing our connection with God is regular worship and prayer. Worship and prayer are a "spiritual oil change."

Does your spiritual power train need servicing? Overhauling?

JULY 9

In 2012, Chick-fil-A made national headlines when its president Dan Cathy spoke out in support of traditional marriage. Reaction by media and some politicians was predictable. Groups tried boycotting the Christian-owned company, but it backfired. Chick-fil-A grew in popularity.

In early 2015, a terrible ice storm hit the south. The press showed miles of cars stranded on frozen interstates, with buses holding school kids up to 24 hours because of the ice. But during that storm, few people heard about the actions of a Chick-fil-A cafe along Birmingham's Highway 280. Owner Mark Meadows closed early and sent his employees home. But they weren't able to get home with all the stranded motorists on clogged roads. Their store was 1½ miles from the interstate and 280 was a parking lot.

So Meadows and his employees fired up the kitchen and made chicken sandwiches as fast as they could, taking hundreds of them out to hundreds of stranded motorists. Some of the drivers tried to pay, but Meadows and his employees refused to take a penny. *"This company is based on taking care of people and loving people before we're worried about money or profit."* said one worker.

But Meadows and his crew weren't done helping. They pushed cars and whatever else they could do to help people. They kept the restaurant open overnight so motorists had a warm place. Some motorists slept in booths or on benches. The next morning, the workers prepared breakfast biscuits, again refusing any payment.

During that 24 hour period, that Chick-fil-A restaurant opened its doors and heart to hundreds of stranded people in need. As one person said, Meadows and his staff lived up to the words of Jesus, **"I was hungry, and you gave Me something to eat; I was thirsty, and you gave Me something to drink; I was a stranger, and you invited Me in."** (Matthew 25:35) None of this was reported in the media.

It's amazing how God's love can be handed out when it's needed.

JULY 10

In 2012, Saeed Abedini, Iranian Christian Pastor, was imprisoned in Iran. He'd become a Christian in 2000 and was immediately subjected to discrimination. He married his wife Neghmeh two years later, and soon became a pastor of an Iranian "house church." He then helped establish 100 more house churches in 30 Iranian cities with over 2,000 members. Because of this, he was arrested, but was given a "light sentence" (8 years) due to international outcry. His crime was *"swaying Iranian youth away from Islam."*

In 2015, his wife Neghmeh was quoted as praising God, not because her husband was released from prison, but because he was able to witness to his father from prison. *"Saeed's father was able to see him in prison today behind a glass window,"* she said. *"It was a wonderful time of fellowship and Saeed got to hear about all of your prayers and words of encouragement that you had shared. Nothing encourages him more than to know that you are all praying for him and that he is not forgotten."* Neghmeh wrote this on her Facebook page.

Neghmeh says the amazing part of the visit was that when Saeed and his father were praying, worshipping and sharing from God's Word together, the guards stood watching, and let the visit last much longer.

"The normal 20 minute visit turned into 40 minutes, which turned into an hour, which turned into a few hours," she says. *"Saeed and his father were shocked the amount of time that they were allowed to visit together. The presence of the Lord was so strong that the guards did not want to intervene and end the visit! Praise the Lord!"*

In Acts 16, Paul and Silas were in prison singing and praying. An earthquake broke open the doors late that night, but Paul and Silas didn't leave. The prison guard was so impressed, he asked about Jesus. **"What must I do to be saved?"** he asked. **"Believe in the Lord Jesus, and you will be saved, you and your household,"** Paul said. (Acts 16:30-31)

God willing, Saeed's guards will learn to trust Jesus, too.

JULY 11

On July 11, 1776, British Captain James Cook began his third trip sailing around the world. He had completed two other successful trips, in 1768 and 1772, but this one would cost him his life. Cook joined the British Navy in 1755, and as explorer, navigator, map-maker and Captain, his rise to fame is legendary. But after 35 years at sea, he died during a fight with Hawaiians at the age of 51.

James Cook married Elizabeth Batts who bore him six children. His voyages took him thousands of miles across largely uncharted areas of the globe. He mapped lands from New Zealand to Hawaii in the Pacific in great detail and on a scale not previously achieved. As he progressed on his voyages, he surveyed and named geographical areas and recorded islands on maps for the first time.

He displayed a combination of seamanship, superior surveying and cartographic skills as well as physical courage and an ability to lead in adverse conditions. Cook was killed during his third exploratory voyage in the Pacific in 1779. He left a legacy of knowledge which was to influence his successors well into the 20th century and numerous memorials worldwide have been dedicated to him. Despite living over 250 years ago, "Captain Cook" is still one of the most recognized names of history.

Jesus of Nazareth was a Jewish Rabbi who never travelled more than 100 miles from Nazareth, His home. He owned no house, wrote no known letters and never married. A dozen or more disciples followed Him during his brief three-year ministry in Judea from 27-30 AD. At age 33, He was convicted before a Roman Tribunal for crimes He did not commit and was crucified in Jerusalem.

Jesus did not, however, remain in His grave. After three short days, His grave was found empty and He appeared to dozens, even hundreds, of His followers. Today, Jesus is the most known and followed person in history. More than that, He is the Son of God.

Jesus was also a "sailor." Can you remember when?

JULY 12

Most of us awake each morning with a plan of what we wish to do that day. But first we start with a certain ritual that will includes washing, dressing and making our bodies ready for the day. Women will put on make-up and men maybe shave. We may include time for exercise, reading the paper and hopefully having a little breakfast with coffee or juice. Then we grab our wallet or purse, start up the car, and out we go to face the day ahead!

Most of this shows we cannot get along without having some help. We clothe ourselves for modesty and warmth. We eat for bodily nourishment and groom ourselves so we appear suitable to others. Some of us add things to help us get by for the day: glasses for seeing, aids for hearing and pills to make sure our body is healthy and strong. We take a wallet or purse for money, ID cards and essentials, including perhaps a cell phone to keep connected with others.

The days are long past when we woke up, left our cave, and went looking for food to kill, but maybe the ritual is similar. We are not self-sufficient; we will always need some things to help us through each day. Even a caveman needed a club to kill his food. Since the beginning of time, people have known they cannot live in isolation. They need companionship and the support of others.

People also seek help from God. Of the seven billion people in the world, three-fourths of us acknowledge the existence of God. We know in our hearts the world and universe did not happen by chance, so we seek help from the One who is greater than ourselves.

As Christians, though, we believe that One to be the God of the Bible, the Creator Father, the Redeemer Son and the Holy Spirit who gives faith. He is the one true God who cares for His creation and wants His creatures to depend on Him. There is nothing weak about trusting God and praying to Him. Folded hands and bowed heads are a far greater sign of strength then prideful, self-reliant heads held high.

"O Lord, our Lord, how majestic is Your name." (Psalm 8:1)

JULY 13

David once write, **"Oh, that I had the wings of a dove! I would fly away and be at rest."** (Psalm 55:6) It sounds like he needed a vacation! My wife and I had a dream of owning some mountain property and in 1986 the dream was achieved. We purchased three acres atop Indian Mountain, southeast of Jefferson, Colorado.

For over twenty years we relished our many mini-vacations at 10,000 feet above sea level, staying overnight in a small trailer and exploring the mountains in our car and on foot. We finally sold it after realizing we no longer had the desire to stay at that altitude for long periods of time. We often took friends with us for a day, and have many wonderful memories of our "time-off" spent there.

I wonder what they called "time-off" back in David's day. In his Psalms he wrote of all kinds of circumstances: violence, oppression, strife and sin that surrounded him. He wrote of betrayal, fear of enemies, and restlessness, as well as love, joy and trust in God. With his many troubles it's no surprise that he wanted to fly away.

But David could not escape, nor could he evade his position in life and his relationship with God. He wrote, **"I call to God, and the LORD saves me. Evening, morning and noon I cry out in distress, and He hears me."** (Psalm 55:16-17) No matter where we are or what we are doing, we can always cry out to God and know He hears us. Whatever is happening to us, God will give us strength to carry on.

Do we have a difficult marriage? God can help renew it. A boring or challenging job? God can give us patience and strength. An illness or accident? God can heal us and give us a second chance. Someone cherished that we've lost? God can comfort us with His love and presence.

If we are willing to trust God with our eternal welfare, we can also trust Him with our daily struggles. Psalm 55:22 says it all, **"Cast your cares on the LORD and he will sustain you; he will never let the righteous be shaken."**

What cares do you need to give the Lord today?

JULY 14

Have you ever wanted to search for buried treasure? In 1795 teenager Daniel McGinnis was wandering around Oak Island, Nova Scotia, when he came across a curious circular depression in the ground. Standing over this depression was a tree whose branches had been cut in a way which looked like it had been used as a pulley. Having heard tales of pirates in the area McGinnis decided to return home to get friends and return to investigate the hole.

Over the next several days McGinnis and his friends dug into the hole. What they found astonished them. Two feet below the surface they came across of layer of flagstones covering a pit. At 10 feet down they ran into a layer of oak logs spanning the pit. Again at 20 feet and 30 feet they found the same thing, a layer of logs. Not being able to continue alone from here, they went home, but with plans of returning to search more.

These three young men are but a few of those who have searched Oak Island in vain for buried pirate treasure. During the 19th and 20th Centuries, groups have dug holes all over Oak Island, but no treasure has been found.

People have always sought treasure. Whether it is buried or in a gold mine, whether it is treasure to be spent or the treasure of scientific discovery, mankind seeks what he does not have. This is as true for gold as it is for peace of mind. It is also true of spiritual treasure.

Jesus once said, **"Do not store up for yourselves treasures on earth, where moths and vermin destroy, and where thieves break in and steal. But store up for yourselves treasures in heaven, where moths and vermin do not destroy, and where thieves do not break in and steal."** (Matthew 6:19-20)

It is a greater treasure to know forgiveness and love than to have gold or silver. God would like us to share whatever we have with those in need. **"For where your treasure is, there your heart will be also."** (Matthew 6:21)

Where is your heart today?

JULY 15

Someone from Iowa once said, *"You can't root for both Iowa and Iowa State. You're either a Hawkeye or a Cyclone. It's either black and gold or red and white. You can't love them both."* I suppose the same could be said of many rivalries, such as the New York Yankees and the Boston Red Sox. You just can't love them both.

Jesus made a point of saying something similar. **"No one can serve two masters. Either you will hate the one and love the other, or you will be devoted to the one and despise the other. You cannot serve both God and money."** (Matthew 6:24) He was not only speaking of money, but of anything that could come between people and God – possessions, power, pleasure, addictions or pride. We must not let any earthly thing come between us and God.

Every day Satan tempts us with rationalizations to do it anyway. He will try to get us to make deals with God and play games with Him. Satan will tempt us to have life both ways. He even promised Jesus, the Son of God, that He'd give Him power and glory if He would only ease up on Satan and give him parts of the earth.

Most tempting must have been when he told Jesus He could avoid suffering and death on the cross if He just knelt before Satan, just a little. Jesus had harsh words for this. **"Away from me, Satan! For it is written: 'Worship the Lord your God, and serve him only'."** (Matthew 4:10) Jesus will never allow Satan to define His purpose in life and neither should we.

In my early rural ministry I worked with many recovering alcoholics. One of them told me when he was drinking he actually (almost) knelt before a new bottle when it was new. Alcohol had become his god. It gave him his feeling of worthiness. He also said it tried its best to kill him. Fortunately, he said, Jesus got to him before it did.

A person can't serve God and the devil. We can be devoted to only one team at a time.

Which team do you root for these days?

JULY 16

During my teenage years I learned to water ski. One of my older brothers was part owner of a sleek red and white speedboat. He kept it at the cabin of the other owner on a popular lake near our hometown. I was 16 years old and my brother Fritz said he'd teach me to water ski, so one Sunday afternoon I took the plunge - literally.

Fritz had said, "It's simple. Hold the rope tight, keep your ski tips together near the surface and let the boat pull you up." Surprisingly, I got up on the water skis the first time. I went around the lake a couple of times and fell once, so I did fairly well. I wasn't very strong, but I enjoyed it.

The next time I came to the lake he showed me something different. Instead of a pair, it was a single ski, a "slalom." "You put both feet on the same ski," he said, "one behind the other. It's not hard." This time he wasn't quite accurate, as it was much harder to keep my balance. But after two failed attempts, I did get up on that single ski and after that, I always wanted to go on the slalom ski.

"You need strong legs, arms and hands to ski," he said when I told him how sore I felt. "It'll probably make you taller – stretch you out," he joked. I also learned I needed to trust the person driving the boat. If he wanted, he could turn the wheel sharply and put the skier into a circular spin at twice the speed of going straight. He could also drive past a ramp in case the skier wanted to jump. I didn't try that.

There are lot of people and things we must learn to trust in life. Whether it's driving in traffic, working at the office, entering a relationship or joining a church, we must learn to trust. Without trust, life is lonely and hard.

In our spiritual journey, God will always be there to pull us up and carry us along. Waves may be choppy and the water cold, but when we trust in Him, we will be safe. **"Trust in the Lord with all your heart and lean not on your own understanding; in all your ways submit to Him, and He will make your paths straight."** (Proverbs 3:5-6)

Lean on the Lord, not on the wind!

JULY 17

A TIME magazine article told of how a CEO of a major coffee company wanted to change the world, beginning with America. The article focused on racial problems and how he felt America was at a tipping point, although I'm not quite sure what he meant would happen it if tipped too far. About 40% of his company's employees were minorities, and many of them had faced problems due to their race.

If he meant that too many more racial incidents would result in riots, that has already happened. *"The country is not going in the right direction,"* he said. *"There is no company you can point to that is as dependent on the human condition as we are."* The article told of several commendable programs his company has instituted to help people get along better.

But it will take more than a coffee CEO to fix what's wrong with our world. It will take faith and trust in Jesus Christ. America and all countries, do need to foster greater respect among races and groups and religions, including more respect for Christians.

I'd thought being a Christian in the 1900s was the most dangerous time, but the 2000s are on their way to being worse. Christian men, women and children worldwide are being butchered and tortured at an ever-increasing rate by vicious people, intent on imposing their beliefs on the rest of the world. Most news outlets don't report this.

The real news is not about minorities being shot by police. It is that village after village worldwide is being slaughtered by self-righteous killers. The CEO's words could be expanded, *"The world is not going in the right direction."*

Yet Christianity continues to grow. With 2.5 billion Christians in the world, faith in Jesus is growing faster than any other religion. God's people have never given up easily. Others may kill, insult and rob us of everything, but still we continue to trust in Jesus as Lord. We pray for an end to the hatred and persecution of Christians, as well as a change of heart for those who wish them evil.

Pray for leaders to help all in need, including Christians.

JULY 18

Back in the 1960's, a popular style of car was the station wagon. It was usually the chosen means of transportation for larger families. Some models came with three bench seats that could hold up to 9 people, so long as they weren't too large. Some came with a bench seat that faced backwards and I always thought that would be an interesting way to travel. Then you could see where you came from, not where you were going. No seat belts, just three bench seats.

One day I got my wish and sat in the rear seat facing backwards with one of my cousins as we rode on a short trip. I didn't like it at all. All the buildings, trees, horses and lakes flew by in a way heretofore unseen, but instead of being fun, it made me nauseous and gave me a headache. I didn't complain because boys that age don't admit getting headaches or upset tummies. I was very glad the trip wasn't longer and made sure another cousin got the privilege of riding back there on the way home.

Life generally looks better looking forward. It can be fun to look back at where we've come from, but more often, we want to see where we are going. We can't know very far what is ahead of us, but looking forward gives us a better chance of seeing it. We can't know the future, but we can know Who holds the future.

In matters of science, we're told, *"Seeing is believing."* In matters of faith, it's the opposite, *"Believing is seeing."* In Hebrews 11, the writer tells of many people who trusted in God for the outcome of their life. Noah, Abraham, Sarah, Jacob, Rahab and many others rode facing forward. They placed their faith in God for what would happen in the future, and God did not disappoint them.

St. Paul made this point when he wrote, **"Hope does not disappoint us, because God's love has been poured into our hearts through the Holy Spirit which has been given to us."** (Romans 5:5) With all great people of faith, *"Believing is seeing."*

Do you spend your time looking forward or backward?

JULY 19

My mother immigrated to America from Germany, crossing the Atlantic just four months after the Titanic sank. Her oldest sister and brother had come to America only two weeks after the Titanic disaster. I once asked Mom if she knew about the Titanic and she replied, *"Everyone knew about the Titanic. But we had our tickets, so we got on the boat and came anyway."* I admire people who take a chance like that. Mom was only 12 years old that year.

Scientists have figured out that a main cause of the rapid sinking of the "unsinkable" ship may have been due to faulty rivets. Since the wreckage of the Titanic was discovered in 1985, researchers have examined parts recovered from the wreck to determine the exact cause of its sinking. One discovery more than others seems to point to faulty rivets which caused the ship's hull to pop open like a torn cloth when it hit the iceberg. This proves the foolishness of spending money on fancy interior trappings and public promotion while neglecting basic and more important parts that hold the ship together.

In a sense, a nation is like a ship, and its people are the rivets that hold it together. Although each rivet may seem insignificant by itself, all together they are essential for keeping the ship strong and making sure it stays afloat. Too many self-centered or missing rivets can weaken the "ship of state" to the breaking point. If citizens seek only their own welfare and do not have consideration for others, everyone will suffer. The same can be said of the Church.

Individual Christians are all important. They are the building blocks of God's Church. If pettiness and jealousy, or envy and pride grow and flourish inside a congregation or the Church at large, it will be weakened in its ministry. James 3:16 says, **"Where jealousy and selfish ambition exist, there will be disorder and every vile practice."**

Our Lord Jesus gave His life that people might learn to love and care for each other, just as He cares for us.

How strong a "rivet" are you in God's House?

JULY 20

Do you have trouble smiling when someone is taking your picture? The practice of smiling for photos is quite recent. Old black and whites always showed grim-faced people, as if a smile was frivolous waste of film.

My parents had a formal family photo taken the year my oldest brother graduated from high school. It is a very nice portrait, but none of us are smiling. The next portrait was taken about twenty years later when all of us were married, and everyone is smiling. I am not sure exactly when or why smiles came into portrait photography, but it seems to be required now that when a camera comes up, so must the corners of our mouth.

My grandchildren were taught to smile on cue by a signal their Mom taught them. When a smile was required she put her index finger on the corner of her mouth, and the little ones quickly showed their teeth in a grin that often was comical. Eventually they learned that whenever they saw a camera pointed their way to give their best smile.

In a few rare places, it is against the law to smile for a photo. Many states require no smile for their auto driver's license photo in case there's a need for use of photo identity matching software. Technology recognizes a face more easily if there is a neutral facial expression.

Jesus told of a good way to recognize a Christian. He said, **"By this all men will know that you are my disciples, if you have love for one another."** (John 13:35) The ways to show love to other people are as unique and varied as people: a smile, visit, shared meal, prayer, listening ear, pat on the arm, greeting card, small gift, cheerful greeting – the list is endless. John further wrote, **"Everyone who loves is born of God and knows God."** (1 John 4:7)

Christians today may not be recognized by the clothing they wear or the work they do. But showing a Godly attitude in word and deed will identify us as God's loving people.

How can you show others you are a believer today?

JULY 21

I rarely watch horse racing, but once or twice a year the major races catch my attention and interest. The "Big Three," Kentucky Derby, Preakness or Belmont Stakes, are interesting to watch especially if one of the horses has a chance to win all three and the "Triple Crown."

But horse racing can be a dangerous business, for horses and also for the jockeys who ride them. Johnny Longden is a Hall of Fame jockey who knew all about this. He rode "Count Fleet" to the Triple Crown in 1943 and won 6,032 races in his career, living to be 96 years old.

But Longden's life nearly ended in the 1930s when the horse he was riding was rammed in mid-race. Longden was thrown sideways, nearly falling off, but another jockey reached out and pushed him back in the saddle. But he pushed so hard that Johnny fell to the other side of his saddle. Still another jockey grabbed him and was able to help him upright. Incredibly, Longden went on to win the race! Helping hands not only kept him from severe injury, they helped him win the race.

As Christians, God's Word is filled with commands and encouragements to help others in need. Proverbs 31:20, speaks of the virtuous woman and says, **"She opens her hand to the poor, and reaches out her hands to the needy."** Psalm 41:1 says, **"Blessed is he who considers the poor! The Lord delivers him in the day of trouble."**

Mother Teresa was a model of helping the poor and downtrodden while refusing anything for herself more than basic essentials. A woman once gave her a new blue sweater because hers was getting threadbare, and Mother Teresa later gave it away saying, *"Give this to someone in need."*

Helping others can be costly to the giver. Jesus gave us all eternal help and it cost Him His life. Jesus **"did not come to be served but to serve and to give His life as a ransom for many."** (Matthew 20:28)

How can you lend a hand in need to someone today?

JULY 22

I like cars and enjoy keeping them in good condition, the car body and mechanical parts. I made a practice of changing my car's oil regularly and keeping a record of other needed servicing. Whenever I wash my car by hand I often recall doing this for my first car, a 1963 Ford Galaxie yellow two-door hardtop. I kept it three years and often wish I still had it. A similar model with a powerful motor in it brought $130,000 at a Barrett Jackson auto auction.

I recall the first time I took my car through an automatic car wash. I put the coins in the slot and stayed inside my car as it was pulled slowly through the line of sprayed water and soap, brushes and swaying soapy leather "fingers" that gently removed dirt and grime. I was afraid the brushes might break off my radio aerial, but it survived intact. When it came to the hot air blow-dryer phase, I realized a hardtop is not very good at being airtight.

Although there was a sense of being at the mercy of a mechanical apparatus, I enjoyed the ride. I'd paid my money and trusted the machine would not wreck my pride and joy, but make its color shine and chrome sparkle when it came out the other end. One thing I learned that day – when I started the wash I had to finish it. I couldn't get out in the middle and take it somewhere else.

There are times when we are in the midst of situations over which we have little control. We commit to things we must trust, and we work at it the best we can: a job, a marriage, buying a house, taking an airplane ride or submitting to surgery.

In Isaiah 43:2 God promises us, **"When you pass through the waters I will be with you; and through the rivers, they shall not overwhelm you. When you walk through fire you shall not be burned, and the flame shall not consume you."** God is with us each moment of each day. He will help us whether we are on the edge of uncertainty or inside the pit of despair. He will not leave us nor forsake us.

Remember, the car wash will come to an end. This, too, shall pass.

JULY 23

People don't keep photo albums like we used to. Today most photos are kept in digital form, in the computer or other electronic "tablet." No longer do we pore over dusty pages of Kodak prints. My wife and I years ago copied all our slides onto our laptop. In a garage sale, I almost had to give away our Carousel projector. No one looks at slides these days, except perhaps those in Powerpoint presentations.

When my first wife died, I decided to go through all our photo albums and make a large album for each of my adult sons. This was a sentimental time for me, but I believe my sons appreciated getting those pictures as a record of their family's early years.

One picture I vividly recall taking was of my oldest son standing in my church pulpit at age 3. He was standing on a chair and looking out at the empty church, trying to look like his Dad did when he was preaching. Many years later, my son, now a Lutheran School Teacher, delivered a fine Good Friday sermon to a full church, and in my mind's eye I could see him as a little 3 year-old again. The following Christmas his six year-old son stood on a chair in the pulpit before a packed church and recited some lines during a Christmas program, again standing on a chair just like his father had done thirty-five years before.

God instructed, **"These words which I command you this day shall be upon your heart; and you shall teach them diligently to your children, and shall talk of them when you sit in your house, and when you walk by the way, and when you lie down, and when you rise."** (Deuteronomy 6:6-7)

Children will observe and remember. *"Little ears are listening"* was a phrase I thought of as I tried to make sure my sons heard good words around our home. Words and deeds of parents are acted out by our children later in life. It is important that parents remember those little ones are watching us big ones.

What will the children around you observe today?

JULY 24

I published several Bible studies one year and writing one of them taught me a lot. The old saying, "The teacher always learns more than the student" (or something similar) was certainly true. It was a 16 week overview of each of the 16 Old Testament prophets which I titled, *Old Testament Disciples*. During my seminary studies I concentrated mostly on New Testament books, thinking the Old Testament books were difficult to apply to modern life. I was not sure there was enough Gospel of Jesus in the Old Testament to warrant much study. I was wrong.

One minor prophet, Zechariah, speaks a great deal about the Christ, the long-awaited Messiah. For example, the book of Zechariah speaks of Christ's humanity in 6:12, His humility in 9:9, His betrayal in 11:12, His deity in 12:8, His crucifixion in 12:10, His return in 14:4 and His eternal reign as King in 14:8-21. Many of these verses are quoted in the Gospels as they related the story of Jesus of Nazareth.

Zechariah 12:10 is an example. Part of that verse reads, **"When they look on him whom they have pierced, they shall mourn for him."** These words are echoed in John 19:37, **"Again another Scripture says, 'They will look on him whom they have pierced'."**

The Old and New Testaments are more unified than we often think. The Old Testament points forward to the Savior, God's Messiah who will come into the world. The New Testament points back at Jesus who is the promised Savior. Old points forward and New points backward, both at the same person, Jesus of Nazareth who is the Messiah. The Old Testament is filled with references to the coming Savior. Read Isaiah 53 and you will be amazed at its mirror image of the suffering and death of Jesus, yet it was written over 400 years before Jesus was even born.

God's Word has many purposes for us, but always to bring us to faith in Jesus Christ. The Holy Spirit works faith in our hearts every time we look at God's Word.

That's a good enough reason to read it, isn't it?

JULY 25

On this day not long ago, my youngest son was first married at age 41. My family and friends were all pleased as he and his bride stood before the altar and pledged their love and faithfulness for life.

It was surely God who brought them together. They barely knew each other in High School, and she left in her Junior year to graduate from another High School. She decided to come to her former school's 20th reunion anyway, but they barely talked to each other there. But they were finally brought together by the Lord. And of all things, He used Facebook! Praise Him for the social media!

As I had done for his older brother 19 years before, I conducted their ceremony. I also practiced more for that wedding than for any other I'd ever done. The years have made me more sentimental and I don't enjoy choking up emotionally in a sermon, so I practiced a lot, and it helped, at least a little. And we were all so happy for them both.

You see, I believe in marriage. It's easy these days to remain single, and marriage is not the social necessity it has been in the past. A man doesn't need a woman to cook and clean house, and a woman doesn't need a man to provide for her and keep a roof over her head as much as in former days. Single folks can do that much far more easily these days than in the past.

But a good and godly marriage makes us better people. I am certain of that. I told my son and his bride that a good woman can make a good man better and a good man can make a good woman better. That's why God has given us marriage. Godly companionship is a great benefit to us all, especially to our children.

I didn't ask her to obey him, but to submit to each other out of reverence for Christ. **"Submit to one another out of reverence to Christ."** (Ephesians 5:21). When godly men and women submit to each other because of Jesus, their marriage will be stronger.

Do you agree? How can people make this happen in marriage?

JULY 26

My eldest son gave me a book of sayings by legendary basketball coach, John Wooden. In one chapter I read that Wooden had an interesting rule for players on his teams. Whenever a player scored, he was to acknowledge the person on the team who had assisted him. When Wooden was still coaching high school, one of his players said *"Coach, won't that take up too much time?"* Wooden replied, *"I'm not asking you to run over and give him a big hug. A nod will do."*

Wooden's reason behind the rule was important. To win on the basketball court takes teamwork. His players were a team, he said, *"not just a bunch of independent operators."* Each member contributed to the success of the others. Wooden's remarkable coaching accomplishments are still the subject of conversations about basketball yet today.

Paul would agree with John Wooden. The Body of Christ, the Church, must work together as one. Each person is separate, yet all are part of the Body. Paul said, **"If all were a single member, where would the body be? As it is, there are many parts, yet one body."** (1 Corinthians 12:19-20)

If a new church building is constructed, is it because of the pastor only? The Building Committee? Or perhaps a few major donors? Success in a congregation always depends on the efforts and accomplishments of many. Whether it's the church leaders (who make decision to build today), or the children in Sunday School (for whose future the church is built), or those who've not yet entered its doors to know Jesus (our ultimate goal), a church is built by many hands.

How many people contribute to the operation of a congregation, or a school, or a family? How many different tasks are there to help a church do the Lord's work effectively? Jesus said in Matthew 18:20, that wherever two or three are gathered together, there He is with them. God uses everyone who comes to do the tasks He gives.

"Take the task He gives you gladly, let His work your pleasure be.
Answer quickly when He calls us, "Here am I send me, send me."
                    (from the hymn, "Hark the Voice of Jesus Calling")

JULY 27

In 1953, a new business was organized called Rocket Chemical Company, and its three workers set out to create a line of rust-prevention solvents, degreasers and other chemicals for use in the emerging aerospace industry. The three men with background in chemistry tried formula after formula to create a solution that would lubricate and separate metal substances.

It took them 40 attempts to perfect the product they were seeking. The substance did its job simply with available chemicals that combined with water. In fact the lubricant displaced water, so they named it Water Displacement 40. Or as we know it, "WD-40". Through their knowledge and persistence, they created an inexpensive product that has been known and used by just about everyone for nearly sixty years. WD-40 is a story of persistence.

Jesus once encountered a woman with bold persistence. She was an outcast Canaanite whose daughter's life was in danger from a demon. She had no hope for her daughter until she heard a Rabbi from Nazareth named Jesus. The desperate mother called after Jesus until she got His attention. Her race, culture, gender and even Satan were against her, but she did not give up. She pushed her way through the crowd and desperation, got what she wanted: Jesus healed her daughter. The whole story of her remarkable faith can be read in Matthew 15:22-27.

What dark valley of need are you struggling through right now? What dark corridor of difficulty or rejection have you encountered? Jesus can and will answer your prayer. He may not give exactly what you want, but He will ease your burden and give you comfort.

Jesus invites us all to come and approach Him with our requests. He bids us to ask, seek and knock on His door to find His solutions. Above all, He will bless us with grace and mercy in our time of greatest need.

"Ask and it will be given you; seek and you will find; knock and the door will be opened for you." (Matthew 7:7)

JULY 28

In Fairplay, Colorado, there is a small wood frame church named after a remarkable man, Rev. Sheldon Jackson (1834 – 1909). As a Presbyterian missionary, Jackson travelled a half million miles and established over a hundred missions and churches mostly in the Western United States.

Jackson wanted to become an overseas missionary, but his church board told the five foot man his weak eyesight and ill health made him be better suited for ministry in the USA. Thus, he began work in the central and western states until after the Civil War. Jackson's first assignment was at the Choctaw mission in Oklahoma Territory. From there he was a missionary to natives in Minnesota and Wisconsin, where he organized or assisted in establishing 23 churches.

With the completion of the transcontinental railroad in 1869, Jackson went on an ambitious missionary tour that often resulted in establishing a church in a day. He soon became the Missions Superintendent for Colorado, Wyoming, Montana, Utah, Arizona and New Mexico, publishing a denominational newspaper and supervising the building of churches in 22 Colorado towns.

The continental US was not his only mission ground. In 1877, Jackson began working in Alaska among the native peoples by founding schools and training centers. He even made two trips into Russian Siberia to help bring reindeer to some of its native people. Though he discouraged the use of indigenous cultures and religions, he still collected artifacts so their cultures would not be lost. He became the First General Agent of Education in Alaska and died in 1909 at age 75 while attending a conference. Churches in Alaska, Colorado and other states are named after him today.

Sheldon Jackson's incredible ministry was to do one thing: teach people about Jesus. St. Paul wrote of the same thing in 1 Corinthians 2:2, **"For I decided to know nothing among you except Jesus Christ and Him crucified."** I'm sure Jackson and Paul have much to discuss in eternity.

Isn't it amazing what some people can accomplish in their lifetime?

JULY 29

I learned to drive in an alfalfa field. Dad took me out there one day in his old Chevy pickup and showed me how the gear shift worked and how to use the clutch and gas pedal. I stalled and jerked a lot at first, but after an hour or so I could operate it better. Until I received my driver's license, I only drove on gravel roads. My brother taught me how to drive on ice on a frozen lake. Learning to turn into a slide has helped me often on slippery roads.

I took one lesson with our school Driver's Training teacher and then failed my driving test with a score of 46. The officer told me to take more lessons, so I did. My Dad drove with me around the country roads and in town until I was better. Two weeks later I passed with a score of 80.

Fortunately, my sons learned to drive better. I did take each of them to a big parking lot and showed them some basics, but they learned to drive from a qualified instructor. The written test is easier to pass than the driving test. A twelve year-old could probably read the book and pass the written test, but getting behind the wheel is harder.

This is also true in our Christian faith. We can learn the basics of the Commandments, Prayer, Holy Communion or the Creed. Having a qualified instructor helps, too. But putting our learning into practice requires a lot more. Knowing the information is basic, but living and making daily decisions from the Word puts our faith to the real test. Living the Christian life requires more than mere knowledge. It requires faith.

In Matthew 11:29, Jesus said, **"Take my yoke upon you, and learn from me."** When we place our trust in Him and try our best to follow His will, we will learn a better way of life. Fortunately for us all, the Holy Spirit will help us put Christ's Word into action.

Today is my daughter-in-law Kersta's birthday. She has been a joy to our son and all our family. We praise God He brought her into Brian's life.

Can you remember the first time you drove?

JULY 30

My father took his one and only driver's license test at age 89. Born in 1898, he got his first driver's license when he was 18 by paying 75 cents for a Minnesota "Operator's License." It was like getting a fishing license. But in 1917 there weren't many cars on the road.

In those days in Minnesota, unless you seriously violated laws or moved to another state, you just kept getting your license renewed. Dad never moved out of the state and he rarely had a citation or an accident. He wasn't required to take a driving test until he was 89 years old. One day he turned the wrong way onto a highway and was met by a state patrolman coming at him. The officer said he only had to take the written test.

Dad was shook up and sure he'd fail. The rest of us prayed he would, since his driving was bad, but Dad was determined. My brother helped him read the book and quizzed him on possible questions. But reading about driving and taking a test are two different things.

The day of the test my brother took him to the testing room and introduced him. Amazingly, the officer gave Dad the test questions orally and he passed easily. When he came home he shouted, *"I did it!"* and smiled all day. The rest of us didn't. We wished Dad wouldn't drive any more.

The Lord took care of that. A month later, Dad got sick and went into the hospital for two months. When he got out, he and my brother went driving one day. When they were back home, he handed my brother the keys and said, *"That's enough,"* and never drove again.

One day each of us will come home and say, *"That's enough,"* and hand the keys of our life over to the Lord. He already said, **"That's enough"** when He died for our sins on Good Friday. When our final day comes, we will step across the threshold of heaven and shout, *"We did it!"* Or better yet, *"He did it!"* Whatever the case, we will be given the prize of eternal life through faith in our Lord Jesus.

Jesus earned salvation for us and that's GOOD ENOUGH!

JULY 31

A young man became a Christian while attending a state University. While so many around him were rejecting the faith in their new-found "academic freedom," he came to realize his need for God and turned to Jesus Christ. He graduated with honors and went on to study the Bible at a respected seminary. Following seminary graduation he accepted a call to a small church for several years and later took another position farther away from family and friends. After twelve years there, he sensed the congregation needed new leadership and stepped down. When asked his plans, he said, *"I don't know where I'm going. I only know God has something in mind for me and I want to find out what it is."*

The pastor told one of his friends, *"A lot of people talk about being called to something, but rarely that they are being called from something. I am sure God has something in mind for me and I want to see what it is."*

In many ways, that pastor was obeying a call similar to one God gave Abraham. He had a good life where he was, but he heard God's call to go to another place that God would show him. The journey was not easy and it was not direct. Abraham journey to several lands, back and forth, until his descendants were given directions to the Promised Land of Israel. Because of his wandering, his descendants were named Hebrews meaning *"wanderers."*

The Bible commends Abraham often for His faith in God. He had all he needed in ancient Ur, family, work, money, loving support and even his family gods for prayer. But when he heard God's voice to go, Abraham followed. The young pastor above sensed the same. God was calling him to follow to a new place he didn't yet know.

Have you ever felt drawn to a place away from family, a place others have questioned? Perhaps it was for a job, or a ministry, or no identifiable reason. Sometimes God just calls us. And when we follow, surprising blessings will come.

When following Jesus' call, remember that He will go with you.

DAY BY DAY WITH JESUS
in
August

+ + +

AUGUST 1

A man hailed a taxi to take him to the airport. They were moving into the right lane when a big car suddenly pulled out of a parking space right in front of them. His taxi driver hit his brakes, missing the other car by inches!

The driver of the other car stuck his head out the window and shouted angry words at them. The taxi driver smiled and waved at the guy. The passenger was amazing his driver was so cool about this, so he asked, *"How could you do that? He nearly dented your car and sent us to the hospital."*

The driver responded, *"He's just a garbage truck. Some people run around full of the garbage of anger and stupidity, and they need a place to dump it, so they dump it on you. The secret,"* he said, *"is don't take it personally. Smile, wave at them and move on. Don't take their garbage and spread it around."*

That taxi driver was a smart man! Contented people don't let garbage trucks take over their day. Life is too short to let the foolish actions of others ruin your day. It's better to avoid the garbage trucks and live the way you want to. Life is half what you make it and half how you take it.

During his three-year ministry, Jesus had piles of garbage dumped on Him, mostly from religious people who should have known better. But instead of reacting with more anger, He usually walked away. When they hassled Him, He ignored them or tossed their words back at them. He had better things to do than walk around in their garbage.

Jesus' main work was to show people God's love. This He did best on Calvary, the ugliest landfill in human history. Instead of dumping the ugliness of sin back on us, He forgave us, and poured out His grace on us from the cross.

That's amazing grace from our amazing God.

AUGUST 2

Newspapers and magazine articles continually warn us about the future and the dangers it may hold due to climate change, economic trends, political possibilities, worldwide terrorism and cultural decay. Such information may move us to wonder how we should prepare for the future. I am inclined to ask that since so much of what is predicted never happens, how can we possibly prepare at all?

Modern intellectuals may truly believe the future can be known, since computerized facts can point us to "definite" outcomes. But anyone looking at the past can surely see that the present has usually unrolled differently due to sudden or unforeseen changes. About all we can surely count on is that the future will probably surprise us.

I have kept this poem for a couple of decades and read it now and then. Not much can be found about its author, Betty Purser Patten, but I think you'll agree with her fine thoughts and find strength in them today. The poet's words remind me of what my college English professor, Dr. Erhardt Essig, often told us in class, *"Poetry - What oft was thought, but ne'er so well expressed."*

"IN HIS HANDS" (by Betty Purser Patten)

We know not what tomorrow brings   Although we plan ahead,
For only God alone can know   The pathway we must tread.

We cannot know the future,   Not one minute nor one hour;
Each circumstance that we must face   Lay only in His power.

It's vital that we live by faith   From minute unto minute,
And trusting that each step we take   He's walking with us in it.

We cannot see the future,   Nor the trials we must face;
But in all things, God promised us,   Sufficiency of Grace.

This alone should give us hope   Whatever be our plans,
In knowing that our future lies   In His great, loving hands.

"There is surely a future hope for you, and your hope will not be cut off." (Proverbs 23:8)

AUGUST 3

Do you ever wish you could change your life, make it different than it was, or at least different in the future? Have you ever considered getting yourself a "reset" in your life? I once had problems with my television receiver. One of the attachments I'd purchased for it was no longer working. I assumed it was broken, when its lights no longer came on.

So I went online and contacted "Chatman" who typed to me not to order a new device, but to reset the old one. He said to make sure all the cords were plugged in. I found one loose and plugged it in, but the light was still out. I followed the rest of his directives, step by step, and the tiny red light came on! No need for new parts, just reset the old ones.

Oh, that life could be so easily fixed! Not our physical life because most of its worn parts can't be replaced. But we can get help for our spiritual life. Through neglect, distraction or following foolish ways we let plugs get loose, live erratically and even become spiritually dead. Our prayer life can be so under-used that we forget we have it.

That's when we need a spiritual reset in Jesus. God wants us to have a tune-up, and getting it done will require help. You can read the Manual but it also helps to visit Pastor Techmann at his spiritual workshop on Sunday. He works for Master Repairman who can make life work better.

A spiritual "reset" is one of God's specialties. There's no cost except time following His directions. I didn't need new parts, just get the old ones working correctly. The light wasn't off because of a dead part, but because the system was jammed. After re-setting it the light came back on, and everything worked fine again.

Mr. Chatman solved my problem quickly. It can take longer. If you're struggling with problems, I urge you to spend an hour a week with Pastor Techmann. His workshops will do wonders for your overloaded or underpowered system. He'll show you how God works best in His own good time with us. Like the Chatman says,

"Hello! How can I be of assistance today?"

AUGUST 4

What inspires us to make changes in life? Is it what we see others do, or is it something in our personality? Can we be a positive influence on others, depending on what they see us do? What causes us to do the things we do?

New neighbors moved in next door. Like us they're a retired couple, so we're glad we'll have others around home during the week. The man is friendly and always greets me. He enjoys being outside and doing something to improve his yard or garage, activities I enjoy also.

On the other side of us live friendly neighbors too, but their yard is not a high priority. He mows the front yard how and then, but their backyard is a wild kingdom. At first this irritated me, but then I realized it was his decision, not mine, and it's better to be friendly than too critical.

So one neighbor is tidy and one is not. I didn't think seeing our yards would influence neighbors, but then my wild kingdom neighbor got married and his yard began to improve. I helped them rake and she brought over food. I offered to cut down a dead tree and he brought us wine.

So, what inspires us to make changes in our life? Is it what we see in others, or what is in our personal nature? Jesus said in Matthew 5:16, **"Let your light shine before others, so that they may see your good works and give glory to your Father who is in heaven."** People may change what they do and even what they believe when they see Christians displaying God-pleasing virtues.

The cul de sac looks better now. I don't know whether or not it will stay that way, but it won't affect how I keep ours up, and it won't change my attitude towards the neighbors. Kind words and friendly acts show a person's faith more than green grass. Being a good neighbor in word and deed will show our faith in action.

How are you letting your light shine in your neighborhood?

AUGUST 5

I've heard it said, *"Never pass up a chance to make amends."* Making amends means being willing to correct something from the past, trying to make right something you've done wrong. It requires being willing to apologize.

Once in High School Shop Class I slugged a fellow classmate. We were all standing in line and someone poked me from behind several times. I ignored the first pokes, then abandoned common sense and slugged the guy behind me.

It was the wrong guy! Someone said, *"He didn't do it,"* and my classmate was on his knees gasping for breath. I pulled him back up and mumbled I was sorry just as the teacher came back in the room, so class went on. I hadn't really apologized, and I never forgot that I hadn't.

Fifty years later, the classmate came to a Class Reunion and I figured it was time to make amends. I told him what I'd done and that I was sorry for it. He looked at me and said, *"I don't remember any of that."* Here I'd thought of it dozens of times, but he'd long since forgotten.

"Never pass up a chance to make amends." If I'd have spoken to him right away, I wouldn't have felt guilty. But I used that incident in teaching my youth classes not to let a offense go by without trying to make amends. It wasn't the only time I taught kids about something stupid I'd done.

Some people try to make amends with God. They'll try doing good deeds to offset past sins or give big gifts to make up for something neglected. Some even enter a life of service to God, trying to make up for something. But it doesn't work. We can never do enough to make up for sin.

But Jesus can. He has already made up for our sins and earned our forgiveness on the cross. He's already fixed up things between us and God. We can't make amends with God, but Jesus has already done it for us.

The Disciple John wrote, **"This is love: not that we loved God, but that he loved us and sent his Son as an atoning sacrifice for our sins."** (1 John 4:10)

"Never pass up a chance to make amends."

AUGUST 6

Who shepherds a Shepherd? Shepherds take care of their sheep. They find them pasture, water and a place to rest. But who takes care of the Shepherds when they become weary and worn? Who shepherds a Shepherd?

SHEPHERDS CANYON RETREAT is a ministry dear to my heart. A few years ago Dave Anderson of Fellowship Ministries began holding retreats for hurting pastors and spouses. In these retreats, a trained staff assists clients to carefully assess their past and future as God's servants. Hundreds have been helped by SCR.

Clients attend an eight-day retreat where marriages have been saved and church workers have been given new hope. Besides individuals, the Church has been blessed. It is the hope of supporters, like myself, that *SHEPHERDS CANYON RETREAT* will attract more supporters, for it is a truly worthy ministry.

SCR has now been blessed with Standing Stones, a ten acre retreat center 15 miles west of Wickenberg, Arizona. It contains a small "Casita" complex for the clients with pool and meeting rooms. Local and national church groups can also rent Standing Stones for retreats and seminars, giving them a much needed income stream between SCR client retreats.

Being a pastor or other church worker is not an easy task today. Changing expectations, temptations and complexities of ministry can wear down the best of workers. It is a costly thing to become a full-time church worker, and it's so much better to help one who has been trained than see them leave and be required to recruit and train others.

People can see what SCR is doing at their website, http://www.shepherdscanyonretreat.org and donations can be made on the link provided. There are also brief videos that explain its ministry and needs. When shepherds become weary and worn, who will "shepherd" them?

"He leads me beside the quiet waters, He restores my soul"
(Psalm 23:2)

AUGUST 7

One day on Amazon I saw a "Clown Bop Bag" for sale that brought back memories. For only $11.29 (plus shipping) you can get a 4 foot inflatable plastic clown punching bag (made in China). It reminded me of one I played with as a child, probably at a friend's house.

It was fun because you could slug it or knock it over and it would always pop back up again. No matter how hard you hit it, it wouldn't stay down. I didn't know the reason right away, but later noticed the bottom was heavy, probably filled with sand or a lead weight.

The bottom "ballast" kept the toy upright when kids like me tried to knock it over. Sailboats have ballast in their keels for the same purpose. When the winds and waves push and pull on the boat above, the ballast gives it a better chance of remaining upright and not be swamped.

Ballast can apply to our Christian lives also. When we are grounded in Jesus Christ, we stand a better chance of surviving the punches of life. Being a Christian doesn't guarantee a better life. In fact it often seems to bring us more punches than ever. But when our faith remains in Jesus, the Holy Spirit helps us get back up.

St. Paul once wrote words about this. **"We are afflicted in every way, but not crushed; perplexed, but not driven to despair; persecuted, but not forsaken; struck down, but not destroyed."** (2 Corinthians 4:8-9) With confidence in our Lord, we can withstand all kinds of storms, problems and "knock-downs" in life.

God has a plan for us that includes improvement. God loves us just the way we are, but He may not leave us that way for long. A friend wrote me that she had lost three people important to her in one month. She wrote that her losses have been, *"a good reminder to show love and thanks to each other while we still have each other on this earth."*

Give thanks today that you have people who love you.

AUGUST 8

There is an Amazon "Fulfillment Center" in Phoenix, Arizona, that ships items to millions of customers across the world each year. A 2015 article in the Arizona Republic said, *"Like bees attending a hive, hundreds of workers, both human and robotic, move with methodical swiftness through the 1.2 million square-foot space, storing, picking, packing and shipping items."*

This enormous buildings is large enough to contain 28 football fields, and there are four of them in Phoenix, fifty nationwide. In one of them, eight miles of conveyer belts move 15 million different items to be shipped to buyers. On Cyber Monday, their busiest day, in Amazon's 50 nationwide stores, 426 items were shipped *per second*. That's 25,560 items per minute, 1.5 million per hour, and 36.8 million items packed and shipped in that one day. 80,000 workers and 15,000 robots do the work, selling over one hundred billion dollars of merchandise each year. All with very few mistakes.

All this by people, and yet many don't believe God can somehow keep track of our prayers! If sinful, weak, mistake-prone mankind can develop and operate a company that can fill and ship 37 million orders per day with few mistakes, God surely can handle all the prayers we send Him.

Prayers are more than "Wish Fulfillment." They carry our hopes, pleas, confessions and thanksgiving. Prayers are our main connection with God who hears our heart's desires, and grants us what we need. If manmade computers can accurately order, track and deliver millions of items each day, our Heavenly Father surely can sort out our prayers and make sure we get what we need when we need it.

In 1 Timothy 2:1, Paul says, **"I urge that supplications, prayers, intercessions, and thanksgivings be made for all people."** Wouldn't it be interesting if we could track the prayers and answers going heavenward and back each day? The figures would make Amazon pale in comparison.

What are grateful for today? I'm thankful to my wife who drew my attention to this story in the newspaper. Today is her birthday.

AUGUST 9

When many people decide to work together towards a common goal, they can accomplish great things. In 1988, Herman Ostry of Bruno, Nebraska, decided to move his barn. Built in the 1920's, it was so close to a small stream that the barn floor was always wet and muddy. Something had to be done or the barn would be unusable.

Ostry contacted a building moving company but their bid was too high. One night around the table, he commented that if he had enough people they could probably pick the barn up and move it to higher ground by hand.

A few days later, Ostry's son Mike showed his father some calculations. He'd counted the individual boards and timbers and estimated the barn weight. He added the weight of a steel frame installed to lift the building, and the total was just under 10 tons. He said it would take 350 people with each person lifting 57 pounds to move the barn.

That year Bruno, Nebraska, was having its centennial, so Herman and Mike presented their barn moving idea to the committee, and its members made it part of their celebration. It would show how people can work together. On the morning of July 30, 350 people, picked up the barn and moved it 115 feet south and 6 feet higher, setting it on its new foundation. The move took less than a half hour.

The two key terms in the project were *"many people"* and *"common goal."* If only a few do all the work, some tasks cannot get done. If they don't have a common goal, the number will not matter. When many people have a common goal, God can make miracles happen. They can build hospitals, churches, colleges, nursing homes, schools and achieve all kinds of worthy ministries.

It is estimated that there are 2.5 billion Christians living in the world today. Imagine the miracles God would bring about if all of them worked together, prayed together and worshipped Jesus Christ together. **"Blessed are the people whose God is the Lord!"** (Psalm 144:15)

Seeing 350 people work together is amazing!

AUGUST 10

Have you ever lost something valuable and couldn't find it? Around our house, I'm usually the one who finds lost things. Whenever an earring is lost, or car keys, or cell phone or whatever, I can usually find it. Over the years I've found several very valuable things, including gems.

I read in an issue of *Reader's Digest* about a woman named Lena who was tossing some stunted carrots from her garden onto her compost heap. Seeing something glitter, she picked up one of the carrots and found it had grown through a ring - her own long lost wedding ring! Sixteen years earlier she had lost the ring which had apparently gotten mixed in some dust that ended up in her garden. She had given up all hope of finding it and had never replaced it. Now it had come back to her wrapped around a carrot!

Four years after we were married my wife and I had gotten some sweet corn from a member's field. Coming into the house, she discovered the diamond from her wedding set was gone. I retraced her steps with a flashlight, beginning with where she was standing and only a few steps away her half-carat diamond glittered on the floor next to our clothes dryer. A half inch and it would've disappeared.

I once conducted a funeral for a member who had an adult daughter in a wheelchair. During the fellowship after the service she noticed the large diamond was missing from her ring and told me. I retraced her steps back to the restroom and found her huge diamond on the floor, right next to the floor drain. Another inch or two and it would have disappeared forever down the drain.

Jesus told a story to illustrate the joy finding the lost. He said, **"There will be more joy in heaven over one sinner who repents than over ninety-nine righteous persons who need no repentance."** (Luke 15:7) No matter how precious a thing may be to us, we are more precious to God. He never wants His children to lose their way, but if one should, He sends His angels out to find him.

I hope you won't lose anything today!

AUGUST 11

During a phone call to a pastor friend in Minnesota I told him how bad our mosquitoes had been in Colorado that summer. Normally our summer has few of those pesky little bugs. But my friend said something surprising: *"Be thankful you have mosquitoes! We don't have any."* I thought I'd heard it all, but not that. I've tried to give God thanks for all kinds of blessings in life, but mosquitoes? I believe I'll pass on that one, and I told him so.

He responded, *"If you've had mosquitoes, it means you've had rain. It's been so dry here we haven't had mosquitoes all summer. I'd give anything if we'd have had mosquitoes like a normal year. There is almost no crop at all, and with grain prices being so high, it's doubly hard. Be grateful you have mosquitoes."* If those pesky critters come along with rain for the crops, I guess even mosquitoes can be a blessing.

One winter our Chorus at Palm Creek, Arizona, sang a Monty Python song that included the phrase, *"Always look on the bright side of life."* Its goofy lyrics mocked life, but that line had a good thought. If we look for good things in life rather than just the bad, we stand a better chance of being content.

With national politics having grown so contentious, our shaky economy, increase of family problems and growing world tensions, it's tempting only to look on the dark side of life. Paul wrote in Philippians 4:11, **"I have learned in whatever situation I am to be content."** He wrote that from prison, not the brightest place! Even there he could be content through trusting in Jesus.

Being content doesn't mean we ignore the presence of evil. But our problems need not control us if we look for the good things God has given us.

Our Lord Jesus came to this earth to give us new life. Until we experience His precious gift in heaven, we have an earthly life of unique blessings where even problems can be a blessing if we look at their place in the big picture. Like St. Paul, we too, can learn the secret of being content.

Yes, even mosquitoes can be a blessing!

AUGUST 12

911 calls are filled with emotion. They are received by a dedicated staff of individuals all over the United States who are trained to help people in need. That need, however, is not always understood by those who call 911.

There are many lists of foolish 911 calls. I looked at several and now give you my list of "Ten Silliest 911 Calls" that actually happened.

1. A timid High School youth called 911 because someone stole his sack lunch.
2. A ten year-old boy called 911 for help solving a math problem. The operator helped him.
3. An enraged man called 911 late at night because a nightclub doorman had refused him entry.
4. An angry woman called 911 because, "My shrimp fried rice has no shrimp!"
5. An obviously lonely and slightly tipsy woman called 911 to help her find a date.
6. An immature, whiny man called 911 because, "My mother took away all my beer!"
7. A "high" homeless man called 911 on a cold night from a house where he was in a hot tub. A squad car took him to a warm cell.
8. A crying woman called 911 to ask how to get out of her locked car. She was inside, right next to the door locks.
9. A frightened man called 911 when he got stuck inside the house he was burglarizing. Another squad car came to his "rescue."
10. A frantic woman stuck in traffic called 911 because she was late for the movies.

Do you think God ever gets weary at some of the prayers sent His way? I don't think so. Always remember that He has told us,

"Pray without ceasing." (1 Thessalonians 5:17)

AUGUST 13

"I left it on the church pew." My wife and I were returning from worship and realized something was missing. I turned the car around, retrieved the missing item and we went home. On the way I asked, *"Why do they call it a 'pew'"?* She said, *"Maybe you should write about it."*

There are many "church words" we frequently toss around - narthex, nave, liturgy - and rarely know their word origin. Here's what I found on a few familiar "church words," although the list is much longer:

PEW *is from a French word (puy), the stand on which statues rested which came to mean the long benches where worshippers sat.*

NARTHEX *is from Greek words for the passage through which early Christians passed during their baptism. It came to mean the lobby outside the Nave.*

NAVE *is Latin (navis) for "ship" and came to mean the central area where people gathered for worship.*

LITURGY *is from Greek words for "work of the people," our songs, prayers and other orderly responses given to God.*

HYMN *is Latin (hymns) for a "song of praise" or thanksgiving to God.*

CHURCH *is Dutch (Kerk) or German (Kirche), translations of Greek (Ecclesia), meaning those "called out" to worship God.*

BIBLE *is Latin (biblia) for "book." Christians used it for the greatest of all books.*

The English language is relatively new and constantly changing, usually due to words taken from other languages. One of the reasons we have so many English Bible versions is due to the continual changes made in our language.

God's Word is God's message to us. John 1:1 & 14 tell us, **"In the beginning was the Word, the Word was with God and the Word was God... The Word became flesh and dwelt among us."** God's Word has its highest expression in the form of Jesus, the Son of God. What He did for us is the message of God's Word.

What "church word" is confusing? Look up its meaning.

AUGUST 14

When an Ohio waitress asked to see a customer's driver's license to prove she was old enough to purchase alcohol, she was shocked when she saw the picture on the license. It was her own photo. The waitress had reported her wallet as being lost weeks earlier and some of her credit cards had been used for over a $1,000 in purchases.

But she never thought she would be handed her own driver's license by the thief. The 23-year-old thief from Lakewood, Ohio, fled the restaurant, but was soon found and charged with identity theft and receiving stolen property. She was arrested at her home in suburban Cleveland and was jailed awaiting a court appearance.

The 22-year-old waitress, whose name was not released, had called police and said she'd been handed her own stolen driver's license by another woman trying to prove she was 21. "The odds of this waitress recovering her own license defy calculation," a local police captain said. This story was aired on CBS in 2006.

It is far more difficult to fool people today than it was in Old Testament times. Rebekah fooled her blind husband Isaac into thinking his younger son Jacob was Esau. Later, Jacob worked for his uncle Laban for seven years to marry pretty Rachel, but Laban fooled Jacob into marrying plain Leah. Jacob then had to work seven more years to marry Rachel. Both Rebekah and Laban felt they were doing God's will while really seeking to get their own way.

A lot of pretending still goes on in the name of God. Using the right "Christian" words, men or women may attend church regularly, pray often and do good things, all to gain the approval of others. But they can never fool God. He sees the heart and knows what is there.

Our Lord Jesus knows we aren't perfect, but He expects us to admit our sins, not hide behind religion. Jesus' harshest criticism was for religious leaders who were merely "hypocrites" (Greek for "actor").

Are there some areas of your life where you are hypocritical?

AUGUST 15

Fyona Campbell became famous as the first woman ever to walk around the world. But her joy in achieving this remarkable feat didn't last. Despite all the notoriety she achieved and adulation she received, she admitted she was a fraud. Overtaken by guilt, she said she had cheated. During her world-wide walk, she broke the guidelines of Guinness Book of Records by riding in a truck part of the way. To clear her conscience, she called her sponsor and confessed what she had done.

World famous golfer Bobby Jones didn't let one of his mistakes become deceitful. Jones, a skilled golfer, was always observant of the principles of sportsmanship and fair play. In the first round of the 1925 U.S. Open, his approach shot to the 11th green fell into the deep grass. As he took his stance to pitch onto the green, the head of his club brushed the grass, causing the ball to move, a USGA Rules infraction.

Jones took the shot, then informed his playing partner Walter Hagen, and the USGA official covering their match, that he was calling a penalty shot on himself. Hagen was unable to talk him out of it, and that extra shot cost Jones the tournament. When praised for reporting it, he said, *"You might as well praise me for not robbing banks."*

God has given each of us a conscience that brings guilt when we do what we know is wrong. In Romans 2:15, Paul says our conscience is either accusing or else excusing us. The obedient follower of Jesus will try to follow his or her conscience despite our sins. Daily confessing our sins to God should be a way of life. Paul said, **"I always take pains to have a clear conscience toward God and man."** (Acts 24:16)

Our worship services usually have a time of confession and absolution. God is glad when we tell Him we are sorry for our sins and then ask His help to do better. Through absolution, we can be assured God does not keep track of our sins, but "clears the slate" each time.

What sin is bothering you right now? Speak to God about it.

AUGUST 16

A man walked into his 40th High School Reunion and hugged and talked to people for 20 minutes before realizing he was in the wrong place. Another reunion was going on that day and he was at the wrong one.

Bill Hustad, a technology writer for the *Atlanta Journal-Constitution* used that experience to illustrate one of his proven axioms of trouble-shooting computer problems: *"Check the obvious first."* Before replacing something big, check the little things – cords connected, volume control turned up, modem reset, etc. Before tossing the old laptop away, make sure the old one is plugged in.

But sometimes the "wrong thing" can turn out to be the "right thing." A single man goes into a church for his aunt's funeral and after twenty minutes finds he's in the wrong church. He is sitting next to a single woman, they laugh at his mistake and a year later are married.

"Check the obvious first" can be a good attitude for one's spiritual troubles. Often people will say *"God feels so far away"* until they realize He hasn't moved, but they have. Feel like it's hard to pray? When is the last time you really sat down and did pray more than a memorized prayer? Feeling lonely? What have you done to be around people who share your values and attitudes?

Faith, prayer and friendships all need your involvement. The obvious may be that you need to try a new approach, including find new friends. Proverbs 13:20 says, **"Whoever walks with the wise becomes wise, but the companion of fools will suffer harm."**

At the risk of being pelted with verbal rocks, I believe some of the Christian "connection" agencies can be good to locate people who share common interests and values. I am speaking primarily to those who are single, of course. But God gives us good friends often in the most surprising places.

Have you needed a good friend lately?

AUGUST 17

Jonathan Wiener has authored *Long for This World,* a book about science's oft-promised feat of radically extending human life. It seems that English scientist Aubrey de Grey is predicting science will one day be able to help people live a thousand years or more. Aubrey claims the molecular biology is nearing the stage of finding a cure for aging, and that it may even happen during our lifetimes.

But who really wants to live a thousand years? Do we really wish to be around to see what will happen in even a few hundred years? And wouldn't it be counter-productive to population theorists that a bunch of young-looking geezers are taking up space in our too-fast growing world?

What is de Grey's point in seeking this? Despite what science may do to make us live longer, we all will still die. Is he trying to work toward the day no one will die, or is he just denying the inevitable? Would not living forever be more of a curse than a blessing?

Holy Scripture, given us by God Himself, tells us over and over again that death is not the end of our existence. Instead of just dying and decaying like an old tree trunk, we are assured that everyone will one day stand before Jesus Christ and receive His judgment – eternal life for believers and their faith in Him, and eternal separation for non-believers and their rejection of Him.

John 5:28-29 tell us, **"Do not marvel at this, for an hour is coming when all who are in the tombs will hear His voice and come out, those who have done good to the resurrection of life, and those who have done evil to the resurrection of judgment."**

That is very plain language. It's not a possibility but a reality. If we trust that Jesus is Himself the Son of God, then He speaks the truth. It might be interesting to know a few things that will happen in the future, but I think few of us would believe what we'd be told. Who of us thirty years ago would have believed what computers do for us even today?

What would you like to live to see in the future?

AUGUST 18

A woman found a wrinkled old baseball card in a drawer. Thinking it might be worth some money, she posted it on eBay and received a few responses. A friend told her it might be worth more, so she took it to an antique dealer who referred her to sports collector. The collector confirmed the photo on the card and said her old baseball card was printed in 1869 showing a player from the Cincinnati Red Stockings, the first professional baseball team in the USA. Her card sold for more than $75,000.

Mike Osegueda, writer for *The Fresno Bee,* wrote an article about the card in which he said even though it was discolored and worn, it still had great value. The most important thing was its authenticity. It was not a copy - it was the real thing.

Being "the real thing" is important. A pastor starting a new church was visited one Sunday by a couple he'd known from another congregation. They said they wanted to help him with his new mission plant. When asked by other people at the church why they came, one of them said, *"We trust him. He has the integrity we like in a pastor."*

A pastor needs to be trusted by his people. It is easy to act like someone you are not, and when it comes to leading people to Jesus Christ, having integrity is important. Integrity is the quality of being honest and having strong moral principles. It doesn't mean a life of no mistakes but honest mistakes. A person of integrity is not a copy – he or she is the real thing.

Jesus of Nazareth was such a man, with the exception that He made no mistakes. He not only avoided the big sins, His nature was holy and without blemish. 1 Peter 1:19 tells us we are saved **"...with the precious blood of Christ, like that of a lamb without blemish or spot."** Jesus was "the real thing." He followed God's Law to the letter. Because He did, He is our substitute with our Holy God. When we trust Him, He makes each of us "the real thing" with God the Father.

Do you know someone of integrity?

AUGUST 19

Does it bother you to see all kinds of public admiration for people who stand for the wrong things? Perhaps it is politicians who "stretch" and even break the law but are excused by their admirers. Maybe it is entertainers, actors or musicians who espouse immoral living or write songs that denigrate marriage, the police, women, the Church or even God. Maybe you pray, expecting God to straighten up the mess our nation and world seems to find itself in.

It is not difficult to be fretful and anxious about life today. We have seen so much progress in medicine with diseases going away that we might expect sinful behavior to go away also. We think freedom should bring moral behavior, but it seems to produce the opposite.

David the king saw evil around him and it moved him to write Psalm 37. He wrote, **"Fret not yourself because of evildoers; be not envious of wrongdoers! For they will soon fade like the grass and wither like the green herb. Trust in the Lord, and do good; dwell in the land and befriend faithfulness. Delight yourself in the Lord, and He will give you the desires of your heart. Commit your way to the Lord, trust in Him, and He will act."**

It's easy to become fretful when the faithful struggle, but the evildoers succeed. Remember that our Lord Jesus Christ, the Son of God, has all things under His control. He will not let evil succeed, nor will the righteous.

David continues, **"Be still before the Lord and wait patiently for Him; fret not yourself over the one who prospers in his way."** Being still and waiting on the Lord is trusting Him to do what is needed at the right time.

We may not like what we see and hear from parts of our society, but always remember that God is in control of our world. As David encourages us, don't fret – don't envy – delight in God – trust in the Lord – commit your way to the Lord – let Him do what is best for us all.

What do you fret about most? How can God help you?

AUGUST 20

Allan Pinkerton (1819-1884) was a Scottish American spy and detective who became well-known in the 1800s when he and his assistants solved a series of train robberies and foiled a plot to assassinate President Abraham Lincoln as he traveled to his first inauguration in 1860.

Pinkerton came to America in 1842 and settled in Dundee, Illinois, 50 miles northwest of Chicago. Becoming an abolitionist, he offered his home as a stop on the Underground Railroad. In 1849 he became Chicago's first detective, and with the help of Chicago attorney Edward Rucker, he later established the Pinkerton Detective Agency.

Pinkerton met Abraham Lincoln, then a young lawyer for the railroad, in the 1850's. He worked many undercover missions for the Union Army, and helped establish the U.S. Secret Service. After the Civil War, Pinkerton's agency worked for the railroad and was unsuccessful in trying to capture the James Gang. At the time of his death, he was working on a system to centralize all criminal identification records, a database now maintained by the FBI.

His Pinkerton Agency logo was an open eye with the words under it, "We Never Sleep." Surprisingly, no agency has been found to use such a logo or slogan, but the thought is rather reassuring. Christians believe God never sleeps and watches over us at all times. It's a nice feeling knowing you are protected both night and day.

Some, though, are anxious. There may be dissention and anger in the home, or worry over a rebellious child, or someone who is seriously ill. Sometimes parents check their children to make sure they are breathing.

Psalm 34:15 says, **"The eyes of the Lord are toward the righteous and his ears toward their cry."** God never sleeps. He keeps watch over us and our loved ones, no matter where and no matter what. He will always make sure our needs are met, whether they are earthly or eternal.

Do you have an alarm system? How has God protected you?

AUGUST 21

A 2015 Reader's Digest had an article by Emily E. Smith titled, *"Happiness: It's Not All It's Cracked Up to Be."* In it she stated that in 2012 the happiness levels in America hit a four-year high. At the same time, a poll showed 4 in 10 people said they had not yet discovered a satisfying life purpose, regardless of how well their basic needs were being met.

She referenced Viktor Frankl, a Jewish psychiatrist who survived a Nazi concentration camp because he had a purpose working as a therapist during his time there. Frankl wrote *Man's Search For Meaning* in which he said, *"He who knows the WHY of his existence will be able to bear almost any of the HOW."* In other words, having a purpose in life increases a person's overall satisfaction.

During the first decade of my ministry it became fashionable to have a "mission statement," a few well crafted words which would tell what your purpose in life was. I decided to make mine simple enough that I wouldn't forget. I eventually settled on this: **"To give people hope."** Most of what I have done in preaching or teaching, leading or listening during my ministry was to find a way to give people hope. That has been and continues to be my purpose. That's why I am so grateful to be writing. Giving people hope in writing continues my life purpose now and can remain so as long as I am willing and able.

Early in ministry I wrote a sermon called, *"Happiness is a By-Product,"* not a very inspirational title but certainly descriptive. I used this theme in many wedding addresses also. In it I said, *"Don't seek happiness first in your life; seek the Lord first and happiness will come from Him."* It has surely worked that way in my married life. As Jesus tells us in Matthew 6:33, **"Seek first the kingdom of God and his righteousness, and all these things will be added to you."**

Jesus put our needs first and earned for us a place with the Father in eternity. If we put Him first, we will find much happiness.

What is your purpose in life? How can you find it?

AUGUST 22

Kids in school often learn some fascinating facts and pass them along to their friends. There was a word going around my high school supposedly the longest in the English language: *"antidisestablishmentarianism."* It had 27 letters – wow! Just being able to say it or count the letters gave a high school kid a feeling of accomplishment.

But what did it mean? In High School I didn't care, but thinking about it now moved me to look it up. A dictionary defines this enormous word as *"opposition to the withdrawal of state support or recognition from an established church, especially the Anglican Church in 19th Century England."* Saying the definition is almost as hard as saying the word!

Evidently during the 19th Century, some British people wanted to remove the Church of England as the official "established" religion of the land. But opposition quickly formed in the hopes of retaining the Church of England for all the people of England, Ireland and Wales.

But it didn't work. In 1871, the Anglican Church of Ireland was "disestablished" and in 1920, the Anglican Church in Wales was "disestablished" and became the Church in Wales. Knowing this probably still isn't as important as being able to pronounce and spell the word. I am sure none of this impresses us now.

St. Paul didn't try to impress people either. He wrote, **"When I came to you, brothers, I did not come proclaiming to you the testimony of God with lofty speech or wisdom. For I decided to know nothing among you except Jesus Christ and him crucified."** (1 Corinthians 2:1,2) Paul wasn't there to show off his knowledge but to share his faith in Jesus.

"Lofty speech" isn't necessary when sharing our faith. We don't need to impress people, just share Jesus with them with a few well-chosen words. Simple terms work best. Paul was a brilliant scholar, but he continued in verse 5, **"...so that your faith might not rest in the wisdom of men but in the power of God."**

Have you ever shared your faith? With whom?

AUGUST 23

On August 23, 1936, 17 year-old Bob Feller pitched his first Major League baseball game for the Cleveland Indians, striking out 17 members of the St. Louis Browns. This amazing athlete was so good he passed up Minor Leagues and spent 18 seasons with the Indians in a career that spanned 1936 – 1956, interrupted by four years in the Navy during World War II as a Petty Officer on the *USS Alabama*.

Feller became the first pitcher ever to win 24 games in a season before the age of 21. "Bullet Bob" set many records and helped the Indians win the World Series in 1948. He was recognized as one of the fastest and best pitchers in the history of the game. Fellow Hall of Famers Stan Musial and Ted Williams both said he was probably the best pitcher of their era. One of his pitches was clocked at 107 mph!

Young Feller was amazing even as a child. He learned to throw a curve ball at age 8 and by age nine could throw a baseball 270 feet! Raised on an Iowa farm, Feller once said his arm strength came from *"milking cows, picking corn, and baling hay."* His father built a baseball diamond on his farm and urged his son and others to form a team. At age 15, Feller substituted for an injured pitcher and found his gift. He was signed by the Indians at age 17 for $1 and an autographed baseball. Feller threw his final pitch in the *Hall of Fame Classic* at age 90. He died in 2010 at the age of 92.

While certain people may stand out in history, God has gifted all of us in some way, through what we can do, what we know, how we deal with people or a special talent. Whatever God has given us, we should use it to give Him glory and to help others. St. Paul said, **"Whatever you do, in word or deed, do everything in the name of the Lord Jesus, giving thanks to God the Father through Him."** (Colossians 3:17)

What gift, skill or talent has God given you? Have you considered how you can use it to help others?

Give thanks today for all that God has given you.

AUGUST 24

Those who served in the Armed Forces for many years, perhaps making it a career, are usually thankful they were able to give those years in service to their nation. When it comes time to leave, they go through a period of service in which they can be referred to as "short-timers."

A short-timer is a soldier who has only a few weeks before being discharged. They often spend their last days "mustering out" which can include easier days of visiting the commissary and the quartermaster's office to return equipment and make sure their accounts are all cleared. The longer a person has served the longer it takes to muster out. A 27-year Chaplain Colonel told me it took him over a year to get everything cleared for his retirement. He said it was a good time with less pressure. He carried out his duties but had fewer worries and stress because he knew he was soon going home.

Now that some of us are "old-timers," we also know that we are "short-timers." It won't be long before we're discharged from our duties here on earth. Because of this, our pace of life is light and cheerful because we know soon we will be going home. St. Paul said in Philippians 1:21, **"For to me to live is Christ, and to die is gain."** When God finally musters us out of this life, we know our home-going will be best.

But what will we do as earthly "short-timers"? We don't stop following the Lord, but rather make sure we are doing all we can to make our time here productive yet enjoyable. There is usually less pressure and worry, and there can be more time for doing tasks for the Lord and His people. We can also take more time to read and learn God's Word because it's message is timeless and precious.

Christians place their hope in the words of Jesus Christ. Our hope means certainty, the firm assurance that we will not merely die, but be raised from the dead as Jesus was and be welcomed home into eternity with God.

A Christian's true home is in heaven.

AUGUST 25

Have you ever called for someone to fix a problem around your home, only to find you could have easily fixed it yourself? Technicians report that up to 30% of their service calls could easily have been avoided had the home owner flipped a switch, pushed a button or tightened a nut. Service calls typically cost $60 to $100. When they are easily fixed, they can cost some embarrassment too.

My older car once didn't run right. I called a mechanic in my congregation who said to bring it over. He listened to the motor, raised the hood and pinched a rubber tube. The motor immediately began running smooth. *"Vacuum hose,"* he said. *"It was crimped, so I straightened it."* No charge for that "repair."

Another time I had an electrician come out because a series of outlets no longer worked. He looked at the problem, went into my workshop and punched a small button in the middle of the outlet there. Everything worked! *"It's called a GFCI,"* he said. *"It is a small breaker we're required to put in houses, and sometimes people don't know they are there."* Since then, I've always known where my GFCI breakers are. The electrician's $50 service fee taught me well!

Our Christian life can be fraught with small things that don't go well. Unrest over a relationship, anxiety over family matters or stress in work can often be traced to something relatively small that we have neglected. If we rarely pray any more, or if we attend worship only sporadically, or if our language has become more coarse, we may feel something is wrong.

And it is! When our relationship with God is neglected, the rest of life can become shabby and bumpy. A decision to return to regular prayer, worship or giving to the needy (instead of only to ourselves) can bring the balance and contentment that we have been missing. It is as Paul said in 1 Timothy 6:6, **"Godliness with contentment is great gain."**

Is something missing is life? Might it be something small?

AUGUST 26

C. S. Lewis wrote an interesting work called, *The Weight of Glory*. It tells the story of a woman who gave birth to a child while confined in a dungeon as a prisoner. Since the child had never seen the outside world, his mother attempted to describe it with pencil drawings. She did her best to portray things of life for the child, and later when she and her child were released from prison, the simple pencil drawings were replaced by the actual images of the real world.

In it he wrote what our world is like, compared to the glory of being with God. *"At present we are on the outside of the world, the wrong side of the door. We discern the freshness and purity of morning, but they do not make us fresh and pure. We cannot mingle with the splendors we see. But all the leaves of the New Testament are rustling with the rumor that it will not always be so. Some day, God willing, we shall get in."*

Another profound thought in this oft-quoted book is this: *"He who has God and everything else has no more than he who has God only."* With so many of Lewis's writings, he clarifies for us that this world is not all there is, and it is surely inferior to the coming blessings of life with God.

If you could, what pictures would you draw to show an infant what the world is like? In many ways this is what the writers of the Holy Bible attempted to do. They could not show us digital photos of life with God, but they left us word pictures of eternity.

We can only see in shadows, pencil drawings of eternal life with God. Paul wrote in 1 Corinthians 13:12, **"For now we see in a mirror dimly, but then face to face. Now I know in part; then I shall know fully, even as I have been fully known."** Our current ideas of the glory of heaven is only a sketch in black and white. But we can have genuine confidence in Jesus who has told us He has gone to prepare a place for us (John 14:1-3). In Jesus, the best is yet to come!

What sketch would you draw to show someone our world?

AUGUST 27

Gerald was an outspoken atheist. He spent much time and energy denying the existence of God with his friends. *"It's all just a waste of time,"* he said. Then Gerald got a terrible disease, one that quickly rendered him helpless and dependent on others just to live. His health became so poor he was placed into hospice and awaited death. No longer did he speak as confidently that there was no God, but he still didn't believe God existed.

During his hospice stay, many of Gerald's family and friends visited him, including some Christian friends he'd known since high school. They told him they were praying for him, but he usually changed the subject. Soon he was too weak to object and he just listened. Yet being closer to death did not make him any more interested in God.

One Sunday afternoon a pastor visited him who had been told of Gerald's resistance. To his surprise, Gerald folded his hands when the pastor prayed for him. He asked the pastor to return and the next day wanted to know how to pray for salvation. *"Are you sincere about Jesus, or are you just hoping there is a God?"* the pastor asked him boldly. Gerald smiled and said, *"Maybe a little of both. My Christian friends have been so good to me, more than I expected. Maybe what they believe is true. Maybe it's time I gave God a chance."* Then Gerald prayed and asked God for forgiveness. A few weeks and several visits later, he died.

Gerald gave God a chance. He had denied Him for years, but spent only a few weeks trusting Him. Because of his faith, he will know God's presence and love for eternity. Some may argue this isn't fair, but according to Jesus, it's not about fairness but faith. In Matthew 20:16, He said, **"The last will be first, and the first last."** Salvation doesn't depend on when but on who. It's not the duration of our faith, but the subject of our faith that grants us eternal life.

Have you known someone who rejects God. What can you do for him or her?

How can you pray?

AUGUST 28

Poison ivy and I are not friends. In fact, if there is any around, it will find a way to let me know. Strangely, I never encountered it on the farm, but I surely did in a couple of cities. I once had taken my boys golfing when they were young and one of them hit the ball into a small ravine. From above I could see his ball together with several others, so I told them to stay and went down to retrieve it and the other balls. Down there I saw a sign that said, "Caution!" but gave no reason, so I cautiously picked up the balls and we finished the game.

That night morning my tummy was on fire! I tried washing it away, then soaking in a tub and some ointments, but nothing worked. I barely slept and went to work but couldn't concentrate. I finally went to see my doctor's nurse who chuckled and said it was poison ivy. I must have brushed some plants when I picked up the golf balls. She gave me some tablets that took away the itch in a few hours. That's what that "Caution!" sign meant.

There are all kinds of "Caution!" signs around us that we may not see or believe. The obvious ones direct our driving in traffic, but others direct our lives. Parents and friends can caution us but we don't always hear them. I once made a major decision and my brother-in-law told me, *"Watch out - don't do it!"* But I did it anyway and lived to regret it.

The Bible is filled with "Caution!" signs. They can be obvious in the Ten Commandments or subtle in the comments of Christian family and friends. They do not always tell us the exact nature of why we're to be cautious, but if we are wise, we will not leap down into the ravine before we've looked.

Proverbs 14:16 tells us, **"One who is wise is cautious and turns away from evil, but a fool is reckless and careless."** Signs are usually there for a purpose, right?

What sign have you seen today?

AUGUST 29

Thomas Moore (1779-1852) was an Irish songwriter, singer and poet. His talents brought joy to many in his lifetime and also to those of us who may have sung one of his hymns. Moore (not to be confused with Sir Thomas Moore, servant of King Henry VIII) became close friends with the poet Lord Byron, often visited with him, travelled with him and in 1830 after Byron's death, published the *Letters and Journals of Lord Byron*.

Moore's many talents as singer, poet and novelist earned him the title of the National Bard of Ireland, similar to what poet Robert Burns is to Scotland. But though he was highly successful in his career of writing, his personal life was not without tragedy. He suffered a number of heartaches including the deaths of all five of his children. A stroke rendered Moore himself disabled from performances for which he had become renown. One of his poems shows his personal faith in trials.

> *Come, ye disconsolate, where'er ye languish,*
> *Come to the mercy seat, fervently kneel.*
> *Here bring your wounded hearts, here tell your anguish;*
> *Earth has no sorrow that heav'n cannot heal.*

This emotionally moving verse reminds us what God can heal the wounded heart and troubled soul, no matter how severe it may be.

The apostle Paul wrote in 2 Corinthians 1:3-4, **"Blessed be the God and Father of our Lord Jesus Christ, the Father of mercies and God of all comfort, who comforts us in all our affliction, so that we may be able to comfort those who are in any affliction, with the comfort with which we ourselves are comforted by God."**

God's presence is our life can transform tragedy into triumph. Even if life should cast us a terrible blow, we need not languish without hope. *"Earth has no sorrow that heaven cannot heal."*

Pray for someone you know has suffered greatly.

AUGUST 30

A longtime friend of mine passed away and it saddened me. I know this will be happening more and more as I age, so it's good to recall Jesus' words, **"Blessed are those who mourn, for they shall be comforted."** (Matthew 5:4)

Life isn't easy. We gain and lose, we find joy and then pain. Jesus reminds us that life isn't only found in the gaining and joy. It's also found in the pain and losing. If we are sad over what we have lost, Jesus is there to comfort us. If we are joyful, He is there to laugh and dance with us. Jesus is with us in all of life.

Mourning means sadness. We may not like shedding tears, but they can clear our eyes, and the sad memories can console us. Finding comfort in mourning usually happens with those we love, next to each other or wrapped in strong and gentle embraces, with the quiet reassurance of others that we are not alone.

It's also good to mourn our sins, to be reminded we still have much to learn and far to go attaining life's wisdom. Mourning our sins can bring us positive changes, or the ability to make choices that will help us live His way, not our own. Jesus promises that mourners will be comforted. Comfort doesn't mean that all is well, or that all wrongs are made right. It does mean we can stand up after falling down, or the knowledge that this sadness, too, shall pass.

It's also good to mourn our world. God created it perfect and rebellious people have changed for the worse. Our world is good, but it is frail and will not last forever. This wonderful planet called Earth is a gift from God, but only until time ends. It is a means to an end, not the end in itself.

When the temporary of this earth is gone, the permanent of heaven will remain. There we will understand and see with an eternal clarity what we can never have here.

God grant you comfort today through growing faith and peace that comes through our Lord Jesus Christ.

AUGUST 31

Rjuken, Norway (pronounced ReYOUken), was founded in 1905 and in 1934 the world's then-largest power plant was built, harnessing the power of a 350 foot high waterfall. It has been a major source of electricity for Norway as well as saltpeter, an important ingredient in fertilizer. It has also become a tourist's destination with its narrow valley and majestic waterfall.

But the cozy village of Rjuken had a problem. Located in a valley at the foot of Gaustatoppen Mountain, the town lies in shadows half of the year. For six months, between September and March, the entire city gets no sunlight. Residents had long considered putting up large mirrors on the mountain to reflect the sun's light down on the town, so in 2005, a local artist started "The Mirror Project" to bring together people who could help make this happen.

Eight years later, in October of 2013 and at a cost of five million Norwegian Kroner, the large mirrors were placed into service. Residents crowded into the center of town to soak up light reaching the town all through the long Norwegian winter as mirrors reflected light from the sun.

Because of sin, much of the world is cast in shadows and darkness. Like in the city of Rjuken, mountains of trouble, sorrow, tragedy and evil keep people in the darkness. They need the Light of the World, Jesus Christ, to give them light. But how will this light come? Only when His followers mirror His light.

Jesus said, **"Let your light shine before others, so that they may see your good works and give glory to your Father who is in heaven."** (Matthew 5:16) Like John the Baptist who came to bear witness to the Light of Jesus, we too can help give light to those who sit in darkness and in the shadow of death.

Sunlight is needed for emotional and physical health. Deprived of it too long, we become weak, but with it we are renewed. Jesus not only renews us, He makes us all new!

How can you help bring light into someone's life?

DAY BY DAY WITH JESUS
in
September
+ + +

SEPTEMBER 1

Have you ever made a mistake on an e-mail address and it caused problems? A Minnesota couple decided to go to Florida one cold winter. They planned to stay at the same hotel where they spent their honeymoon twenty years earlier, so it would be fun.

Because of their different work schedules, it was difficult to come on the same flight. So the husband flew to Florida on Thursday, and his wife had a ticket to fly there Friday. The husband checked into the hotel, saw a computer in their room and decided to send his wife an email.

However, he omitted one letter in her email address, so the message was not sent to his wife, but to a widow in Houston who had just returned from her husband's funeral. The widow checked her e-mail, expecting condolences, but after reading the first message, she screamed and fainted. Her son rushed into the room to help and saw the e-mail:

To: My Loving Wife
Subject: I've Arrived   Date: July 19, 2014

I know you're surprised to hear from me. They have computers here now and you are allowed to send emails to your loved ones. I've just arrived and checked in. I've made sure everything has been prepared for your arrival tomorrow. Looking forward to seeing you! Hope your journey is as good as mine was.

Your loving husband
P. S. It sure is hot down here!

Just one mistake took this nice note to the wrong person with the wrong message. God's Word will not do this. When we let the Bible speak to us, we will hear of God's clear message of love and forgiveness in Jesus. We will know it is from God who will help us understand his message.

Did you ever get an email message that was so confusing?

SEPTEMBER 2

When bad things happen, it's important to maintain a good perspective. One Colorado day in early September we had a hailstorm, and not just our usual hail with small slushy ice balls, these were big chunks of ice that hammered our roof. The strangest part was that it happened at 10:30 at night and lasted 2-3 minutes at the most. The next day I found out hardly anyone in town had hail, just a small area, perhaps a half mile long and a quarter mile wide. But everyone there got huge hail for a few minutes, and nearly every one got a new roof out of that storm.

My roof had been hailed many times in the years we'd been there, but each time the adjuster came out he'd say the roof was still good. This time I called the insurance company, and when I told them our address, after a few moments the man said, *"Call a reputable roof company and have them send us a bid. You will probably get a new roof."* I ask how he could say this when he hadn't seen the house and he said, *"We've heard of that storm in Castle Rock last night. It was severe hail. Every house there will probably get a new roof. In fact, we knew how bad the storm was right after it hit. Computers tell us everything these days."*

God's plans for us are always best. My son once had hail and called the insurance only after a friend urged him. He, too, received a new roof. Somehow the last storm had done just enough damage to bring him a new roof.

God provides us with our needs, especially when the bad storms in life can bring damages. His provision is more than the replacement of insurance; it is the replacement of life. When our earthly life is over, we are promised a new body and life in eternity with Him. He who blesses us with life on this planet will bring us even more when we trust His Son for forgiveness.

"I praise You [O God], for I am fearfully and wonderfully made. Wonderful are Your works, my soul knows it very well." (Psalm 139:14)

How wonderful to know our new life will be even better.

SEPTEMBER 3

On September 3, 1967, Sweden changed its law of changing driving on the left side of the road to be on the right side. It was chaos on a scale rarely seen. The change of directions had been advertised as "H" Day for over a year in advance "H" stood for "Högertrafikomläggningen" which translated into "The right-side traffic conversion."

The day the law was implemented, the traffic jams were numerous and humorous. Swedish drivers snarled traffic in cities and smashed into each other on country roads. Accidents happened because drivers had forgotten about the change, or because they hadn't heard of it. Still others because they resisted the unwanted change.

A logo had been designed that was a large "H" with an arrow inside it moving from the left to the right. The country had been attempting to implement this change for over 40 years, and some had even composed traffic-theme songs played on media so the people would know about it. Despite the preparations, there were accidents and traffic mayhem in the cities as the people struggled with the new law.

People usually resist change or new customs. We grow accustomed to our ways. Even the word "accustomed" tells us how important "customs" are to us. Changing worship customs can drive members to another church, and change of leadership can cause people to be resistant to new laws.

The Jewish leaders in Jesus' time resisted new things, often violently. Early Christians were punished, jailed and sometimes killed for speaking of Jesus. Jesus Himself was condemned to crucifixion by Roman and Jewish leaders because His new message undermined the old ways.

Jesus said, **"No one puts new wine into old wineskins… But new wine is for fresh wineskins."** (Mark 2:22) Christians may struggle with change that is needed, but we do not change what is essential – faith in Jesus Christ – just to conform to the world's fickle changes.

What are you often tempted to change that is essential?

SEPTEMBER 4

Have you ever felt like you were adrift in life? Carol and I attended a church in north Denver and the pastor's sermon was about that. I took notes and found them the other day under a pile on my desk. These days I often take sermon notes, not for use in preaching, but for devotions.

His message reminded me of a time when we owned a canoe and were learning how to use it. Another couple was with us in their canoe on a river near our North Dakota home. Our afternoon of learning how to handle a canoe quickly turned into a Splash Fest of laughter and getting wet. At one point my wife and I both lost our paddles, and we were drifting *"up a creek without a paddle."* We tried paddling with our hands, but our experienced friends retrieved our paddles for us. It's a fun memory to recall.

The pastor spoke of four reasons why people might find themselves adrift in life. 1) We may be blaming God for our problems, or 2) we are succumbing to life's negative influences, or 3) we are giving in to harmful temptations that *"everyone else is doing,"* or, 4) we are loving the things of this world way too much. All four reasons will drive a wedge between us and God and eventually cast us adrift in life.

Having shown us God's Law that reflects our sins, the pastor then showed us the Gospel of forgiveness in Jesus Christ who died on the cross for our sins and rescued us from being adrift. The pastor then told us how to keep from drifting through 1) God's Word, 2) God's Sacraments and 3) God's Prayer Line that holds us to Him in all kinds of trouble. Making regular use of these three will keep us from drifting and help us stay connected to God in life. I don't recall he used the phrase, *"up a creek without a paddle,"* but his fine message brought that past incident to mind.

The sermon reminded me of a favorite Bible verse, **"Commit your way to the Lord, trust in Him, and He will make good things happen."** (Psalm 37:5)

Are you adrift in life right now? What will you do about it?

SEPTEMBER 5

A farmer was stopped by a stranger who drove up in a new car. He wanted to know if the old barn by the road was for sale. The farmer said he was crazy for wanting that old thing, but the man was from the city and when he saw that old barn by the road last week he'd wanted to buy it.

The farmer said he had a funny idea of beauty. True, the old barn was a handsome building in its day, but a lot of winters had passed with their snow and ice and wind. The sun had beaten down on it until its paint was gone and its wood was a silver grey. It leaned a lot because its walls were weak and its roof leaked. The old barn was just plain tired, yet the stranger called it beautiful.

The farmer named his price and the man paid it on the spot. He said he planned to have it taken down and the lumber used to line the walls of some rooms in a new home he was building. He said that you can't buy paint to make wood that beautiful. Only years of weather, with its storms and scorching sun could produce beautiful wood like that.

Some people are like that. As they age they get to looking rough on the outside, but it's what's in the heart that's a person's true beauty. Most of us eventually turn silver-grey too, and even lean a little more than we used to.

But the Good Lord knows what He's doing. As the years pass He uses the weather of life, the dry spells and storms, to beautify our souls like nothing else can. People may think life should be easy with no struggles, meanness, poverty or even skinned knees. But that's foolish thinking. A life without hardships makes a person soft and prideful.

Jesus said, **"In My Fathers House are many rooms, and I go there to prepare a place for you."** (John 14:2) People took down the old man's barn and hauled it away to beautify another man's home. One day all believers will be taken to heaven to do whatever the Lord has for us there. There we will surely be more beautiful than we are here.

There is often great beauty in aged things and people.

SEPTEMBER 6

Several decades ago two boys were selling newspapers on a Detroit street corner. One of them shouted, *"Read all about it!"* and then shouted a headline like, *"President elected! Read all about it!"* The other boy just said in a loud, whiney voice, *"Ain't it awful?"* He held up an open newspaper and shouted in a pleading voice, *"Ain't it awful?"*

Which boy do you think sold the most copies? The second one, of course, the one who "awfulized" the news. People stopped to see what was so "awful" about the news and more bought from him than from the other boy.

Most of us agree that newspapers and news programs *"awfulize"* the news to get our interest. There's a saying, *"No News is Good News."* But today's journalist says the opposite: *"Good News is No News."* The nasty story is always on the front page, while any good news is buried in the back.

Perhaps that's because there is so much news that is awful, wars that never end, evil killing of the innocent, world disease, drugs, murders, politics, planet destruction and death. What will tomorrow bring? *"Ain't it awful?"*

Jesus was no stranger to the awful side of life. He saw brutality and depravity around Him, but He didn't spend His life preaching about it. His life message was God's marvelous plan that we can have a better life than this world gives us. Jesus "marvelized" our awful world with His love and forgiveness, His mercy and hope. No matter how ugly life may look, with Jesus life can be marvelous.

St. Paul wrote something marvelous: **"The wages of sin is death, but the free gift of God is eternal life in Christ Jesus our Lord."** (Romans 6:23) Because of Jesus death and resurrection, we are promised life with God – FREE!

Sin has made our world and its people wallow in the "awful," but Jesus has a solution. He gave His life on the cross so that all who trust Him will not perish, but have eternal life. Sin and Satan "awfulize" life, but Jesus "marvelizes" it.

Pardon my grammar, but "AIN'T THAT GREAT!"

SEPTEMBER 7

We had a hard rain a few days ago, and while driving through a new subdivision nearby, I saw dirt and clay from earth movers as they shaped new streets and lots. Trucks delivering materials left muddy tracks, construction sites had dumpsters filled with lumber, paper, rocks and all sorts of trash, a real mess. Even the newly started houses looked ugly, their insides exposed as they were framed together.

Yet this mess is necessary to have a finished product. When completed, the homes will be beautiful. Landscaping will make them look as if they are pictures in a home design magazine. Everything will be clean and neat for the new homeowners when they move in. During construction, however, the mess makes beauty unmanageable, and we can't wait for it to end.

Our walk with God can be much the same. In life we must occasionally go through a messy period of confusion or disharmony. It is in those times that God is building a new part of life for us. He might be removing some old boards of life and replacing them with new ones. He might be adding another room or even be changing the shape of our life altogether. But unless a messy time takes place, we will never see the new and improved version.

The Lord's goal is for us to become more like Himself. To achieve a change for the better will require removing all that is not from Him. It can be a painful and messy process, but in the end it will be worth it. You don't have to like the mess or revel in it, but you can accept it and not consider it a tragedy, because it will bring something better.

It's up to us to learn from what is happening in these confusing times so that we might see the fulfillment of His purposes. If God is allowing a mixed-up period in your life right now, remember that this time may be necessary in order to ensure something better for you. Like one woman said, *"I embrace the mess, because it won't last forever!"*

"My help comes from the Lord, Who made heaven and earth." (Psalm 121:2)

SEPTEMBER 8

In 2013, 20,000 Colorado homes and buildings were damaged or destroyed due to a storm system that stalled over the area for days. The flooded Platte River cut farms and towns in half, including Ft. Morgan. Fortunately, their old "Rainbow Bridge," built in 1923, stood while the new bridge next to it quickly became unusable.

Flood waters don't stand still but are terribly destructive. Damage is not caused by rising clean water. The debris, trash and mud do that. Floating branches, broken buildings and floating cars destroy things as the flood moves along. Roadbeds are torn apart, hillsides and culverts are washed out. Sewers pollute fresh water and homes are ruined. Rising clear water would be bad enough, but it's what the flood waters carry that does the damage.

How very much like life! It's not merely time or age that can hurt us, or even illness and accident. It's the garbage we carry with us and release along the way. Bad decisions, hurtful words, destructive habits and evil acts can turn a secure life into a raging torrent that destroys individuals and families. Trash let loose during the storms of life has hurt us more than the storms themselves.

What can we do about it? For one, we can make sure we have as little buildup as possible. We can start by confessing the garbage of sin along the way. Ask for forgiveness rather than gloss over or hide bad things. Stop doing what we know is unhealthy or immoral. Most importantly, we can call in the Trash Man to haul all the bad stuff away.

Jesus is our Trash Man, the Holy One who removes life's garbage whenever we ask Him, removing it from us as far as the East is from the West. He does so by taking it to a landfill called Calvary where He will bury it forever. We may not be able to avoid all floods, but Jesus is our lifeline, our "Bridge Over Troubled Waters" who can not be torn down. So long as we are in contact with Him, we'll be okay.

"The Lord is my shepherd, I will have everything I need."
(Psalm 23:1, NLV)

SEPTEMBER 9

On September 9, 1942, Nobuo Fujita of the Japanese Imperial Navy surfaced in a Japanese submarine off the coast near Brookings, Oregon. His tiny seaplane was attached to the deck of the submarine, and his mission was so secret that it was a total surprise to American military.

Still smarting from Doolittle's bombing of Tokyo five months earlier, Japanese strategy was to cause enough damage to induce U.S. leaders to withdraw their ships from the Western Pacific and reduce pressure on Japan's Navy. Fugita's mission over Oregon was to start a giant forest fire with bombs to ignite the forest and spread to the cities. Fujita flew over the Oregon coast dropping incendiary bombs near Brookings. After his bombing run on Mt. Emily, they came under attack by U.S. aircraft which forced the submarine to hide on the ocean floor. Later Fujita was able to launch additional bombing sorties there until he returned to Japan, the only Japanese ever to have bombed the USA

After the war Fugita become a successful businessman, but he was bothered by his wartime duties. He tried to build a bridge of peace and respect between Japan and the United States and in 1962 was invited to Brookings. He took with him his family's 400-year-old Samurai sword and if the Americans were hostile, intended to commit suicide with it.

However, they received him warmly. The sword was placed in the mayor's office, where it remains today. He was later host to some Brookings High School students at his home in Japan. He was an honored guest at the 1990 annual Azalea Festival in Brookings. The City Council declared him an honorary citizen and his ashes now rest on the same spot where his first bombs landed east of Brookings. *"He was so very sorry and had deep regrets,"* said Ernie Bowers, 61, a close friend of Fujita's. But he was greatly impressed at the kind reception he received from whose he had injured.

"Love your enemies and pray for those who persecute you, so that you may be sons of your Father who is in heaven."
(Mathew 5:44-45)

SEPTEMBER 10

SIX TINY STORIES WITH SIX BIG LESSONS

> 1) Once upon a time, all the villagers decided to pray for rain, and on the day of prayer all the people gathered, but only one boy came with an umbrella. That's **FAITH**.
>
> 2) When you throw a baby in the air, she laughs because she knows you will catch her. That's **TRUST.**
>
> 3) Every night we go to bed without any assurance of being alive the next morning, but still we set our alarms to wake up. That's **HOPE.**
>
> 4) We plan big things for tomorrow in spite of zero knowledge of the future. That's **CONFIDENCE.**
>
> 5) We see the world suffering evil, but still we get married. That's **LOVE.**
>
> 6) An old man's shirt read, *"I am not seventy years old. I am twenty with fifty years' experience."* That's **ATTITUDE.**

Those are six very good lessons to learn. Sadly, so much of our life is spent wondering six (or more) other things:

1) Will I succeed? 2) Will I be loved? 3) Will evil prevail? 4) Will I have enough? 5) Will people ever learn? 6) Does God really exist and love me?

God helps us understand by the little lessons we learn in life. True, the big occasions will teach us some things, but the small ones shape our learning, reason and faith as we meet them each and let the good lessons seep into our soul.

We humans will always see life as a series of small daily acts, but God sees the Big Picture. He knows where we are headed and how we will get there.

He gives us **FAITH** to see each day as a gift and helps us **TRUST** that He will never leave us nor forsake us. He gives us **HOPE** that we may not despair and **CONFIDENCE** to face each day without fear. He shows us His **LOVE** in Jesus Christ on the cross and gives us the **ATTITUDE** of joy in knowing what faith in Christ will bring us.

"Rejoice in the Lord always; again I will say, rejoice!"
(Philippians 4:4)

SEPTEMBER 11

A TV show was about a young woman who's family was killed by a drug-crazed man when she was six years old. The murderer was caught and sentenced to life in prison. Twenty five years later the murderer asked to see her so he could tell her he was sorry. She met with him but said she'd never forgive him and the only way he could show he was sorry was to kill himself. She left the prison smiling.

I was left with a feeling of disappointment. The writers gave us their view of forgiveness, *"Don't do it! Hurt him back!"* I have no idea how she would have felt, but it seemed that evil had won the day. Satan made bitterness her solution. Forgiveness was withheld and we were supposed to feel the woman was vindicated.

Forgiveness is not excusing what another person has done, but giving up all claim on the one who has hurt you. It is surrendering one's right to hurt the offender. Forgiveness is choosing a new way to live. It is a conscious decision not to let the offender or the offense control your life.

Forgiveness does not need the offender's repentance. After the 1999 Columbine High School massacre, some said that since the killers both were dead, it wasn't necessary to forgive them. That's a mistake, because the offender may not be sorry or available. Forgiveness is an act of free choice by the offended to the one who has caused offense.

Forgiveness can also be for the offender, but it's first for the offended. Forgiveness is decision made so the offended can go on living. It's also a way to show mercy. Withholding forgiveness locks us into a prison we don't deserve or need.

When Jesus hung on a cross, it was after a night of arrest and confinement, a morning of betrayal and beating, the humiliation of the crowds and the pain of crucifixion. Yet His first words were, **"Father, forgive them, for they know not what they do."** Jesus knew forgiveness was needed, and so He did it. He did it for sinners, and as a human being He also did it for Himself.

Who do you need to forgive?

SEPTEMBER 12

Yesterday was the anniversary of the terrorist attacks of September 11, 2001, on the United States. It's hard to think of that day without thinking of the images of falling towers, dust-covered people and memorials that have been erected to remember that day.

In the brief time after the plane crashed, US airspace was closed, and airplanes had to land at the closest airports available. Nearly forty planes landed the small airport at Gander, Newfoundland. The small Canadian community was nearly doubled in population as thousands of frightened passengers deplaned, wondering why they were there and whether their loved ones in the US were okay.

In a show of humane support and kindness, the people of Newfoundland quickly opened their homes and officials worked to convert high schools, churches and meeting halls into places for them to stay. The stranded passengers were overwhelmed with the caring and generosity shown them. A few years later Gander held a "reunion" of those days and dozens of the passengers returned to greet and thank once more their friends from those days who had helped them so kindly.

God's people have always sought to help people in distress. The Bible tells us, **"Do not neglect to show hospitality to strangers, for thereby some have entertained angels unawares."** (Hebrews 13:2) The writer may have been referring to the three men Abram greeted and "entertained" during his journeys (See Genesis 18:1-16) Two of those "men" were angels and one of them, the "Angel of the Lord," was possibly Jesus Himself. Among Jews and Christians, Abraham is regarded as an example of faith and fellowship.

God calls all of His people to show their love and gratitude to Him through good works and hospitality to people in need. As the hymn says,
Hark the voice of Jesus calling, who will go and work today?
...Who will answer gladly saying, "Here am I, send me, send me".

How might you answer His call today?

SEPTEMBER 13

Much of what passes along the internet is not worth reading, but sometimes an item comes along that is. I gleaned these words from a PowerPoint presentation which had many much nicer thoughts than some of its pictures.

> **"The Secrets of Old Age"**
> (source unknown)
> *Before middle age, do not fear, after middle age, do not regret.*
> *As long as physically possible, visit places you wish to see.*
> *When there's opportunity, visit with classmates and friends.*
> *Treat yourself well when old; when it's time to spend, spend!*
> *Eat what you feel like eating; it is important to be happy.*
> *Treat sickness with optimism, whether you are poor or rich.*
> *Every day you smile and laugh a little.*
> *Life ends when you stop dreaming.*
> *Hope ends when you stop believing.*
> *Love ends when you stop caring.*
> *Friendship ends when you stop sharing.*
> *One never knows what tomorrow will bring us.*
> *The nicest place to be is in someone's thoughts.*
> *The safest place to be is in someone's prayers.*
> *The very best place to be is in the hands of God.*

The last line to me is most meaningful. Being in the "Hands of God" is nicest, safest and best place to be, for there is where God shows me His blessings.

I strive to use my hands like my parents' did. With them they were used to congratulate, to soothe, to help, to caress, to greet, to hold, to comfort and to rescue. Many adults use their hands to punish, fight and grab. God uses His to lift us up to eternity.

"The hand of our God is for good on all who seek Him."
(Ezra 8:22)

SEPTEMBER 14

We have lovely back yards in both of our homes. In Arizona my cactus garden borders the edge of our small but well kept golf course. In Colorado, our house is surrounded by shrubs and trees – twelve or more varieties – that make for good exercise trimming, raking and bagging at various times. Yes, these make for some extra work, but they are also pleasant to have.

We also have a little wildlife to enjoy, mostly birds and rabbits. In Colorado the rabbits have taken away any chance of having a garden. In Colorado I've seen a half dozen adult rabbits nibbling grasses and lying in the backyard cool grass on hot days. In Arizona my cacti are not food for the desert bunnies, but they provide dens and safe shelter from predators with their dense needles.

We've had deer wander off the nearby Green Space and check out our yards for morsels to munch. I have a photo of three that our neighbor captured on film lying on the lawn on a Sunday morning while we were off at worship. No bears here yet, but they have been known to come around in the fall looking for berries and nuts.

I usually feed only the birds. I am not sure I trust anyone who feeds rabbits and squirrels, although I may toss out stale chips from the pantry or wilted veggies lost in the back of a refrigerator drawer. That's allowed.

Why all this "nature stuff" in a daily devotion? To express gratitude. God keeps plants and animals close at hand to show us His wisdom and grace. We live together with all manner of God's earthly creatures, and although mankind has been given dominion over the earth, we must never destroy what God has entrusted to us.

I will never believe mankind is the scourge of the earth as many environmentalists do, but we surely make our mistakes. We are stewards of all that is on the earth.

"Even the sparrow finds a home, and the swallow a nest for herself, where she may lay her young, at your altars, O Lord of hosts, my King and my God." (Psalm 84:3)

SEPTEMBER 15

I am often asked, *"Are you keeping busy these days?"* It's usually asked by people trying to be friendly and interested in my life after full-time ministry. I suspect, though, that they are hoping I will say I am bored and wish I was back working. Or it may be they hope I will rattle off a whole list of things I am currently doing, so that they can agree that retirement is something good for them to anticipate.

There might be a third reason, though, that my list of current projects might give me some kind of value in their eyes. With many people, if you're not doing lots of worthwhile things, you aren't worth very much. I actually find myself thinking this as I see some of my fellow retirees do little more than golf or sit outside and read.

Human beings tend to associate value with activity. If we hear someone who is involved in all kinds of activities, inside and outside their career, it may make us feel they are living a more worthwhile life than we are. It might even inspire us to take on additional activities in our own life.

I wonder whether God sees us of more value based on how busy we are. There is a saying attributed to author John Milton, *"He also serves who only stands and waits."* This implies activity alone isn't always measure by what is being done. Think of the Buckingham Palace Guards who stand at their post, day after day, disregarding all the touristy prods and pokes, standing at attention. They are good examples of Milton's words.

Jesus' words in Matthew 11:28, **"Come to me, all you who are weary and burdened, and I will give you rest,"** are proof it isn't necessary to be active all the time. We are God's valuable people even when we are resting or taking a break from work. Jesus and His men often sought rest from their work, although the needy crowds kept them from doing so.

What are you busy with these days? Does it accomplish very much? Would you invite Jesus along with you in your task, or would you be embarrassed that He showed up?

Do you need some rest?

SEPTEMBER 16

Have you ever forgotten to turn your cell phone off and it rang while you were in church or other important place? I did and it was during a funeral I was helping with. I wasn't up front in my gowns but helping a fellow pastor with the sound system when my phone went off – loudly! I hurriedly shut it off and was as embarrassed as I've ever been in church. I heard of a groom whose phone went off during his own wedding service on an ocean beach. He grabbed the phone out of his coat and threw it into the ocean, to the cheers of his friends there. A gallant but expensive recovery to an embarrassing situation.

Who hasn't forgotten to turn their phone back on and missed a call? I forgot to turn mine back on once on my own birthday. There were quite a few messages and texts waiting when I realized it. One lesson learned from the first instance is that a cell phone doesn't care who is listening when it rings. In the second instance, I learned if you can't hear your phone, what good is it?

In some ways this is like our Bible. If we don't read it, what good is it? I guess we could also say a Bible doesn't care who is listening when it is read. The point is communication. A Bible isn't meant for decoration, but for the message it has, divine and holy information so the reader of God's will and ways.

I once heard the Gospel in the shortest form ever: *"God loves you, but you're a sinner. That's why He sent Jesus, so praise the Lord!"* That's even eight words shorter than John 3:16, although not as accurate or memorable. But let's make sure:

> **"For God so loved the world, that he gave his only Son, that whoever believes in him should not perish but have eternal life."** (John 3:16)

Definitely better! Remember – it may be in the Bible, but if you don't read it, what good will it do you?

Keep your phone on when needed and read your Bible often.

SEPTEMBER 17

One of the more difficult tasks in ministry comes when a pastor must inform a family member that a loved one has died. The first time I did this, I was not yet a pastor, but working at Lutheran Hospital as an ER tech. Miss Kubler, the Head Nurse came over and said, *"Mr. Tasler, I have a job for you."* As we walked she explained I would be telling the family their loved one had died. When I asked why she wanted me to do this, she said, *"When you are a pastor, you will do this many times. You should start learning this now."* I did my best in kindly telling them of the death, and Miss Kubler told them the medical reasons. I always appreciated her giving me that opportunity.

If I recall, the death had occurred because someone was driving the wrong way and struck another vehicle head-on. It happened during a rainstorm and the victim was elderly. Not long ago, I drove onto a wide boulevard at night and got into the wrong lane. Fortunately, traffic was light and I got squared around and into the right lane quickly. It was also a rainy night.

We need to live life going in the right direction. Jesus' Disciples discovered this when some decided to leave Jesus. John 6 tells us of Jesus explaining difficult lessons to His Disciples, so difficult that **"After this many of his disciples turned back and no longer walked with him."** (John 6:66) Jesus asked the others if they'd also like to leave Him, and Peter said, **"Lord, to whom shall we go? You have the words of eternal life, and we have believed, and have come to know, that you are the Holy One of God."** (John 6:68-69)

Peter may have made mistakes at other times, but he got it right that time. He and those who stayed kept going in the right direction. They didn't reverse course, but rather "stayed the course."

Whatever you may face today, remember the words of Peter and be encouraged to follow Jesus as He takes you on the right path. With Jesus, you're going the right direction.

Pray that Jesus will give all the strength you need today.

SEPTEMBER 18

For a time years ago, "journaling" was all the rage. It was touted to *"help people to clarify their thoughts and feelings, thereby gaining valuable self-knowledge."* Journaling was not to have people keep record events such as in a diary, but to keep a daily log of one's feelings and thoughts. I tried it awhile, but was not good staying with it. Somewhere there is a Journal with my name in it that has a dozen or so written pages in it, but the rest is all blank.

While ministering in a large city, I tried with some success to keep notes on a small voice recorder. As I drove the busy freeways, when I thought of something, I'd pick up the small black device and talk into it about some thought, plan or reminder I could use at a later time. That didn't last much long than my Journal.

A friend once old me he used a voice recorder quite a lot, but not for what one usually thinks. After his day of work he had a long commute home, so he talked into his voice recorder about the events of the day, his feelings and perhaps ideas for the future. Then he said, *"When I came to my driveway, I hit the "erase" button. I had no desire to take my day's problems with me into the house."* A wise man!

It's easy to rehearse one's disappointments and troubles, but it rarely helps to do it very long. During one frustrating period of my ministry I talked with a friend about it so much that one day he told me, *"I have an idea. Let's go get a gun and shoot them all. Maybe that will help you feel better."* I must have given him a startled look because he then said, *"Just kidding, Pastor. Feel better now?"*

In Psalm 62:8, David wrote, **"Trust in Him at all times, O people; pour out your heart before Him. God is a refuge for us."** God always has time to listen to us. He won't get tired of our prayers, no matter how we complain, whine or rehearse things. He is our rock and comfort in all times of distress. As a youth song goes, *"Jesus is the rock of my salvation and His banner over me is love."* (Author unknown)

To whom do you talk when you get frustrated?

SEPTEMBER 19

One autumn during my seminary days, I had a job taking care of a person's yard in Ladue, Missouri, a wealthy St. Louis suburb. The yard was about two acres and had an abundance of trees, shrubs and vines growing among large portions of the lawn. Besides mowing the grass, I trimmed the trees and bushes according to the owner's wishes.

The owner warned me to stay clear of poison ivy. He showed me its leaf shapes and said it was easy to spot this time of year because the leaves were turning red and gold. *"They're attractive but toxic,"* he said. *"During the summer, they blend in with the other leaves and when you least expect it, that's when they can really hurt you."*

Some people are like toxic plants. They look harmless and blend in with others, but sometimes when not expected, they can really hurt a person if they decide to do so.

Acts 8 tells us of a man named "Simon the Sorcerer." He blended in with other followers of Philip, even being baptized into the name of Jesus. But then he showed his hand. He asked if he could buy the ability to lay hands on people and heal them or give them the Holy Spirit.

Peter heard of this and was appalled. *"May your silver perish with you, because you thought you could obtain the gift of God with money!"* (Acts 8:20) Peter demanded he repent of his attitude with such force that Simon begged forgiveness so that he would not be punished. Nothing is mentioned of him after this, so it is assumed Simon took his practice elsewhere.

Sometimes people use the church as a place for selfish purposes. Like poison ivy among flowers, they can cause much misery and distress when they disguise their motives and take advantage. Their evil intentions usually come to light but not before they can harm the Body.

Jesus told His followers, *"You will recognize them by their fruits."* (Matthew 7:16) He warns us not to take the toxic fruit, but to follow Him in righteousness.

Can you think of some "toxic people" in society?

SEPTEMBER 20

When Dr. Vernon Grounds, former president and chancellor of Denver Seminary, went to be with the Lord at age 96, tributes poured in from all over the world from friends, students, colleagues, theologians and others who knew him. Almost all recalled a time they had met or been personally touched by something he had said.

I only heard him speak once, at a pastor's luncheon, and his text was John 21:22 when Jesus spoke to Peter after He had forgiven him for his denial. Dr. Grounds quoted from the King James Version, **"If I will that he tarry till I come, what is that to thee? Follow thou me."** The "he" Jesus spoke of was the youngest disciple, John.

In this chapter Jesus had just told Peter he would suffer for his faith, saying that people will take him where he does not want to go. This bothered Peter and so he wondered if he would be the only one to suffer. He saw John and asked Jesus, **"Lord, what about this man?"** That's when Jesus said, **"If I will that he tarry till I come, what is that to thee? Follow thou me."** Peter need not worry about others, just that he continue to follow Jesus.

Dr. Grounds said that we, too, should not worry about what happens to this or that servant, but that we should follow Jesus, no matter what. It is easy to be wonder about others in their relationship to the Lord, but our main concern must be if we are following Jesus.

Dr. Grounds' wisdom and counsel grew out of his relationship with Jesus and the grace of God. His warm character and exemplary Christian life was a product of humility brought on as a fruit of the Holy Spirit. He ran his race of life well and finished with grace. As it is written:

> *"Life's truest heroes never carve their name*
> *On marbled columns built for their acclaim;*
> *They build instead a legacy that springs*
> *From faithful service to the King of kings."* (Gustafson)

May we always honor those who have shown us Jesus.

SEPTEMBER 21

My grandson was born today, a tiny preemie who required much care and many prayers. He has grown into a fine young boy with warmth and charm that attracts many friends and loved ones. What a blessing he has become!

Today is the first day of autumn and in many places the leaves are already turning. Do you ever wonder why some tree leaves turn red, orange, yellow or maroon in the fall? Trees are green in the summer because chlorophyll, the green pigment in the leaves, absorbs red and blue light from the sun. Amazingly, we still see green in the leaves as it does.

But chlorophyll is unstable, and bright sunlight causes it eventually to decompose rapidly. Because of this, plants and trees must continually regenerate it and make more. The shorter days of late summer and fall interfere with this process, so the chlorophyll breaks down and the green color fades. Some trees change from green to yellow, orange or gold, as chlorophyll breaks down. Sugar in some trees can make its leaves turn bright red, maroon or purple as the chlorophyll fades away.

Another question might also be, why do we have color at all? It seems to serve no practical purpose, none that scientists have been able to determine. And why do we have eyes that enable us to see color?

Even if there might be no scientific answer to this question, Christians have an idea God did it because He loves His creation. Color enhances joy in human life like no other single element. The Bible says, **"The LORD is good to all; He has compassion on all he has made."** (Psalm 145:9)

Children love color, children of all ages, that is! The Bible also says, **"In Christ Jesus you are all children of God through faith."** (Galatians 3:26) God colored the world for the delight of His children.

The Bible says, **"I have covered my bed with colored linens from Egypt."** (Proverbs 7:16)

I wonder if he got them at "Bed, Bath and Beyond?"

SEPTEMBER 22

On September 22, 1529, Cardinal Thomas Wolsey was stripped of his office as Lord Chancellor of England. King Henry VIII had demanded that Woolsey secure a divorce from his first wife, Catherine of Aragon, so that he could marry Ann Boleyn. Despite her total faithfulness to the king, Catherine had been unable to bear him a son and heir to the throne that lived, so Henry wanted a new wife.

Through the efforts of his advisor, Thomas Cromwell, Henry finally got his wish, but only due to England's break with the Church of Rome, and the creation of the Church of England, over which the King was head. However, the new queen Ann was also unable to bear him a son, only a healthy red-headed girl. In 1580, Henry had both Ann Boleyn and Cromwell beheaded, both for treason.

Despite having married six wives, King Henry VIII died in 1547 leaving only a sickly young son who ruled six years. The English throne was eventually assumed by Henry's very capable daughter, Elizabeth I, who ruled and reigned over England for forty-five prosperous years. In this case it is true when said: *"If you want a good man for the job, get a woman."*

Great things happen when God brings the right person to the task. He raised a shepherd boy named David to be Israel's greatest king and a cowardly fisherman named Peter to lead the early Church. People may make their plans for greatness, but God makes His plans come true.

In Mark 9:35 Jesus said, **"If anyone would be first, he must be last of all and servant of all."** Greatness in the new kingdom is granted to those willing to wash the feet of others, like Jesus, **"who came not to be served, but to serve and to give his life as a ransom for many."** (Matthew 20:28)

History is filled with great people, but all died in due time. So did our Lord, but after three days He arose, **"the first-fruits of those who have fallen asleep."** (1 Corinthians 15:20) And because He arose, we too shall rise.

Praise God this day for the resurrection He promised us.

SEPTEMBER 23

My neighbor was moving and showed me some things he said I could have so he wouldn't have to move them. I was walking away with a couple of iron bars when he asked, *"Do you want a nice flat screen TV?"* "Why are you giving that away?" I asked. *"You could sell it."* He took me to his basement and turned it on. *"See those lines across the screen?"* he said, pointing to several large ugly lines on one side. *"They're a gift from my little grandson. We were watching a program about tools, and when I came back into the room he was pounding on the TV screen with his toy plastic hammer. The TV's great, except for the lines."*

I politely declined and chuckled on the way home at the thought of a four year-old mimicking a "TV man" and ruining an expensive television. Our children and grand children learn by watching us more than we realize. As has been said, *"Little eyes and ears are watching and listening."*

Big ears are listening, too. As Christians, we are under observation by others who seek to see how we live. When we speak, our words are measured by our faith. If we gossip, lie, curse or use vulgarity, it will be noted as a measure of whether or not we are living by our faith.

James 1:22 tells us, **"Be doers of the word, and not hearers only, deceiving yourselves."** What we do should mirror what we say we believe. Our faith should show itself in similar deeds. James later says if a person claims to be religious but does not "bridle his tongue" from evil words, he religion is meaningless.

Such observation can have great impact. An African tribe accepted a missionary and his family into their midst, heard their message of Jesus' love and forgiveness, but tortured and killed them. Years later, descendants of the missionary returned to the village and found a church there, and a missionary gaining many converts. A tribal elder told them, *"The first man of God forgave us as we killed his family. We knew then his teachings were true."*

"By their fruits you shall know them." (Matthew 7:20)

SEPTEMBER 24

I've always wanted to become a pilot and fly small airplanes. I've flown in small planes many times and it feels like you're really flying, not like on the big planes that feel like you're sitting in a crowded room with hundreds of others. Most people I've told about this have said they distrusted small planes, but I loved them.

In 1971, right after we'd come to our first church, I came home one day and announced to my wife that a member of our church would teach me to fly and I could get my pilot's license for only $1,000 - amazing! My dear wife looked at me and said, *"You told me we barely have enough money to get new car tires!"* Her comment brought me back down to earth. But it was fun thinking about flying here and there. I later found out how expensive it is to rent a plane for even a few hours a month. Hadn't thought of that, either.

David the King could do all kinds of things. He was a man of wealth and power and people wanted to please him and give him things. Yet even he felt a little like I had. He wrote, "Oh, that I had wings like a dove! I would fly away and be at rest." If he said within his wife's hearing, she may have said, *"Fly? You sometimes fall off a donkey!"* (Wives often have a way with words.)

David often wrote about the many circumstances he dealt with being king. Violence, oppression and strife surrounded him and his kingdom from all sides. Friends were not always loyal and anxiety entrapped him so that he couldn't sleep some nights. His own weakness caused him no small problems, either. More than once the head of this powerful man of God was turned by temptation.

Still, David never abandoned God like kings after him. He also wrote in Psalm 55, **"But I call to God, and the Lord will save me. Evening and morning and at noon I utter my complaint and moan, and He hears my voice."** (22:16-17)

Whatever our burdens may be, we can give them to the Lord like David did. As he said in Psalm 55:22,

"Cast your burdens on the Lord and He shall sustain you."

SEPTEMBER 25

I love a loaf of fresh bread. Every time I see one and smell its freshness I think of my mother's fresh loaves sitting on the counter waiting for one of us to cut a slice or two with butter and jam. Although some "experts" say bread isn't good for you, I have a hard time believing them.

It also makes me think of the story of Jean Valjean, the poor Frenchman who was imprisoned nineteen years for stealing a loaf of bread to feed his starving family. Valjean's escape and relentless pursuit by Inspector Javert is the basis for Victor Hugo's classic novel, *Les Miserables*.

While this immense novel contains many smaller stories, there emerges a Christian message of forgiveness and grace. After his escape, Valjean is given a night of food and rest at the Bishop's residence, but during the night he steals a set of silver candlesticks and runs away. When he is caught, the Bishop does not press charges, but rather tells the police he gave Valjean those valuable items so that he could start over anew in life. After so many years of horrible confinement, Valjean is overcome by the Bishop's mercy and dedicates the rest of his life to showing mercy to others, eventually even to his nemesis, Javert.

It is never easy to forgive, but it is especially difficult when it involves pride and dedication to wrongful pursuit. Javert does not deserve forgiveness, but that is precisely why Valjean forgives him. He who had also been shown mercy must be merciful to his fellow man. He cannot deny another man, no matter how terrible he may be, this unnatural and yet necessary act of forgiveness.

Our Lord Jesus was the object of the wrath of sinful people. He was scorned and rejected by those He came to save, but He did not let their rejection and hatred deter Him from why He came. Instead, He laid aside all malice and showed mercy. Because of it we, too, may show mercy.

In the Beatitudes, Jesus said, **"Blessed are the merciful, for they shall receive mercy."** (Matthew 5:7)

And this, just from seeing a loaf of bread!

SEPTEMBER 26

Baseball season is nearing its end again and fans are either hopeful or have come to the realization that their favorite team isn't going to the playoffs this year. Despite some scandals and changes in the game, baseball still remains America's favorite sport.

In the 135 years of Major League Baseball, only 20 pitchers have thrown a "perfect game," meaning a victory with no batters reaching base. This means there can be no runs, hits, walks or hit batters on the opposing team. In a perfect game, 27 men come to the plate and 27 are retired.

In 2010, that number could have been 21. Armando Galarraga of the Detroit Tigers had pitched a perfect game until an umpire's mistake put the last batter on base. A video of the play showed the truth, that the man should have been called out, but there was no Video Replay rule, so the call could not be changed. The umpire later acknowledged his error and apologized to Galarraga but the decision on the field could not be altered. He was denied a perfect game.

All through the controversy Galarraga maintained a calm attitude and even expressed sympathy for the umpire, never criticizing him. His refusal to retaliate amazed fans, players and sportswriters alike. It was unlike much of the prideful demands made by some in professional sports.

When people insist on getting fair treatment for ourselves, it is easy to become angry and demanding. But when we embrace the Bible's wisdom, we will react differently. Proverbs 1:2-3 tells us **"to know wisdom and instruction, to understand words of insight, to receive instruction in wise dealing, in righteousness, justice, and equity."** Life is not always fair, but God is always faithful.

The insightful Christian writer Oswald Chambers once wrote, *"Never look for justice, but never cease to give it. And never allow anything you meet with to sour your relationship to men through Jesus Christ."*

If you experience unfairness today, handle it with God's love.

SEPTEMBER 27

When Carol and I were young and first married I was concerned at the amount of pills she took each day. It wasn't that many, but since I took none, hers seemed too much. Now in my (somewhat) advanced age I take more pills each day than she does because my doctor advises me to.

My doctor and I have an interesting relationship. For awhile he and his wife attended my church and gratefully received my sermons. That ended when I retired, but I know he still worships most every week and reads his Bible often. When I come for my annual checkup or other appointment he is interested in my health and also my work.

Now and then he will urge me to start a program of care or a diet and I question it: *"I've been reading about that online and perhaps there's a better way."* Hearing this one day he said, *"You should do what I tell you, not what you read about online."* I joked that he probably didn't always do what I said in my sermons and our discussion got lively. But I do try to follow his advice and always take my medicine.

Most laws and rules are for our benefit. God's Ten Commandments certainly help us when we observe them. They will not address every possible situation, but they give us a standard framework for most choices and behavior.

But people today are less willing to follow God's Law than in previous generations. Perhaps it is the supposed wisdom of modern life or the massive information we have at our fingertips. People no longer accept God's Word without questioning. They're like Thomas who said, **"Unless I see it with my own eyes, I will not believe."** (John 20:24, par.)

But Father knows best. He has given us rules and standards of behavior far better than we set up ourselves. Mankind's laws are formulated by self-interest, but God's laws come from His love and goodness. His rules may seem harder, but our easier ones are rarely better.

Jesus offered up His life on the cross as the most complete prescription for sin, We need to take His medicine.

Have you ever argued with your doctor? Who won?

SEPTEMBER 28

After Carol's mother died, we returned home to Colorado with her parents' wall clock, the mechanical kind with chains and weights that has a gentle "tick, tock" as the brass pendulum swings back and forth. It has a lovely wooden box with carved decorations. We often hear it's pleasant chime at night, and we miss it when we're in our Arizona winter home. Her parents' old clock always tells us what hour it is.

I attended Country School my first six grades and learned many quaint, old songs, including Henry Clay's "My Grandfather's Clock," written in 1876. The song tells of a large floor model clock belonging to his grandfather that faithfully ticks away the owner's life. From childhood to adulthood to old age, the song shows the relationship of the old man's beloved timepiece to his life. The refrain says:

> *Ninety years without slumbering -*
> *Tick, tock, tick, tock*
> *His life's seconds numbering –*
> *Tick, tock, tick, tock.*
> *But it stopped! Short! Never to go again,*
> *When the old man died.*

The old song tells us something about life. It reminds us that our time on earth is limited and no matter what else happens, time keeps marching on. For the Christian, all the time we have on earth is a gift from God and a chance for us to learn of God and His will.

Psalm 90, which was my mother's favorite Psalm, says in verse 12, **"So teach us to number our days that we may gain a heart of wisdom."** How can we do that? How can we learn to be more like Christ? Can we read His Word more and spend time with His people in worship and fellowship?

No matter what phase of life we are in, whether childhood, youth, middle age or senior years, we can always grow in our wisdom through Jesus Christ.

Do you have a clock that ticks in your house?

SEPTEMBER 29

I recently experienced an embarrassing moment. I'd gone out to do a few errands and decided to have a cup of coffee at a convenience store. It was a busy place with many gas pumps and it had my favorite cappuccino, "Pumpkin Spice." I spilled a little, so I grabbed a napkin. After drying the cup, I walked right out the door without paying! It didn't occur to me until I was home and saw the coin purse on the car seat. I drove back to the store and explained to the young man behind the counter who smiled and said, "Thanks."

Somewhere on the way home I remembered reading that "Honest Abe" Lincoln walked three miles to a store when he found the owner had given him too much change. Maybe I remembered that because I was driving a Lincoln.

It would have been easy to let it go, but I knew the memory would not let me go. I considered taking it back at another time, but it was worth driving those three miles to pay up. Taking what does not belong to us is theft and no one deserves to have things stolen, no matter how wealthy or crooked they are, or any other justification we may use.

My father told me he once stole a tiny file from a store. He was in town for his weekly shopping and needed the file for repairing a motor. He realized he had no money in his pocket, so he put it in his pocket and walked out the door without paying. It bothered him all week until he went back and paid the shop owner - 4 cents!

All we have is a gift from God, but people steal from Him, too. In Malachi 3:10, God tells the people they are robbing Him by not giving what they had promised in their tithes and offerings. He said, **"Bring the full tithe into the storehouse, that there may be food in my house. And thereby put me to the test, says the Lord of hosts, if I will not open the windows of heaven for you and pour down for you a blessing until there is no more need."**

God promises to give us our needs when we honor Him and trust in His Son Jesus Christ as our Lord.

How can you honor God today?

SEPTEMBER 30

I spent six fun and wonderful years in Country School in southern Minnesota. Memories of those days stay with me and I can talk about life in Country School for an hour if you have the time. I had three teachers during those six years, and they all made a positive impact on my life.

Great Bend District Two really was a one-room school, although there were two coat closets in front, one for boys and one for girls, and a library off to the side. The big cement floor basement was our play area in winter when it was too cold outside. We had a furnace with a stoker to push crushed coal into the firebox. It was always warm downstairs in the winter time.

Except for getting drinking water from a farm, we were never to cross the road. I can't recall ever seeing someone get spanked during school time for disobedience, but I'm sure justice was meted out by parents after they read some of the notes our teacher sent home with us after school.

There were usually about 15-18 students in six grades. Older students helped the younger by listening to their reading or helping them learn their arithmetic tables. I think I learned cursive writing more from showing the little ones how to do it than from my teacher. We all ate from lunch boxes at noon and then listened for twenty minutes as she read to us from "Little House" books by Laura Wilder. We learned the basics, and that's what people still need to know.

God has some basics for us to learn also: He created us and the world, He knows we are sinful but loves us anyway, faith in Jesus is the only way to eternal life and it's better to follow the "boring" Ten Commandments than it is to break them.

Isaiah 2:3 tells us, **"Come, let us go up to the mountain of the Lord, to the house of the God of Jacob, that He may teach us His ways and that we may walk in His paths."** Jesus taught children of all ages with His stories of God's love and mercy. May we never forget our greatest Teacher.

Did you enjoy your elementary school? I hope so.

DAY BY DAY WITH JESUS
in
October
+ + +
OCTOBER 1

"I have learned that there is nothing more satisfying than the love of those who come after us," said Dr. Leonore Goldschmidt, a brave Jewish teacher who defied Hitler.

In 1935 when the Nazis began their policy of officially persecuting the Jews, most Jewish children were locked out of German schools. Rather than run or despair, Dr. Goldschmidt began a school of her own in Berlin with an estate and funds from a deceased cousin. "The Leonore Goldschmidt Private Jewish School" quickly expanded into four buildings with over 500 students and 40 teachers. In plain sight of Hitler and the Nazis, it became a refuge of safety in the midst of systematic Jewish persecution.

With the aid of Walter Huebner, a German official who risked his career, her school was granted a license by the German State. Knowing persecution would increase, she insisted all students learn English to enable them to emigrate to other countries. She got her school licensed by the University of Cambridge and started a chapter there. When her school was shut down by the Nazis in 1939, she and her family emigrated to England with 80 students and teachers. She taught in London until 1968 and died in 1983, always being dedicated to those who came after her.

All capable people, especially Christians, need to be dedicated to those who come after, not just themselves. Our children and grandchildren are those for whom we work and serve. It is only natural that we should value and love them so they will come to know Jesus and walk in His ways.

Psalm 127:3 says, **"Children are a heritage from the Lord."** God loves His children and bids us do the same.

Who has shown you love in your life?

OCTOBER 2

A Sunday newspaper contained an article about songwriter and musician Paul Simon who had his seventy-second birthday. As I read this my mind wandered back to my college days. In the 1960s, I joined the Columbia Record Club and proudly received my initial albums for a few pennies. A couple of LPs were classical, but most were by pop groups protesting war, promoting distrust of older generations, or proclaiming what a good society we'd have if we followed peace and love.

One memorable album was called, *"Bookends."* It was sung by Paul Simon and Art Garfunkel and contained songs like *"Mrs. Robinson," "At the Zoo,"* and *"Save the Life of My Child."* I can still remember the words to some of those songs. Their signature number, *"Bookends,"* had a haunting melody and some of its words were: *"Old friends sat on their park bench like bookends. Can you imagine us years from today, sharing a park bench quietly? How terribly strange to be seventy. Preserve your memories, they're all that's left you."*

Now the songwriter is past seventy, and I wonder if he thinks about those words he wrote fifty years ago. I wonder if he would know that I and many others really do try to preserve our memories with photos and writings. I would hope he now realizes memories are not *"all that's left you."*

We leave behind who we are, the life examples we've lived, and the faith in God we've come to believe. We leave behind our influences on the young, aspirations that moved us, challenges we've left for future generations. Christians leave behind the mark our faith in God has made on us.

We look forward to a new life with God, a complete life we can only fully know when it comes, an eternal life that comes to us by faith in Jesus. The most precious thing we can take with us from this life is our faith in Jesus. Without Him, all the rest is only memories that will fade and die.

As St. Paul wrote, **"Thanks be to God who gives us the victory through our Lord Jesus Christ!"** (1 Corinthians 15:57)

Do you have a special memory of a song? Were its words helpful?

OCTOBER 3

"What are the advantages? What's in it for us?" People will ask this as they hear a salesman urging them to make a purchase, join a group or donate to a cause. *"You will get the bargain of a lifetime, and have special privileges as a Premier Member,"* says the announcer. *"But will the advantages be worth the cost?"* There is always a cost of joining a group, even if that group is the Christian Church.

On Facebook I enjoyed several baptismal photos of a little girl born to a Christian couple I know. They were so proud to show friends their tiny baby who had just received God's eternal blessings in the waters of Holy Baptism. It brought back memories of baptisms when I was Godparent and also the host of little ones I had held as I sprinkled water on their little heads in Holy Baptism. I remember especially baptizing my two sons and later my three grandchildren.

"What are the advantages of Baptism?" I was asked in an adult instruction class. The man had a good question. He had said if it was a mere formality, that he wasn't sure he wanted it. But when I told him that God provides eternal blessings of forgiveness, life and salvation through the water and Word, he became interested.

"Must I be baptized to be saved?" Another good question. *"No,"* I said. *"Faith in Jesus is what saves you, not a holy ceremony. But if you trust Jesus as your Savior, would you not want to do what He asks?"* *"Yes, of course,"* he said. So I continued, *"Jesus commands us to baptize all nations, and that includes you and me. The advantages of Baptism are eternal."*

When we are baptized we have special privileges in the Body of Christ. Our cost of membership in God's family has already been paid. Jesus' death on the cross covered everything. Nothing more is required than what Jesus has already done for us. **"Whoever believes and is baptized shall be saved, but whoever does not believe will be condemned."** (Mark 16:16) That little baby possesses God's Riches At Christ's Expense, what the Bible calls GRACE.

Welcome to your Premier Membership in Jesus!

OCTOBER 4

I've read *KILLING JESUS* by O'Reilly and Dugard. It is quite good in its historical and factual narrative, as well as its respect for Jesus. I read a lot these days, but only what's enjoyable. If I don't like a book, I don't finish it. But this book, as well as their others, held my attention.

The authors treated Jesus and His times quite factually and used more biblical references than I expected. Some readers were upset because he didn't state Jesus was the Messiah and treated Him as merely a historical figure. But that wasn't the book's purpose.

The book is neither theology nor exhaustive history. It is a presentation of their findings for the public to examine. Readers may benefit by circumstances surrounding Jesus' lifetime and what He endured at the hands of jealous people.

What we say outlasts us. I'm often asked if I enjoy writing my books, and I appreciate the question. People write for a reason, to inform, entertain, express personal views or to leave something of themselves behind.

Some people like to write. It gives me pleasure to craft words into sentences that express my thoughts. It's surely not for the money. Between expenses and the books I give away, there's rarely more than pocket change left over.

There is much online or in print that hasn't been well thought out and I see a lot of spelling or grammatical errors. All writers make their mistakes, but I enjoy articles well written and accurate. I encourage you to write, if you feel so inclined. It's nice to know some of your thoughts may be passed on to people today or future generations tomorrow.

New authors rarely have much success, but that's to be expected. Knowing you have written a few worthwhile thoughts can be reward enough. God's Holy Bible is the best book of all, as Psalm 119:105 tells us, **"Your Word is a lamp for my feet and a light to guide me."**

Give thanks we still have freedom of speech in our nation!

OCTOBER 5

Today on a lovely Colorado autumn afternoon I've just finished a project and rewarded myself with coffee and a great caramel roll at a local bakery. I read awhile in a little book I had along, and part of the story was about a farmer feeding cows.

It reminded me of a Sunday afternoon in my first church in rural North Dakota. My wife and our little boys were visiting Art and Peggy and their older kids at their farm on a chilly October afternoon. The little ones had fallen asleep so Art asked, *"Want to help me feed the cows?"* We put on our caps and coats and went outside.

Art started up his truck and we lumbered down the road a half mile with a load of hay bales to a gate where he stopped and unlatched it. The pasture looked empty so I asked, *"Where are the cows?"* He said, *"They'll come."* He drove in about a hundred yards, turned off the truck and honked his horn. In less than a minute his cows came running over a hill. Not walking, running. They were hungry and it was cold. *"They know my horn,"* Art said. *"They know it means lunch."*

John chapter 10 says, **"My sheep hear my voice and they follow me."** I told Art that, and he said with a grin, *"I don't care for sheep."* I can still remember the way he said it, like it was yesterday.

Art is gone to be with the Lord now, but I exchange Christmas cards with Peggy. Our kids are all grown up with families of their own, but we still have our memories. I can still see those cows running over the hill and hear Art's laugh. And I'm eternally grateful that our children and their families know the voice of the Good Shepherd Jesus and follow Him. I'm thankful they, too, regularly receive His holy meal.

Do you have a favorite memory of former days?

OCTOBER 6

No matter how lofty a thought may be, there's always something to bring us back to earth. I have written Bible Studies on New Testament books and also an overview of the Major and Minor Prophets of the Old Testament titled, *OLD TESTAMENT DISCIPLES.*

The Old Testament prophetic books are difficult to understand. Book after book records God's disappointment with His unfaithful people and prophecies of punishment. His grace and mercy are always there if they repent, but that seems to happen infrequently. Each book has its rich Hebrew name, Ezekiel, Obadiah, Habakkuk and Zephaniah to name a few, and each is a record of God's attempt to turn the hearts of His sinful people before it's too late.

The prophet Haggai is interesting. His prophecy to Judah came fifteen years after they had returned from exile in Babylon. The people were busy rebuilding homes and businesses, but things weren't going well. Haggai told them it was because they'd been busy with the wrong things. If they would put God's work first and their own needs second, he said, life will be more productive. Haggai was saying, *"First things first!"* Great idea for a sermon!

I came out of the office and shared this with my dear wife who listened patiently and then said, *"Check the pork chops."* *"Did you hear what I said?"* I asked and she said, *"Every word, Now check the pork chops or they will burn."*

As I begrudgingly checked them, I realized she had a point. No matter how wonderful an idea may be, if the food is burning, we'd better tend to that first. Even the most exciting revelation has its proper place in the line of human need. She was saying, *"First things first!"* just like Haggai.

Jesus put us first when He went to the cross. He came to serve us, not to be served. On Calvary He lived the axiom, *"First things first."* Later I wrote a sermon on this theme.

Check out www.bobtasler.com to see if there is a good book for your personal or group Bible study.

But don't forget to check the pork chops!

OCTOBER 7

There is an amazing word in the English language that can have five separate uses: noun, verb, adjective, adverb, and preposition. It's a two-letter word with more meanings than just any other word in our language. That word is UP.

It's easy to understand UP, meaning toward the sky or the top of the list, but when we awaken in the morning, why do we wake UP? At a meeting, why does a topic come UP? Why do we speak UP, and why are officers UP for election? Why is it UP to the secretary to write UP a report? Do people still drive UP town?

Listen UP everybody! We call UP our friends, brighten UP a room, warm UP the leftovers and clean UP the kitchen. We also lock UP the house and fix UP the car. We may might even tell someone to hush UP.

If we are confused, we're UP a creek without a paddle. At various times, people stir UP trouble, line UP for tickets, work UP an appetite, and think UP excuses. To be dressed UP is special. Why is a drain opened UP? It was stopped UP.

We're all mixed UP about UP! We open UP a store in the morning, then we close it UP at night. In order to know the many uses of UP, look it UP in the dictionary. It probably takes UP a page and can we add UP the definitions.

If you are UP to it, try building UP a list of the many ways UP is used. It will take UP a lot of time, but if you don't give UP, you may wind UP with dozens of uses. The sun comes UP in the morning, and the moon comes UP at night. When it threatens to rain, we say it is clouding UP and when the sun comes out, we say it is clearing UP. When it rains, it soaks UP the earth, and when it doesn't rain, the earth dries UP.

One day God will take all His faithful people UP to heaven because Jesus rose UP from the dead. There in His presence we will lift UP our voices and sing praises to God who has raised us UP. I could play "One UP" with you on this, but I think I'll wrap it UP, because my time is UP!

"Lift UP your eyes and look to the heavens." (Isaiah 40:26)

OCTOBER 8

Tim Conway, comedian and actor, grew up in Chagrin Falls, Ohio, a safe and happy town where nearly everyone went to church. God was a mysterious presence in his life, and even though he had no proof God existed, everyone said He did, so Tim figured He must.

Every year at the annual Blossom Festival a carnival came to town. A magical mini-village sprang up with its giant ferris wheel, booths and the smell of popcorn. Ten year-old Tim had fifty cents as he made his way to the midway, five dimes he'd earned on his paper route. After buying a coke and ticket for the ferris wheel, he decided to try his luck at a game booth where he saw a white plastic cross that glowed in the dark. Tim decided he wanted it.

All he had to do was snag one of the plastic ducks with a fishing pole and get the prize named under it. First dime, he missed the ducks entirely. Second dime, he hooked a duck but got a cheap charm. Third dime, another cheap thing. Tim wanted that cross, but he was out of money.

Sad faced, he started walking home when he spotted something shiny next to the sidewalk - another dime! Tim grabbed it and went back for another chance at the midway.

This was a big moment, so he sat down under a big maple tree and prayed, *"Lord, I would really like that white cross, the one that glows in the dark."* He spoke his little prayer slowly, got up and went to the booth. He handed over the dime, concentrated and snagged the first duck with the pole hook. It won him the cross!

"I kept that cross under my pillow until I went to college," Conway later said. *"and I still have it."* In his later years of uncertainly, from college exams to casting calls, Conway was bolstered by the assurance he'd gained that day when he prayed. He never forgot God's answer to his prayer.

Does God ever seem mysterious and intangible to you? Are you not quite sure He exists? Watch for a small sign from Him that He does, a sign of His love shown by a cross.

Jesus never fails!

OCTOBER 9

Despite the fact that we all grow old in the same basic biological way, we don't all age the same. Some of us remain young in heart long after our bodies have grown older. Others of us find our mind aging more quickly than our body. We cannot escape growing older, but perhaps we do have some control over how we do it.

As she celebrated her 100th birthday, Lenore was asked what was the "secret" for her long and active life. She said, *"Laughter, the Lord and little things."* Each day she found enjoyment by talking with people, taking a walk and reading the Bible. She said, *"I don't know how long the Lord will let me stay here on earth, but I surely thank Him for what He's already given me."*

Few of us may live to be a hundred years old, but we can learn from Lenore how to enjoy the days we are given.

Laughter: In Genesis 21:6, Sarah said, **"God has made laughter for me."** There was delight in being with child at age 90. God has given us joy, knowing, **"A merry heart makes a cheerful countenance."** (Proverbs 15:13)

The Lord: Psalm 111:10 tells us, **"The fear of the Lord is the beginning of wisdom."** I chose this Psalm to be read when we were married, and that verse has remained with me. When God is central to our life, we learn and grow.

Little Things: Proverbs 13:17 tells us, **"Better a dinner of herbs where love is than a fattened ox and hatred with it."** Telling someone you love them, helping someone cheerfully, smiling at someone unexpectedly, all these cost only effort, but they bring joy to others. They're worth more than riches.

A lifelong friend of mine died recently. We grew up together and both became Lutheran pastors. Harley was my age and he served the Lord with sincerity and faith, doing the best he could wherever the Lord placed him. Praise God He forgives us in Jesus and allows us time on this earth, serving Him and sharing life with others while doing the best we can among the people where God has placed us.

May you find joy today in laughter, the Lord and little things.

OCTOBER 10

According to some historians, the ancient Greeks and Romans thought kneeling was beneath them. Regardless of how they feared their gods, they would not kneel before them in worship. Kneeling was not considered a worthy act for a free man and was suitable only for slaves. Plutarch and Theophrastus regarded kneeling as an act of superstition, and Aristotle thought it a barbaric act.

People who worship the God of the Bible, however, have never held this view. In Psalm 95:6, David wrote, **"O come, let us worship and bow down. Let us kneel before the Lord our Maker."** In this verse he uses three different Hebrew words that speak of the attitude a worshipper can take in relation to God.

First, he uses the word *worship*, which means to fall prostrate before God as a sign of honor and allegiance to Him. Then David uses the word for *bow*, which meant to sink to the knees and to lower the head, giving respect and worship to the Lord. The third word David uses is *kneel*, which means to be on one's knees while giving praise or worship to God.

David was king at the time of this writing, and kneeling in God's presence was a sign of his reverence, not of superstition. The important thing of worship is not our physical position, but the humble attitude of our heart in relation to God who gives life and all its blessings.

James *the Just*, half-brother of Jesus and first Bishop of the church at Jerusalem, was reported to have spent so much time in prayer that his knees looked like a camel's knees. He is the author of the Epistle of James and was martyred in the year 62 AD.

The most important aspect of worship is that one's heart be centered on humility toward God. This is not easy in our world of distractions, but God does know our hearts. He will accept our worship however we offer it in faith.

The most important thing about worship is that we do it!

OCTOBER 11

(The following was written by Ben Stein, journalist, economist and humorist. He spoke these words on CBS Sunday Morning News.)

+ + +

I don't like getting pushed around for being a Jew, and I don't think Christians like getting pushed around for being Christians. I think people who believe in God are sick and tired of getting pushed around, period. I have no idea where the concept came from, that America is an explicitly atheist country. I can't find it in the Constitution and I don't like it being shoved down my throat.

Or maybe I can put it another way: where did the idea come from that we should worship celebrities and we aren't allowed to worship God as we understand Him? I guess that's a sign that I'm getting old, too. But there are a lot of us who are wondering where these celebrities came from and where the America we knew went. This is not intended to be a joke. It's not funny, it's intended to get you thinking.

In light of recent events, terrorists attacks, school shootings, etc., I think it started when Madeleine Murray O'Hare complained she didn't want prayer in our schools, and we said OK. Then someone said you better not read the Bible in school. The Bible says thou shalt not kill, thou shalt not steal, and love your neighbor as yourself. And we said OK.

Then Dr. Benjamin Spock said we shouldn't spank our children when they misbehave, because their little personalities would be warped and we might damage their self-esteem (Spock's son committed suicide). We said an expert should know what he's talking about, so we said OK.

Now we're asking ourselves why our children have no conscience, why they don't know right from wrong, and why it doesn't bother them to kill strangers, classmates, and themselves. Probably, if we think about it long and hard enough, we can figure it out. I think it has a great deal to do with, 'We Reap What We Sow.'

Funny how simple it is for people to trash God and then wonder why the world's going to hell. Funny how we believe what the newspapers say, but question what the Bible says. Funny how you can send 'jokes' through e-mail and they spread like wildfire, but when you start sending messages regarding the Lord, people think twice about sharing. Funny how lewd, crude, vulgar and obscene articles pass freely through cyberspace, but public discussion of God is suppressed in the school and workplace. Are you laughing yet?

My best regards, honestly and respectfully, Ben Stein

May our country and its people always respect our God!

OCTOBER 12

On June 6, 2015, Judge Loren A. Smith of the United States Court of Federal Claims, issued his final opinion in *Hage vs. United States*, awarding the estates of Wayne and Jean Hage $8.6 million in compensation for 17 years of legal fees and expenses. Unfortunately, neither Wayne nor Jean Hage were able to savor the victory, since both had died.

It was a battle for water rights, who owns them and what rights the state has in taking them over while a case is being decided. Even though earlier court proceedings determined the Hages owned those rights, still the federal government prohibited the Hages from using them.

"This is an important legal victory," said Hage's attorney. *"Federal agencies have used their regulatory power to drive ranchers out of business with no regard for their property rights, and now the court has set limits on the agency's actions."*

In addition to being a rancher, Wayne Hage became a public advocate and legal scholar whose pioneering research has impacted the American legal system. *"My parents pursued this case so that... future generations of ranchers would have the security of their property rights."*

When asked if he and his father thought the battle was worth it, Wayne Hage Jr., said, *"Yes. Dad said, never ask for an easy life, just for the strength to get through it."*

That last statement struck me as helpful for all of life. *"Never ask for an easy life, just for the strength to get through it."* Life can be remarkably difficult. Physical, emotional and financial problems can weaken the strongest person. They can make a weak person stronger. Wayne Hage's pursuit of what is right made his family strong also.

When faced with gigantic odds, it is tempting to take the easy way out. Jesus in Gethsemane prayed for relief, but also for the strength to do God's will. *"Father, if it's possible, take this away, but Your will be done."* (Matthew 26:42 paraphrased)

Today, if you are faced with a huge problem, decide what is better – to fight it, or let God take care of it for you.

"Thy Will be done on earth as it is in heaven."(Matthew 6:10)

OCTOBER 13

God brings people into our life when we need them. When Paul Villiard was a boy, his family had one of the first telephones in Seattle. Young Paul discovered that somewhere inside that wooden phone box lived an amazing person named "Information Please" and there was nothing she did not know. Ask her for anyone's number or what time it was, and "Information Please" had the answer.

He once hit his finger with a hammer and because there was no one home, he called on the phone and Information Please told him to put ice on his finger. *"Don't cry,"* she said, *"You'll be all right."* After that, Paul called Information Please for all sorts of things, help with geography and arithmetic, and once she even soothed him when his pet canary died. She said quietly, *"Paul, always remember that there are other worlds to sing in."*

Eventually nine-year old Paul moved across country. His old wooden box phone was replaced, but he never forgot how Information Please helped him. Years later as he was passing through Seattle, he called for Information Please and asked, *"Could you tell me, please, how to spell a word?"* There was a long pause and then a soft answer. *"I guess your finger must be healed by now."*

"I wonder," she replied, *"if you know how much you meant to me? I never had any children, and I used to look forward to your calls. Silly, wasn't it?"* Years later Paul heard Information Please had died, but she had left him an message: *"Paul, always remember that there are other worlds to sing in."*

Truly, God does place people in our lives when we need them. When we are struggling with problems of life, He sends us friends to counsel us and loved ones to console us. He sends us honest people to tell us hard truths and He sends us gentle people to comfort us.

God sends us Someone to forgive us our sins and give us hope for life. When we feel we can no longer sing, Jesus reminds us, *"There are other worlds to sing in."*

Thank You, Jesus, for sending people I need into my life.

OCTOBER 14

"Signs Found Along the Roadways of Life"

Beauty is only a light switch away. (North Carolina)

At the feast of ego, everyone leaves hungry. (New Mexico)

It's hard to make a comeback when you haven't been anywhere. (Arizona)

If pro is opposite of con, then what is opposite of progress? Congress! (Indiana)

A man will pay $20 for a $10 item he needs. A woman will pay $10 for a $20 item she doesn't need. (Colorado)

A woman worries about the future until she gets a husband. A man never worries about the future until he gets a wife. (Idaho)

A successful man makes more money than his wife can spend. A successful woman is one who can find such a man. (Florida)

To be happy with a man, you must understand him a lot and love him a little. To be happy with a woman, you must love her a lot and not try to understand her at all." (Michigan)

Woman marries man expecting he will change but he doesn't. Man marries woman expecting she won't change but she does. (Iowa)

A woman has the last word in any argument. Anything a man says after that is the beginning of a new argument. (Missouri)

Notice how most of these sayings deal with men and women? You would think after years of relations between the sexes, it would no longer be such a mystery. But it still is!

This is part of the reason God made us male and female. Not only is it not good to be alone, our spouse helps us. We learn in Ecclesiastes 4:10, **"But woe to him who is alone when he falls and has not another to lift him up."**

God made male and female so different to keep us interested in each other. If we always understand each other perfectly, will we not quickly get bored? Part of the great mysteries of life are found between man and woman.

"A cord of three strands is not quickly broken." (Ecclesiastes 4:12)

OCTOBER 15

When I attended the seminary in the late 1960's, I worked two years at St. Louis Lutheran Hospital as an orderly in the Emergency Room and Clinic. One of my periodic tasks was to clean, wrap and sterilize packages of surgical instruments in the autoclave. After being trained and tested, I learned which instruments went with which procedure and was taught how to sterilize the instruments and store them in their proper places on the surgical cart.

When assisting doctors with minor surgical procedures, I would open the packages and place the instruments in the correct order on the stainless steel surgical tables. Details of cleanliness and order were important for each procedure.

The most important part of sterilization is to wash the instruments clean with soap. If you try to sterilize dirty instruments, you've not done your job. First clean them, then sterilize. If they weren't first washed, they were all considered dirty.

People may think all they need to do is make their outward life better. If inwardly they think sinful thoughts and bad things, so what? So long as they don't act on these bad things, they are being good, right?

Wrong! Sinful people still have sinful motives, and such motives need to be forgiven and changed. Our nature taints what we do and why we do it. If we continually cover up bad motives with acceptable actions, we are still doing it wrong and need forgiveness. If we teach others to do the same, we are doubly wrong. When our Lord forgives us and makes our heart right, then our actions will also be right.

All of us depend on people doing things right. If we enter a hospital, we expect those present not only to know what they are doing, but that they will do what they know is right. God grant that we, too, are willing to learn what is right to do and to follow through by doing it.

May the Holy Spirit guide our hearts, so that our actions also may be according to God's will.

OCTOBER 16

When problems occur in life, the first thing we should try to do is fix them. If there's water in the basement, we must grab a bucket or shop-vac and clean it up. Later we can find the leak. Sometimes we have to do both at the same time. It there's water leaking out of a pipe, first shut off the Water Main, then find a way to fix the leak.

Thinking back to those days when I worked at Lutheran Hospital, St. Louis, I recall coming home and my wife was in tears. She, too, had just returned from her work and our new 1969 Volkswagen "Beetle" car had stalled in the middle of a busy intersection. It was a standard shift transmission and she was unfamiliar with it.

Coming home during rush hour, she drove into a busy intersection, stalled the motor and couldn't get it going again. With cars all around her, a man finally came over and drove the car to the side of the road. She said didn't want to drive it again, and I made sure that she didn't. That night we went to a Lutheran car dealer I knew from a church I was serving and traded for a larger 1968 Ford, a year older with more miles on it, but it was an even trade. It wasn't the cute brand new VW, but it was much safer and easier for both of us to drive.

When problems occur in life, the first thing we should do is try to fix them. But sometimes we can't. We cannot fix most illnesses we have without medicine or therapy or a day or two of bed rest. We cannot change another person's personality if it clashes with ours. We can, of course, change how we react to that other person, providing we realize we are part of the problem.

We also cannot fix our sinful lives without realizing we are the problem and we need God's intervention. We can and should realize we are doing wrong and stop doing it, but we still need God to repair the damage of sin. Without Jesus and His forgiveness, we are headed for huge trouble.

Ever stalled your car in a bad place? How did God help you?

OCTOBER 17

A "paraprosdokian" is a figure of speech in which the latter part of a sentence or phrase ends in such a surprising or unexpected way that the reader or listener must reframe or reinterpret the first part. For example:

> *I could agree with you, but then we'd both be wrong.*
> *I used to be indecisive. Now I'm not so sure.*
> *Some cause happiness where they go. Others, when they go.*
> *A clear conscience is usually the sign of a bad memory.*
> *We never really grow up; we only learn how to act in public.*
> *I didn't say it was your fault, I said I was blaming you.*
> *The voices in my head aren't real, but they have good ideas!*
> *Borrow money from a pessimist. He won't expect it back.*
> *You're never too old to learn something stupid.*
> *Nostalgia isn't what it used to be.*

Jesus was the Master teacher, and His stories are not only memorable, they give us eternal truths. Some of His parables contain unexpected elements, such as when the Master of the Vineyard paid all his workers equally, whether they came in the morning, at noon or just one hour before quitting. We'd expect those earlier to be paid more, but the Master pays all equally the same.

Another example is the account of Jesus healing the Ten Lepers. Luke 17:15-16 tells us after they were healed, **"One of them, when he saw that he was healed, turned back, praising God with a loud voice; and he fell on his face at Jesus' feet, giving him thanks.** *Now he was a Samaritan.*"

Noting that the only grateful man was a Samaritan makes his gratitude a greater event. The other nine were Jews and should also have been grateful, but only the "foreigner" Samaritan (Jesus' words) gave God public thanks. Noting this makes the ingratitude of the other nine inexcusable. God's Word is life-changing and life-giving. In Jesus ministry we see God active and alive in the world.

Look around today to see how God is active in the world.

OCTOBER 18

I've watched with interest the development of the electric car. If one can be made economically and be able to travel far enough to make it comparable with a fuel driven car, it should be a good idea and benefit us all.

While several electric brands have already come and gone, the *Tesla* seems to have found a place. It is expensive and has received federal subsidy, but it has produced a car that might be viable in today's auto market. Perhaps part of my interest is that its name is so much like my own.

Its success will involve many things, including how *Tesla* assembles its cars. One *Tesla* video shows an assembly plant with 3000 workers and 160 robots turning out 70 cars per day. While huge machines press out the frame and fenders, robots assemble the major parts, welding, riveting, painting and aligning parts. It then installs doors, drive train, glass, seats, and other interior items as it completes the exterior with tires and trim. Human workers install the technical or smaller details to make the final product run.

Watching the process reminds me of how God has given us His Holy Christian Church. By His design and plan, trained church members assist, teach, support, comfort, encourage and help its members receive the blessings God intends them to have. It takes many people to keep the Church going, all this to help them receive eternal life. But the Church uses people for this, not robots.

Psalm 100:2 urges us, **"Serve the Lord with gladness! Come into his presence with singing!"** God made human beings to praise Him and to serve each other. We are living, breathing creatures, not metallic, electronic robots. God did not want a robotic church, but a living Body of Christ. Certainly it is good that we employ new and good methods to do His work, but we always deal with people made of flesh and blood, not metal, batteries and plastic. God gives us the ability to make choices, and the Holy Spirit helps us make the right one, that Jesus is our Savior.

"Me and my house will serve the Lord." (Joshua 24:15)

OCTOBER 19

While autumn is a favorite season of mine, I can see why some do not like it as much as I do. Its changing lovely colors, crisp blue skies and unique smells are a "rush" on my senses. But they also signal the rapid change from verdant life to the seeming lifelessness of winter.

Each season has its positives and negatives, and I welcome the changes. Living in a tropical climate where there are only two seasons, wet and dry, or living in a Pacific island where the temperature rarely changes 20 degrees during the year would seem uninteresting.

The changing seasons of nature challenge our minds and bodies to adapt to our surroundings. Temperature extremes require us to create things that will help us live and thrive. True, extremes of cold or heat can make us invent heaters or coolers. Or we might move to other areas for a time. But those of us who have lived most of our lives in four seasons enjoy and even look forward to the changes the seasons bring us. Variety in life is a blessing from God.

Variety in worship is also a blessing. Psalm 150 is a song of joy and variety in our worship of God.

> *"Praise the LORD! Praise God in His sanctuary; praise Him in His mighty heavens! Praise Him for His mighty deeds; praise Him according to His excellent greatness! Praise Him with trumpet sound; praise Him with lute and harp! Praise Him with tambourine and dance; praise Him with strings and pipe! Praise Him with sounding cymbals; praise Him with loud clashing cymbals. Let everything that has breath praise the LORD! Praise the LORD!"*

Note the variety of ways of worship God gives us in Psalm 150. Not all will be included in all church services, but the joy and exuberance noted here show how God appreciates the variety of ways people can praise Him. The means of worship is not as important as faith and attitude of the heart.

What do you prefer in worship? Has it changed during your life?

OCTOBER 20

In my life I have had the privilege of being friends with many good people, the best of which has always been my wife. Not every husband can say this, but those who can are doubly blessed. Best friends don't always get along perfectly because of our human weaknesses, but they still care for each other when disagreement occurs.

Cicero, one of Rome's most skilled orators, as well as politician, linguist and writer wrote this: *"Friendship improves happiness and abates misery by the doubling of our joy and the dividing of our grief."* That is a good understanding of the benefits of friendship on the road of life.

Wise King Solomon wrote in Ecclesiastes 4:9-10, **"Two are better than one, because they have a good reward for their toil. If they fall, one will lift up his fellow. But woe to him who is alone when he falls and has not another to lift him up!"** He continues the benefits of friendship by saying two can keep each other warm and also can ward off enemies if they approach.

When God said in Genesis 2:18, **"It is not good that the man should be alone; I will make him a helper fit for him."** He was not referring only to marriage, but also to friends. A life without friends makes our journey lonely and hard to bear. Friends are important. They serve as confidants and counselors and can share our burdens.

Think about your friends. It isn't necessary to have only a "best friend" because several friends can bring benefits by their various gifts they can share. In my High School yearbook a friend wrote, *"To my best friend, Bob."* Until then I didn't realize he gave me that honor. As a result of his note, we remained friends until his death.

Jesus considered His Disciples as friends. He told them in John 15:15, **"No longer do I call you servants… but I have called you friends."** May you find joy in your friends, and especially in your best friend, Jesus.

What a friend we have in Jesus,
all our sins and griefs to bear! (from the hymn)

OCTOBER 21

Names can often be confusing. We may think we are talking about one person when we discover there was another person by that name. On October 21 of 310 AD, a man named Eusebius died, ending his one-year reign as Pope of the Catholic Church. *"Ah,"* you may think, *"that was Eusebius the Church historian."* But this is untrue.

Pope Eusebius is not the same man as Eusebius of Caesarea, the famous historian, Bible scholar and writer who lived around the same time, but died 30 years later in 340 AD. The practice of using a first name and a last name (surname) or family name, is a recent invention.

Surnames were added to help identify people. A person might be given the name of family or the area in which he lived. Scandinavian cultures gave the surname of the father, such as "Johnson" which meant "son of John." Europeans added surnames by location or trade. Peter was called Aufdemberge (from the mountain) or Martin was called Miller (grinder) or Bauer (peasant). Only in the past two hundred years have western cultures adopted uniform first and last names to keep our identities separate.

Jesus was a common name in His day, and our Lord was probably known by the town where he lived, Jesus of Nazareth. Some were known by their stature. Apostle Paul was named Saul but later was called "Saul Paulus" meaning "Little Paul," which was shortened to Paul. Jesus gave Simon Peter his second name to distinguish him from others. Most of us today are unable to determine why we have our surnames, but it helps to identify us.

Names are important. God told His ancient people, **"Fear not, for I have redeemed you; I have called you by name, you are mine."** (Isaiah 43:1) In our baptism, God gives us a very important name, Child of God. We are a child of our parents, but also a child of the Living God. Some people don't like their name and some even change it. But a Child of God is grateful for his or her sacred name.

Do you like your name? Why or why not?

OCTOBER 22

Money is a wonderful blessing but a terrible master. It has no inherent value of its own except what it can bring us. You can't eat it, build a house with it or find happiness by it, but we all need at least some of it to gain those things. Money cannot bring us happiness, but the lack of it can certainly make us miserable.

By the grace of God I have more of it right now than I did when I started in ministry in 1971 and had none. Some has come through work, some by investment and some by marriage. Some has been lost but more gained. Much has been given away to worthy causes or people in need, and all that has been returned and then some.

I've learned a person cannot out-give the Lord. Whatever is given in gratitude for His work has been given back, and more. The words of our Lord are so true in Luke 6:38, **"Give, and it will be given to you. Good measure, pressed down, shaken together, running over, will be put into your lap. For with the measure you use it will be measured back to you."** I can't count the times my lap has been full of His unexpected blessings.

One must take care not to give merely to get back. That is surely deception and borders on theft. God still knows our motives. But when we provide to others in need, He assures us our needs will be satisfied also.

It is satisfying to have money, yet the satisfaction is short-lived. It's a relief when your bills are paid with something to spare, but other bills are certain to show up. Jesus urges us not to worry about what we do not have. He said in Matthew 6:31-33, **"Do not be anxious, saying, 'What shall we eat?' or 'What shall we drink?' or 'What shall we wear?',...Your heavenly Father knows that you need them all. Seek first the kingdom of God and his righteousness, and all these things will be added to you."**

May God give you contentment this day, even if you are short of needed funds. The Lord will always provide!

How has the Lord provided for you in the past?

OCTOBER 23

German pastor and theologian Helmut Thielicke continued his ministry during some of the worst days of World War Two. Educated at humanist universities, he earned both the Doctor of Philosophy (1932) and Doctor of Theology (1934) degrees, despite suffering health problems.

Interrogated and persecuted by the Nazis, Thielicke maintained his preaching and teaching whenever possible. During the 1944 bombing of Stuttgart, he preached to a small gathering of Christians who had to change locations several times when their meeting room was destroyed. His series of sermons on the Lord's Prayer are memorable in that he realized the people may have no Bible to read, but they still knew the Lord's Prayer from memory.

Thielicke once said to his small congregation on a Sunday evening while hearing bombs explode nearby, *"Isn't there a comfort, a peculiar message in the fact that, after all the conflagrations that have swept through our wounded city, we can continue our study of the Lord's Prayer? We don't need to interrupt and search the Bible for texts appropriate for catastrophe. The Words of the Lord's Prayer are immediate to every situation of life. The farmer can pray it at close of day's work, the mother can pray it with her children in the air-raid shelter, the little child seeking fatherly protection or the aged person in the trials and pangs of his last hour, both can pray it. It can be prayed by everybody in every situation, without exception."*

Helmut Thielicke and his family survived the war and he went on to teach at the University of Tubingen. He later helped organize the theology department at the newly formed University of Hamburg where he remained until his death at age 77.

Throughout history and in all situations, good and bad, God brings us His Word of comfort and strength. The Words of our Lord Jesus are timeless. The Psalm says, **"Your word is a lamp to my feet and a light to my path."** (Psalm 119:105)

Praise God He is with us in all the storms and wars of life!

OCTOBER 24

On October 24, 1931, Chicago gangster Al Capone's reign as crime boss ended at age 33 when he's sent to prison for tax evasion. There he was diagnosed with several serious illnesses and was barely able to do his work in the prison shoe factory. Only the protection of seasoned prisoner Red Rudinsky kept him from being beaten to death. Released in 1939, the mighty and feared crime boss spent the rest of his days a broken man and finally died at age 49 of disease and dementia. His gravestone epitaph reads, *"My Jesus, Mercy!"*

In 2 Samuel 1:27 David laments the deaths of King Saul and his son Jonathan with the words, **"How the mighty have fallen, and the weapons of war perished!"** The same end always comes to the mighty. Whether the "mighty" are good or evil during their lives, they all face the grave. No matter what the words on their epitaphs may read, they all have passed from this life. And so shall we all.

But the Child of God knows that is not all there is. By the grace and mercy of our Creator God who made heaven and earth, He has another place prepared, a new heaven and a new earth where there is no suffering and pain, no tears or sadness. Revelation 22:4 says of the blessed living win the presence of God, **"They will need no light of lamp or sun, for the Lord God will be their light, and they will reign forever and ever."**

It seems depressing to know we all will die. Even if we realize the reason (sin and human frailty) the prospect of our death lurks in the shadows of our minds and tries to darken any light of joy or happiness. But Christ is between us and the shadows. He has overcome death and will bring us over the bridge between this world and eternity with God.

When living in North Dakota I recall a Bismarck bank advertisement that ended, *"Cross over the bridge!"* The bank was by a river, and to get there we must *"Cross over the bridge!"* Jesus helps us cross the bridge of sin to the presence of God. We cannot thank Him enough for His promises.

Those old ad slogans can really stick with us, can't they?

OCTOBER 25

Truth alone doesn't make a fact important. My son is an excellent teacher to his 8th Grade students. He teaches them what is important as well as what is not. One of his usual daily class routines in giving the students useless facts. Nearly every day he tells his class a small bit of information that has little or no value. Examples:

- *Israeli people consume more turkeys per capita than any other country.*
- *A "quidnunc" is a person eager to know the latest news and gossip.*
- *There are more than 10 million bricks in the Empire State Building.*
- *Human thighbones are stronger than concrete.*
- *A herd of hares is called a Husk.*

Each of these bits of fact may be true, but they have little or no value. Unless, of course, you are an Israeli turkey farmer gossiping about bricks while standing on concrete surrounded by a Husk of hares. But I doubt there is anyone in the entire world who fits that description.

Contrast those statements with these:

- *"No one comes to the Father except through Jesus."* (John 14:6)
- *"The Truth will set you free."* (John 8:32)
- *"He that endures unto the end shall be saved."* (Matthew 24:13)
- *"God is light, and in Him is no darkness at all."* (1 John 1:5)
- *"I, the Lord, do not change."* (Malachi 3:6)

Do you see the significant difference? Each set may be factual, but the truths of the second set are hugely important while the truths of the first set are of little importance to anyone. Truth alone doesn't make a fact important.

Isaiah 49:16 tells us an important truth. **"I have engraved you on the palms of my hands."** This is important not the process, but the words and where they are engraved. When Carol and I were married the pastor read to us from the Song of Solomon 8:6, **"Set me as a seal upon your heart, as a seal upon your arm."** During the first month we were married, she burned her arm in the oven, a mark she still carries. Its truth will always be important to us.

What truth will always be important to you?

OCTOBER 26

Today is my daughter-in-law Debbie's birthday. She is a very intelligent woman who was high school valedictorian and had a 4.0 GPA in college. Debbie has a very good memory and is even able to remember how many times I tell certain stories. That's too bad…

Does God ever forget anything? The Bible reminds us over and over how God does not forget us in our troubles, i.e., **"He does not forget the cry of the afflicted.** (Psalm 9.12), **"He remembers that we are dust** (Psalm 103:14) **"He remembers his covenant forever."** (Psalm 111:15)

But does God ever forget? Being divine, He should always remember and never forget anything, even the smallest detail. But being merciful there need to be times when He forgets; otherwise our sins would become a roadblock between Him and us.

My son and I once took a road trip, driving a thousand miles in one day back home from his brother's wedding in Arizona. Fourteen hours is a long time in a car, but it went by quickly as we both recounted stories from the past. Some of mine were about my youth, and some were from his. He has his father's memory for details, so he, too, shared stories of his youth, some of which I'd never heard. And some of them I should have heard long before then! But the "statute of limitations" usually runs out on things we did when we were kids, so he was safe.

I once asked my aged father if he remembered any bad things I did when I was young, and he said, *"If I did, it wouldn't matter."* I believe that's how it is with our gracious God. He knows what we did, but because of Jesus, it no longer matters. When we have faith in Jesus, the "statute of limitations" no longer applies to our past sins.

Memory can be a deterrence. If we're reminded of our past sins, we may stop whatever wrong we're doing. Give thanks that God always remembers His mercy towards us.

For that we can be eternally grateful!

OCTOBER 27

During World War Two the British Isles were the last line of resistance against the powerful sweep of Nazi forces bent on controlling the world. Fortunately the Channel Islands off the western coast of Normandy were the only British land to be occupied by the Germans.

Under relentless attack and danger of collapse, Great Britain lacked the resources to see the conflict through to victory. For that reason on February 9, 1941, British Prime Minister Winston Churchill went on the BBC radio and appealed to the allies saying, *"Give us the tools and we will finish the job."*

Churchill knew that without the necessary manpower and armaments they could not endure the enemy assault they were facing. But if their allies pitched in with men and materials, they could prevail over the powerful enemy. Ten months later Pearl Harbor brought the United States into the war, and then Great Britain and the world knew our men and materials would now be available.

Life is much like that. There are often times we feel inadequately equipped for the troubles life drops on us, and we need help from the outside. Being part of the Body of Christ, we can help each other when we need it.

Paul said in Romans 12:13, **"Contribute to the needs of the saints and seek to show hospitality."** Again He said in Galatians 6:2, **"Bear one another's burdens, and so fulfill the law of Christ."** God made us to praise Him and to help one another. As some pastors include in the wedding ceremony, **"We are to bear one another's weaknesses, comfort one another in sickness, trouble and sorrow, and are to minister to one another in Christian love."**

The business of being a Christian is never finished until we leave this earth for eternity in God's presence. But, as Churchill said, if we give each other the tools, we can finish the job!

What tools can you share to help others in their Christian life?

OCTOBER 28

The name Ponzi is forever associated with fraud. In 1920 Charles Ponzi began offering investors a 50% return on their money in 45 days and 100% return in 90 days. Though it was too good to be true, people poured their money into his scheme. Ponzi then used money from new investors to pay prior investors and fund his lavish lifestyle.

By the time his fraud was discovered six months later, investors had lost 20 million dollars and five banks had failed. Charles Ponzi spent 3 years in prison and was later deported to Italy. He died penniless in 1949 at the age of 66. His name will always be associated with financial schemes and breaking the law.

Ecclesiastes 7:1 tells us, **"A good name is better than precious ointment, and the day of death than the day of birth."** While we understand the first part of this verse, the second may seem puzzling.

Certainly a good name is a precious possession. In a collection of poems by Ellen Bailey is one called "Your Father's Name" and its first two verses are:

> *You got it from your father, It was all he had to give,*
> *So it's yours to use and cherish For as long as you may live.*
> *If you lost the watch he gave you, It can always be replaced;*
> *But a black mark on your name Can never be erased.*

My father committed much of that poem to memory and I recall him quoting it. A good name is better than precious ointment, no matter how much the ointment costs.

Second part of the above verse might be puzzling only if we forget that the "day of death" for the believer ushers in a new life with God in eternity. The birth of a child is surely a precious event, but that child must face a lifetime of sin and struggles. The death of a Christian is the birth of new life, so **"the day of death than the day of birth."**

When my eldest brother died, he was buried on his birthday. His family gathered after the service at home and sang, *"Happy Birthday to Dad."* It was a tender moment.

Praise God we have a better life ahead with Him.

OCTOBER 29

Of all the disturbing words that Jesus spoke in the Gospels, His statement in Matthew 24:12 has always bothered me the most. Seeing Herod's great temple in Jerusalem and speaking of the End Times, Jesus told His disciples, **"And because lawlessness will be increased, the love of many will grow cold."**

Christians don't want the kingdom of God to shrink; we want it to grow. But Jesus said the future Church will shrink because evil will get so great in the world that people will fall away. Lawlessness will increase until believers will grow weary and embittered by sin and fall away from the Lord. I believe this has already started to happen.

Whether it's the spread of evil due to drugs and unpreventable murder, whether it's the breakdown of the family and the spread of deceit and selfishness, whether it's the deaths of a thousand people who committed suicide under the influence of Jim Jones and his *"People's Temple"* in 1978, lawlessness seems to be increasing. Despite what many statisticians quote to us to the contrary, the love of God's people appears to be growing cold.

Despite our great advances of technology, people increasingly ignore laws and forget common sense. Rather than resist growing evil deeds, they embrace them in the name of progress and inclusiveness. Christians are not exempt from this influence. Because of it their love for God grows cold and they are deserting Him, especially in the developed Western Nations.

What do you see around you? Are the marks of lawlessness already here? Can anything be done to turn things around in our world? Jesus meant to warn His Disciples, so His words are a warning to us also.

Be prepared for the spread of evil. Prevent what you can, at home and in your personal life. But know *"Satan's Little Season"* is close at hand, so do not forsake your Lord. Cling to His Word and urge your loved ones to do the same.

O God, help us remain steadfast to You always. Amen

OCTOBER 30

Despite the gloom of yesterday's devotion, Jesus also gives us hope. Right after telling His disciples about the coming loss of love by the spread of evil, Jesus gives them words of hope, **"The one who endures to the end will be saved."** (Matthew 24:13) If we hold fast to Jesus and trust Him to rescue us, we have nothing to fear. If we endure through all the coming trials and temptations, God will take us to our heavenly home.

But what if we don't? And what if our loved ones don't either. How can we endure? There is so much around us that tries to tear us away from our faith in Jesus. Government authorities and trained intellectuals tell us we're better off being a secular society. The wealthy control us with power and the poor want to control us in order to solve their problems. How can we hold fast to Jesus when we're pulled this way and that?

To be saved means to be spared from destruction. It does not mean we will not see problems, or that evil will not touch us. Evil is a reality. Both believers and non-believers are affected by it. While we won't escape the affects of evil, trusting in Jesus with faith will save us from eternal death and separation from the goodness of God.

Those who bring evil into the world will suffer a fate worse than death. While we cannot fathom what hell will be like, we know it will be the complete absence of God, and that in itself is terrible. Those who abandon Jesus and those who seduce others to follow will experience pain that defies imagination. Hell is no place to joke about.

But if we endure and not give up Jesus, we will be saved. The Holy Spirit will help us endure. By the gifts and power He gives, believers in Christ Jesus will be able to hold on. They will be able to cling to their faith, held close by God Himself.

Holy Spirit, keep me faithful to Jesus, and help me endure so that I will not fall away. Amen

OCTOBER 31

I never experienced the reality of total darkness until one October 31 night in North Dakota. I had scheduled a German Reformation service for Sunday night, October 31, Halloween, but also Reformation night, and my church was filled. Lutherans, Baptists, Methodists, Catholics and even some Adventists all came because they wanted to sing German hymns and see if that new preacher really could preach in German.

The first part of the service went well, as we prayed and heard lessons *"auf Deutsch."* During the sermon hymn, I stepped into my front office and when I opened the door to return, all the lights went out! Every one of them! It was a cloudy, moonless night and it was dark!

For a few moments all was silent. Then my organist asked quietly, *"What happened?"* A flashlight came on, and another and then a lighter. *"We are in blackout."* said someone. *"The whole south side of town has no lights."*

I told the people to remain calm and we'd think of something. Then I remembered the box of Christmas Eve candles in my office. I got a flashlight, found them and we passed out the candles. Then I went into the pulpit to preach my German sermon with a flashlight. Halfway through, the lights came back on. Later we learned a snowmobile had struck a support wire on a light pole and knocked out a transformer. Half the town was in blackness, but now the lights were back on.

People are afraid of the dark. It doesn't matter where we live or what period of history, we're all "hard-wired" to fear total darkness, perhaps because we fear what we can't see. Light is good, but darkness is bad. Why? Because we feel helpless and defenseless in darkness. Darkness takes away our control and douses us with fear of the unknown.

Jesus said, **"I am the Light of the World."** (John 9:5), and He really is! Satan tries keeping us in darkness and often succeeds. But the Light of Christ can't be extinguished.

When were you last in total darkness?

DAY BY DAY WITH JESUS
in
November
+ + +
NOVEMBER 1

In the early 1900s, Fort Bragg, California, residents threw their garbage over a cliff to a deserted beach. For decades people dumped refuse there into the ocean, cars, metal, furniture and mostly garbage, with innumerable glass containers. In the 1940's they called it "The Dump." Finally in 1967, city leaders closed the area to dumping. Cleanup programs tried making it better, but without much success.

Over the next thirty years the waves pounded and cleansed the beach, breaking down everything except the glass. Ceaseless waves disintegrated the trash but only broke up and smoothed the tons of glass, moving it back and forth along the shore. Glass shards remained by the millions, polished by the ceaseless waves until an amazing thing was formed the locals called "Glass Beach." Its sea glass tumbles in the water, 24 hours a day, bumping and grinding against each other, fashioning the surfaces frosty and glistening. Sand joins to smooth the glass into precious gems.

In 2002 Glass Beach became part of MacKerricher State Park and now attracts large numbers of tourists. Where decades ago people illegally dumped their refuse, now it is illegal to remove even a piece of it.

Maybe at some time you have felt like trash, left behind, dumped overboard or abandoned as worthless. Hopefully the bumps and bruises of life have shaped you as well and made you realize you are more valuable. Life may try to dump and grind us, but God considers us His treasures. He believes we are so precious that He gave the life of His only Son that we might be with Him forever. **"How precious is your steadfast love, O God!"** (Psalm 36:7)

Because of Jesus, we are all God's gems!

NOVEMBER 2

At the end of the Korean War in 1953, a group of POWs emerged from the darkness carrying a crucifix of firewood and wire made, amazingly, by a Jewish soldier. More amazing was the man in whose honor it was made.

Fr. Emil Kapaun was chaplain to the American 8th Cavalry Regiment. He drove hundreds of miles ministering to the men all over the battlefields, helping the wounded, hearing confessions and celebrating Eucharist from his Jeep. He worked with little sleep, baptizing, cleaning latrines and ministering to the sick and dying.

At the Battle of Unsan, Fr. Kapaun ran into "no-man's land" to minister to the dying. Although told to evacuate, he stayed to help the wounded. Among the men he saved was Sgt. Herbert Miller whom he carried and helped him walk for 80 miles, urging others not to lose hope. In prison Fr. Kapaun gave his food to the starving, smuggling in needed drugs and boiled water for the sick. He organized them to get wood and clean the camp and led them in daily mass.

The communists punished him for the hope he gave the men, forcing him to stand naked for hours in the bitter cold trying to "re-educate" him. When he got sick, he was taken to a "death house" where no one came out alive. As he was taken, he comforted them saying, *"Boys, don't worry about me, I will pray for you."* In his final act they saw him praying for enemy soldiers. He died May 23, 1951.

Fr. Kapaun is the most highly decorated military chaplain in history with fifteen medals and commendations including the Medal of Honor awarded in 2013. Nine of the men from that POW camp were there, including Sgt. Herbert Miller, the man whose life he'd saved 63 years before.

When human history is over, it will not be the forces of evil which will have the final word. It will be God's love in Jesus Christ, the force that moves people like Fr. Kapaun to such self-sacrifice. The wood and wire crucifix stands today in the Fr. Kapaun Memorial Chapel in Seoul, South Korea.

"I will fear no evil, for You are with me." (Psalm 23:4)

NOVEMBER 3

Aphorisms are terse sayings which express a general truth, principle, or astute observation, and spoken or written in a humorous or memorable form. They may include known phrases that are changed at the last moment to convey an opposite outcome.

A Few Examples of Aphorisms:
* *It's not whether you win or lose, it's how you place the blame.*
* *Money isn't everything, but it sure keeps the kids in touch.*
* *If at first you don't succeed, skydiving is not for you.*
* *We are born naked, wet and hungry, and then things get worse.*
* *Red meat is not bad for you, but fuzzy green meat is.*
* *Ninety nine percent of the bad lawyers give the rest a bad name.*
* *Artificial intelligence is no match for natural stupidity.*

The Bible rarely shows humor like these aphorisms, but it does give us many astute observations in memorable form. The Old Testament book of Proverbs is filled with terse bits of wisdom that can guide a person in Godly living.

Consider these Proverbs:
1:7 - "The fear of the LORD is the beginning of wisdom."
1:9 - "My son, if sinners entice you, do not consent."
3:9 - "Honor the LORD with your wealth.
3:35 - "The wise will inherit honor, but fools get disgrace."
6:6 - "Go to the ant, O sluggard; consider her ways, and be wise."
8:33 - "Hear instruction and be wise, and do not neglect it."

Jesus our Lord gives us much more to ponder:
John 8:7 - "Let him who is without sin cast the first stone."
Luke 11:28 - "Blessed are those who hear the word of God and keep it."
John 14:6 - "No man comes to the Father except through me."
John 13:34 - "Love one another just as I have loved you."
John 3:16 - "God so loved the world that he gave his only Son."

What is your favorite Bible verse?

NOVEMBER 4

In 1880 Richard was a young telegrapher in a northern Minnesota train station when a crate arrived from the East. It contained dozens of pocket watches, and because no one came to claim it, Richard telegraphed the manufacturer offering to sell the watches for half the profits. They agreed.

He sent a wire to every train station agent in the system asking them if they wanted a good pocket watch cheap and was surprised how quickly the watches sold at a profit. He ordered more and encouraged his fellow telegraphers to set up a display case in their stations offering quality watches for a low price. Word spread and before long both travelers and local people came to the train station to buy watches.

Richard rented a building, hired a man named Alvah to help him with the orders and added dry goods and other items for sale. Richard and Alvah did so well that they left their jobs and moved their company to Chicago where it still is in operation today, a hundred thirty-three years later.

It was all started when Richard Sears left his job as a telegrapher to sell watches, and Alvah Roebuck left his job repairing watches to work for Richard. We know their business today as Sears, Roebuck and Company.

We may look back and see we missed an opportunity. Maybe we really wanted to try a certain thing, but never felt courageous enough. Maybe it meant leaving our job for another, but we didn't want to take the risk. No one should feel guilty for not taking such a chance. Not everyone has the vision of Richard Sears or the skills of Alvah Roebuck. Rather than feel bad about what we didn't do, lets trust in God for what He gives us and give Him thanks for what He's done for us. Then do the best we can as we are able.

Proverbs 3:6 says, **"Remember the Lord in everything you do, and he will show you the right way."** (Good News)

Trusting God may mean stepping out in faith to do what you never thought you could. But it also might mean staying where you are and doing your best.

For some people, this is their life's motto, and they don't know it.

NOVEMBER 5

My computer told me that there were software updates awaiting installation. All I had to do was hit the right button and new things would come to make my clever and useful laptop even more clever and useful. One thing we learn quickly from our electronics, there is always something newer or better out there. No matter how good the machine or software, there is always room for improvement.

That's how it is in life also. No matter how hard we try, there is usually room for improvement. That might seem discouraging, but it should give even more reason to give thanks to God that our life depends on Him, not on us. How could we ever get everything so right that God would accept us into heaven based only on our effort?

My computer is already old. Newer versions never cease being produced. There are rumors one day that they will all have "touch technology" a concept I don't comprehend. Technology is obsolete the moment it is put on sale. Our "new and improved" model already has a newer version being created.

But some things are unchangeable. I once officiated at the burial of a retired Air Force Chief Master Sergeant. His family said his favorite Scripture was the old and beloved John 3:16, so my message was titled, "The New Old Gospel." I shared with them God's simple plan of salvation, that all depends on Jesus. He paid the price for our sins and lays salvation into our hands as a gift. We merely receive it.

How much newness do we really need? Jesus said, in Revelation 21:5, **"Behold, I am making all things new."** The world tells us we must continually upgrade. "Download our updates lest you be left behind." The Bible says getting to heaven isn't complicated at all. Because of Jesus there will be no more pain or anger, suffering, tears or discontent. We will be in the presence of our loving God experiencing eternal joy, peace and contentment. Sound boring? Not to me!

Are you ready for your heavenly upgrade?

NOVEMBER 6

What makes you afraid? Terrorists? Politics? A bad relationship? Sickness? Death? Maybe it's bugs. I once saw a T-Shirt that said, *"The Only Thing We Have To Fear Is Fear Itself – and Spiders!"* Sometimes we get fearful when things come to an end, but the end is when we trust God most.

God is our fortress and our strength, and He is always there to help us, in our sickness, trouble and pain. If God can protect us from sin or even from hell, how much more will He not care for us now, today? Because God is our fortress, we need not fear. David said in Psalm 46, **"God is our refuge (fortress) and strength, a very present help in trouble. Therefore we will not fear."**

I see there is a "NO FEAR" brand of clothing. It was created in 1989 by the Simon brothers and Marty Moates, and it was inspired by extreme action sports. NO FEAR sponsors Martial Arts matches, Motocross Racing, Big Wave surfing and that incredibly dangerous sport, "Cage Fighting." It even offers a NO FEAR energy drink made by Pepsi. But on February 25, 2011, NO FEAR filed for bankruptcy. Maybe they were afraid of losing their shirts!

Despite our fears, today we have more money, better healthcare and are safer than at any time in human history. Many of our fears are irrational.

A doctor was making a house call. He gave the sick man medicine and instructions, and as the Doctor was leaving, the man asked, "I'm afraid to die. Tell me what lies on the other side." The doctor said, "I don't know." "You, a Christian man, don't know what's on the other side?" As he spoke they both heard scratching from the other side. As he opened the door, a dog leaped into the room. The doctor said, "This is my dog. He has never been in this room before. He didn't know what was inside, but he knew I was here and that was enough. Like him I know little of what is on the other side of this life, but I do know one thing: my Master is there and for me, that knowledge is enough."

Lord, show us Your presence, Lord, and make it enough!

NOVEMBER 7

One Sunday we were attending a contemporary worship service at our son's church to hear our youngest grandchild sing with her preschool class. Looking around the gym at the 500 adults and children, it occurred to me that I could not pastor that church. The energy level there, the activity of parents and little ones, as well as the music and technology would require an energy level I no longer had.

The pastor preached right to our needs. He walked back and forth, making biblical point after point about three words, "Repent, Forgive, Oneness," how God calls us to repent of our sins, be forgiven and to forgive each other, so that we can become One with each other and also One with God. Great thoughts in a fine message

Then came the moment many were there for, when the little ones came up front to sing. With them came an armada of parents and grandparents, bearing that bane of modern Worship, cameras to capture their little ones as they sang. Oh, how I dislike cameras in church!

But as the little ones sang and wiggled their fingers and jumped up and down, I did something totally unplanned. I turned on my iPhone camera, held it up and took pictures for myself! Me, the old Pastor, icon of propriety, became wrapped in the joy of the moment and took pictures.

The following weekend I led worship at our church with its pews full of gentle, retired folks. A few children attended with parents, but there were no cameras. Yet I still found joy there, the joy of God's people smiling, singing, praying as redeemed and forgiven Christians do so well. Then came a revered Lutheran tradition, a Potluck!

In the Gospel of Matthew Jesus speaks of the great feast His People will enjoy in heaven. I hope it will feature my favorite foods, as well as friends and family and the joy of children singing their delights in Jesus. No cameras will be needed because we will remember the moment forever. **"Sing to the Lord a new song!"** (Psalm 98:1)

Smile! God's camera is pointed at you!

NOVEMBER 8

Can you still remember your first bicycle? I can. I don't remember its brand, but it was a one-speed balloon tire model, and it was brand new! I got it when I was in seventh grade. I treated it with care, although I did leave it outside one fall and had to paint the fenders and replace the chain. But that was okay – I am a fixer!

I remember wanting to ride it to school on the last day when I was in the eighth grade. I made it about three miles on the gravel road and finally decided to turn back. I had three more miles of gravel, then four miles of blacktop, and wasn't sure I could do it. Then my chain came off and Dad came to take me the rest of the way to school, and he hauled my bike back home. It was just one of many times he helped me when I'd made a poor decision.

Over the years I've had many new bicycles, a three-speed, a ten-speed and others. I bought a new one when I retired and a few years later sold it after I fell off and narrowly escaped serious injury. Now I only ride on things with four wheels. No sense dealing with broken bones at my age if I can help it.

It's important to learn lessons in life. The best lessons are those we learn without getting hurt, but sometimes it takes an injury to help a person realize some things aren't good to do. I've helped several marriages sort out their troubles and have escorted several addicts into treatment centers so they could turn their lives around. No sense in living a broken life if there's help out there to mend it.

Sometimes God lets us get hurt because it's the only way we'll learn. He allowed His ancient people of Israel to be defeated by their enemies so they would return to Him. He let Peter get caught in some lies so he could repent and truly follow the Lord. He lets us fall off our bikes so we will call out to Him for help.

As God tells us, **"Call upon Me in the day of trouble; I will deliver you, and you shall glorify Me."** (Psalm 50:15)

What are you calling on God for these days?

NOVEMBER 9

History books list November 9, 1938, as *"Kristallnacht"* the "Night of Broken Glass," resulting from a series of coordinated attacks against Jews throughout Nazi Germany and Austria. It was carried out by paramilitary forces and non-Jewish civilians and German authorities looked on without intervening. The name comes from the shards of broken glass that littered the streets after Jewish-owned stores, buildings, and synagogues had windows smashed.

Hundreds of Jews were also attacked and killed, and while the true number will probably never be known, it was certainly many times greater than the published *"96 or more were found dead,"* published in some newspapers. With the dozens of Jewish men arrested and brutally beaten, and the 300 or more suicides caused by the despair it caused, the Jewish death toll was perhaps a thousand.

Additionally, 30,000 were arrested and incarcerated in Nazi concentration camps. Jewish homes, hospitals and schools were ransacked with sledgehammers. Over 1,000 synagogues were burned and 7,000 businesses destroyed or damaged. The accounts of this from the foreign journalists working in Germany sent shock waves around the world.

Centuries before then, the events of Good Friday and Easter Sunday sent far greater shock waves throughout the world. In the days that followed the discovery of the empty tomb and later when His followers saw Him alive, the shock waves of Jesus Christ continued, eventually bringing Rome's Empire to its knees and Jesus Christ into the hearts of two and a half billion believers, one third of the world's people, such as we have today.

God's plans always trump those of mankind. No world leader lasts long. There are no "thousand year reigns" such as Hitler proclaimed. There is only the King of kings and Lord of lords who reigns in the hearts of His people.

"And He shall reign forever and ever." (G. F. Handel, "The Messiah")

NOVEMBER 10

In November 10, 1972, my wife and I experienced a wonderful event, the birth of our first child. I was a pastor in a small rural community, and hospital and doctor were sixty miles away. We knew her time was near and so was the fall deer hunting season. A longtime friend was coming and I'd arranged for him to hunt on a member's land. Early in the morning of the first day of hunting season, my wife went into labor. We drove to the Bismarck hospital, and that evening she presented me with a dark-haired chubby little boy. I returned home with her instructions to go hunting so she could rest and get to know her baby son.

The next morning I shot my first and only deer. My hunting season was over, so my friend and I went to see my wife and son. Afterwards when we stopped to eat, it occurred to me I had no sermon for the next day's service. So I jotted some thoughts on a café napkin about how life changes when God brings us great blessings. The next morning I preached my sermon off those napkin notes. Some members said it was my best message since coming there.

Jesus was the Son of Man who came into the world to redeem sinful people. Our chubby little boy grew to be an accomplished athlete, scholar, teacher, husband and father of three precious little ones, our grandchildren. For him and his brother who came 18 months later, we are indebted to Jesus, Son of God and son of Mary, our Savior.

One day we will all hear the trumpet call of God and gather before God's throne as children of the Heavenly Father. Meanwhile, we live grateful lives for the blessings of family and friends, vocation and freedom.

God recently blessed us in the marriage of our second son. He and his wife have made our family a busy and exciting place to be as we watch God's blessings unfold all around us. **"The LORD bless you from Zion! May you see your children's children!"** (Psalm 128)

If you have been so blessed, do you recall first seeing your child?

NOVEMBER 11

November 11 is Armistice Day, also called Veteran's Day and Remembrance Day, and it marks the end of World War One. The Armistice was signed on the "eleventh hour of the eleventh day of the eleventh month" in 1918. While this official date reflects the ceasefire on the Western Front, hostilities continued in other regions, including Russia and in parts of the old Ottoman Empire.

The date was declared a national holiday in many allied nations to commemorate those members of the armed forces who were killed during war. An exception is Italy where the end of the war is commemorated on November 4. The Netherlands, Denmark and Norway do not commemorate this because those countries remained neutral.

World War One resulted in 36 million casualties (16 million dead and 20 million wounded). Stories of terrible death include the use of mustard gas which was outlawed internationally after this worldwide conflict.

One tragic story involved "The Lost Battalion," nine companies of the United States 77th Division, 554 men so named when they became isolated by German forces after an attack in the Argonne Forest in October 1918. The Battalion was left to fend for itself and suffered terrible hardships, with 360 men killed in action, missing or taken prisoner. The remaining 194 men were rescued by a message delivered by carrier pigeon. The Battalion was led by Major Charles Whittlesey who received the Medal of Honor, along with two of his enlisted soldiers. Sadly, Major Whittlesey committed suicide after the war. Seeing his men die in such hopeless conditions was more than he could bear.

After terrible events, what keeps some people alive and others wanting to die? God gives most of us a strength to look past the evils to see Him as a caring provider who will give us a better life here, as well as a new life with Him there. We are not all equally strong, but we all have a God powerful enough to help us overcome the worst adversity.

"We trust in the Lord our God," (Isaiah 36:7)

NOVEMBER 12

There seems to be no lack of advice that authorities are willing to give us in every aspect of human life. Our Government is bloated with bureaucratic agencies that seek to tell us what we can and cannot do, how we should live and even what we should say and think. Everywhere we turn there are labels. Labels warn us, inform us and advise us. This is especially true in the foods we eat. I could go on and on, but I am sure you know what I mean.

The past Tuesday I did something that several agencies would probably say is absolutely wrong. I sat down with friends and had a donut! *"Live dangerously,"* I thought as I drove to the local Wal-Mart. They serve Sr. Citizens free coffee and donuts every Tuesday and I enjoy that.

Life is more than following the rules. Proverbs 16:8 has some good words here: **"Better is a little with righteousness than great revenues with injustice."** Now, I don't intend to go off on a harangue here about government waste and foolishness, I'll save that for the next time I go for coffee and a donut. But I do think we need to worry less about the length of life and more about the quality of life.

The words of Psalm 90:10 have a sobering thought, **"The years of our life are seventy, or even by reason of strength eighty, yet their span is but toil and trouble. They are soon gone, and we fly away."** I recently reached the seventy mark and I must confess I have begun to feel some of that bodily "toil and trouble." Some might attribute this to too much riotous living and too many donuts, and perhaps rightly so. But I have learned enough about physiology to realize no one can live forever.

And who would want to? This earth, as wonderful as it is, surely is the not the best place to live for eternity. Because of sin, the world will always have its problems. But because of our Lord Jesus Christ, there is a better place, a peaceful place with God that will be better than all this world can offer. So live dangerously today – have a donut!

"Better joy with smiles than obedience with boredom!" (PBT 1:9)

NOVEMBER 13

My wife came home the other day smiling. Often in the afternoon while I'm doing something very important like writing or taking a nap, she will drive to the store to get groceries, including something for our next meal. This particular day she put down her plastic grocery sack and also a paper sack from a local fast food store. This was her story:

"I had a coupon for a Wendy's "Buy-One-Get-One Free" chicken sandwich, so I stopped there and ordered two sandwiches to go. It was no problem until I went to pay and showed my coupon. The man at the counter looked at it and said, 'This coupon isn't for Wendy's, it's for Burger King down the street.' I stammered and must have looked confused, so the young man said, 'But I will honor it anyway. And I don't need to ask the manager, because I am the manager.'" My wife ended her story, *"He was such a nice man to do that for me. Despite being wrong, I got the "Buy-One-Get-One Free" food we wanted!"*

Years ago when I received my first "Sr. Citizen's Discount," I felt a little depressed that I had reached that milestone in life. But not any more! Sometimes it's just plain fun when they look at my grey hair and deduct ten percent from the bill. If it's their policy t and my privilege to receive it, I approve! And it makes me never want to darken my hair like some older men do.

God offers us a place at His heavenly banquet because of Jesus Christ. There's nothing to buy. It's all free because His Son has paid the price. We don't need to do something to get something else. Jesus has done it all, and He invites us in faith with no coupons or gimmicks. Trust in the Lord Jesus, and it's all yours.

Jesus told a story about a Master who held a banquet in honor of his son, but none of those invited came. So he invited others until his Banquet Hall was filled. God invites us all to come with faith in Jesus. It will be a great time!

"Tell those who have been invited that I have prepared my dinner… Come to the wedding banquet!" (Matthew 22:4)

NOVEMBER 14

I have a workbench in my garage and enjoy making or repairing things there. I have a fairly good assortment of power and hand tools and most of them hang from a peg board with metal hooks. Some cupboards and shelves hold all kinds of trays and containers for things too good to toss.

There is a chain of stores that is growing in popularity among people of all ages. "Harbor Freight" offers all kinds of inexpensive (and some very expensive) tools for all kinds of jobs. They have used a clever method to bring people in by offering free items with any purchase made there. Whether it's a cheap flashlight, tape measure, screw driver or rope, just come in and buy something and they'll give you it free. Sometimes it's free without buying anything.

One week the flyer advertised a free magnetic tray, so I got one. It was a round metal tray with a magnet on the back, and whatever iron metallic product you put into it, it stuck there until you put it in another container. Nuts, bolds, screws or washers, if they were made of magnetic materials, you could just toss it in and it stuck. It's a good for when you have odds and ends on your work bench.

That tray is somewhat like the church. It contains an assortment of people who need to be there for various reasons, and they're all brought together by the magnetic draw of Jesus. Some need spiritual food and others need earthly food. Some are the helpers and some are being helped. All have their peculiar shapes and needs, but they are drawn together by faith in Jesus. God knows what each one needs and provides it for us in Jesus.

The good stuff is all free. God's grace and mercy in Jesus Christ comes without cost. We don't have to buy something. God just forgives us when we ask and feeds us with His Word when we need it. Isaiah the prophet tells us, **"Come, everyone who thirsts, come to the waters; he who has no money, come, buy and eat! Come, buy wine and milk without money and without price."** (Isaiah 55:1)

What are we waiting for? Let's go get some!

NOVEMBER 15

Garry was tired and disappointed. A nice clock had been donated to Orphan Grain Train's Garage Sale and no one bought it. He'd been told this kind of clock was selling for hundreds, but a local clock repairman had offered only $25. Surely the clock was worth more than that.

A friend suggested he take it to Rocky Mountain Clocks in Denver. As he drove there, he wondered why he was spending so much time and fuel to sell something probably not worth much. And on his birthday! He found the shop and met a man who said he'd owned the place 44 years.

Garry explained who he was and gave him an Orphan Grain Train business card, explaining how they pack clothing for people in need and ship it all over the world. He told how his group personally had packed and sent 1 million pounds in 12 years. He told him about the new pillowcase dresses sent to girls in Nicaragua. He said the clock was donated and asked what it would cost to repair.

The shop owner said it would be at least $700 or $800, but for Orphan Grain Train he would repair it for $400 plus parts, and then they'd be lucky to get $400 for it and have to pay eBay a commission. The man asked more about OGT, so Garry told him of their next shipment, where it was going and that they had to pay all its shipping costs. The shop owner said he appreciated his enthusiasm about helping others and that he'd buy the clock. He wrote OGT a check for $225. On the way home Garry smiled. His birthday today had turned out pretty good after all!

When we do the Lord's work, we don't always know how it's going to turn out. God doesn't require that we be successful, only that we be faithful. If we follow His will, He will make our efforts turn into something good. Agencies like Orphan Grain Train are based on helping others in need. When we give God our time and treasures, He will bless others greatly. He will bless us, too.

"Give, and it will be given to you." (Luke 6:38)

NOVEMBER 16

Have you noticed that nearly every transaction you make is followed up with a survey? Whether it's a major purchase or buying groceries, there's a line on the receipt to give your opinion on their product or service. Some even offer you an incentive to do so, like a drawing or a reduced price the next time you patronize that company.

Most of these are done online. My wife has answered a few and found them detailed and time consuming. Several companies I call even ask if I'd like to give them a survey at the end of the call. *"For Yes, please press one. For No, press 2".* I always press 2. Perhaps you have been tempted to shout, "Opinion surveys – they're everywhere!"

Some may be helpful, especially if you've had a bad experience. After one of my recent rare appointments at a hospital, I received an "Outpatient Services Survey" that was nearly as long as my patient registration.

An accompanying letter stated my feedback would *"help us to evaluate our services and understand how we might focus our improvement efforts."* I guess everyone wants to be as pleasing in their services as possible. It's probably far better than the old method where *"The customer is always right,"* or *"Who's going to listen to you?"*

Have you ever wished you had one of these surveys in your relation to God? Has there been an incident when you would have enjoyed giving Him low marks? I suppose we all have. But then I'd hate to think what kind of survey He might give us in a "Faith & Prayer Survey."

Actually we already have this. Prayer is our easiest way to register our feelings towards Him or what is happening in life. And God doesn't mind it if we complain. He can handle anything we send His way, even our anger and tears. God listens and He answers. He doesn't ignore our "God Performance Survey." He will help us know how it will help us in the long run.

"Ask and it shall be given to you, Seek and you will find, knock and the door will be opened to you." (Matthew 7:7)

NOVEMBER 17

One day in the local newspaper there were articles about two national trials involving multiple murders. One case involved a young man accused of killing over a dozen people in a movie theater, and the other a young man accused of killing three and injuring nearly 300 with a bomb set off during a marathon race.

I was struck right away at how both trials involved young men accused of doing terrible and random killing of people they did not know. Another aspect, however, was how the attorneys for each one was handling their cases with opposite tactics.

In the case of the bombing suspect trial, his attorney stated from the outset, *"It was him – he did it."* However, in the movie theater case, even with dozens of eyewitnesses who could identify the shooter, his attorneys were cautious never to admit his guilt. *"Nothing that took place there is contested by the defense,"* the article reported his attorney as saying. But neither did they say their client was involved.

It's apparent this strategy is used to leave open the possibility that someone else was responsible. "Don't blame me!" the young person says. "It's my parents fault!" Another says, "This neighborhood is the reason!" Or, "Rich people caused this!" Or, "America is to blame!"

Ever since Adam blamed Eve and Eve blamed the serpent, mankind has sought to justify wrong actions by what someone else has done. Cain killed Abel because God liked his sacrifice better. Contrast that with David. The minute Nathan the prophet pointed the finger of blame at him for his adultery with Bathsheba, David admitted his guilt. Lying or denying always makes the crime worse.

If we are wrong, we should admit it. **"If we say we have no sin, we deceive ourselves and the truth is not is us,"** says John 1:8-9. **"But if we confess our sin, He is faithful and just to forgive our sins and to cleanse us from all unrighteousness."**

Was there a time you blamed someone else for what you did?

NOVEMBER 18

Two young men plunged to their deaths recently from the top of El Capitan mountain in Yosemite National Park. Dean Potter, 43, and Graham Hunt, 29, were both experienced at flying in wing-suits, one of the most extreme forms of BASE jumping. B.A.S.E. jumping, is parachuting or wing-suit flying from a fixed structure or cliff. "BASE" stands for four categories of fixed objects from which one can jump: Building, Antenna, Span, and Earth.

Potter and Hunt were planning a mutual jump off El Capitan mountain to fly from on their descent. After about fifteen seconds of flying, both struck a rocky outcropping and were killed.

In a sport so dangerous that they keep list of the dead, some called the two athletes an inspiration while others called them fools. The jumpers considered themselves artists and searchers of spiritual pursuit, but most of us shake our heads at why they'd do it. *"It's fly or die,"* said Potter in a documentary. The suits give them power to fly. *"It's an amazing place in history, that man actually has the skills to pull it off,"* he said. But this time their skills weren't enough.

While I would never wish athletes failure, I do wish they would realize the risks when they're too great. A gust of wind just strong enough probably took them off course to strike into the rocks in the notch.

A "gust of wind" can come any time in life, and when one is taking a great risk, it had better be worthwhile. Men and women of history have always taken great risks to life and limb, but usually because of something greater, such as personal survival or the life of a loved one. When we take on deadly forces, we should do it for a greater good than expressive art or so-called "spiritual pursuit."

Jesus went to the cross knowing He would die. He jumped off the cliff of sin and soared to His death so that we might have life. His choice gave us our life for His. The open grave gives us new life also, and for that, we worship Him.

"No one comes to the Father except through Him." (John 14:6)

NOVEMBER 19

We purchased a new wash machine when the motor on our older one broke and was too expensive to repair. The new one is very nice and so quiet we weren't sure it was working the first few times we used it. But this is not only a quieter model, it is safer. Once the door is closed and the cycle begins, the door locks and you can't get inside without pushing a button and waiting a few minutes. For safety reasons, the door locks during the cycle and you must wait before being able to open the door. We presume this is so that we won't be tempted to put a hand inside and get it injured by the agitating motion.

Jesus once told of being locked out. In Matthew 25 is recorded His story of the ten young women waiting to go to a wedding. They were ready and waiting to be called in, but when the call finally came, five of them discovered they had run out of lamp oil. When they went to get more lamp oil, the wedding couple came and the doors were shut behind them. The young women who were prepared were able to get in, but those unprepared were locked out. And it wasn't for safety reasons, either.

A lot of success in life depends on timing. A young woman couldn't get her car started and was late to the airport, so she missed her flight. Air Asia flight 8501 left an airport in Indonesia and went down in the Pacific, killing all on board. I once avoided an accident on snowy roads, making a turn at the last minute which kept me on the road instead of going into a deep ditch.

We the living all have a story of being spared. But for many others the story is being too late, or being the one that didn't live in the auto accident. Yet God had reasons for that, too. A wall plaque my immigrant mother had said, "Gottes Zeit ist die allerbeste Zeit," *"God's time is the best time."* But we can still be late, so we need to pay attention to His time. **"Behold, now is the favorable time; behold, now is the day of salvation."** (2 Corinthians 16:2)

Did you have any wall memorable plaques in your home?

NOVEMBER 20

Do you ever feel like our world is just a huge mess? Does it feel like nothing will ever get any better? A recent magazine article tried to answer these questions with a resounding "No!" The writers said that despite all the news about poverty, crime and violence, the facts are that these have not gone up, they have gone down. Freedom and democracy in the world have actually increased. Hence the article's title, "The World is Not Falling Apart."

The article is both right and wrong. While the percentages of bad things happening have gone down, the actual numbers have gone up. In 1980, the world's population was 4½ billion people. Today it is 7 billion. While the major crime rate in the USA has decreased in percentages, the actual numbers of crimes have increased. One reason everything seems worse is because we hear of it happening. News that comes 24/7 assaults our ears and can frighten us if we think that crime is in our neighborhood. Some of it may be, but it seems worse than it is.

It is true, however, that as the world ages, it will become more and more difficult to keep our eyes on Jesus. The Bible urges us, **"Fix your eyes on Jesus, the pioneer and perfecter of faith. For the joy set before him he endured the cross, scorning its shame, and sat down at the right hand of the throne of God."** (Hebrews 12:2 NIV)

God's Word tells us that evil will increase and because of it, the love people have for God will grow less and less (Matthew 24:13). So the article is both right and wrong; right because the percentages are going down, wrong because the actual numbers are going up.

But so are the numbers of Christians going up. Today 1/3 of the world's people claim to be Christian men, women and children of all nations, people who hold in faith that Jesus Christ is the Son of God and Savior of the world. We praise God that Jesus is still honored and God is worshipped as the Creator and Provider of all.

Does it surprise you there are that many Christians?

NOVEMBER 21

Each morning like clockwork, around 500 of them board the subway, off to their daily routine in the city. After a hard day working the streets, they hop back on the train and return to the suburbs where they spend the night. But these aren't human daily commuters. These are stray dogs who live in the outskirts of Moscow and commute on the subway to and from the city in search of food.

For decades the subway dogs have figured out how to use the city's subway system, getting on and off at the stops they need. They recognize the desired station by smell, announcer's voice, or by time intervals. Usually they ride the first or last car to keep away from crowds. Experts say they work together so they get off at the right stop at night.

In Soviet times the dogs were barred from subway, but today's passengers are accustomed to them. They behave with friendly manners to the passengers. They have good instincts about people, greeting the kind ones and avoiding the intolerant, and they always find someone who will share food with them.

Decades ago when they were no longer being chased away from the subways, these dogs began hopping trains into the city. Once there, some positioned themselves outside butcher shops and waited for dog lovers coming out of the shop to toss them a bone. Others sneaked up behind people who are eating and surprise them with a loud bark, hoping they'll drop what they're eating. Packs are not led by the strongest or most dominant, but by the most intelligent.

God has enabled the subway dogs of Moscow to learn to live among people in order to survive. Some might say it's instinct, but God gives animals and people certain abilities. If He pays attention to the needs of these creatures, will He not also see that each of us has what we need?

Psalm 84:3 says, **"Even the sparrow has found a home, and the swallow a nest for herself, where she may have her young, a place near your altar, Lord Almighty."**

How have you seen God's hand helping His creatures?

NOVEMBER 22

Our son once bought some small items at a local store and tried to pay for them with a couple of $2 bills he had in his wallet. The young cashier looked at them and refused to accept them. "I think these are counterfeit," she said. Our son said, "They're real. $2 bills have been used for decades." Our son then said, "If I wanted to counterfeit anything, why would I choose the $2 bill?" But the girl still refused and called for her manager. The manager heard the situation and said the same as my son, "Why would he want to counterfeit a $2 bill?" He accepted the money and my son left, wondering if she'd still have her job at the end of the day.

A slightly different story happened in Georgia when a woman tried to pay for $1,500 in jewelry with a million dollar bill that was obviously counterfeit. When questioned, the woman claimed she was misled by her ex-husband, a coin collector, who gave her the bill and said it was good. The size of that monetary bill would make anyone realize it wasn't real. It's a good illustration of how foolishly deceptive people may try to be.

The Old Testament prophet wrote, **"The heart is deceitful above all things, and desperately sick. Who can understand it?"** (Jeremiah 17:9) He expresses a sense of amazement that the heart can move people to commit such foolish acts. He is saying not that *some of us* have a problem with this, but that *all of us* do. Thankfully, God knows the human heart and helps us see our need for His grace.

We are approaching our annual special observance of Thanksgiving in America. This is a time when Christians often help others in need with food baskets, funds or other items they may not be able to afford. Does your church or work place have a Holiday Basket program where you can bring food items? Have you ever taken a basket to a family in need? See if you can help in such a program near you.

"Give thanks to the Lord, for He is good." (1 Chronicles 16:34)

NOVEMBER 23

When I am writing, perhaps a daily devotional like this one, or a sermon or a presentation, I spend long amounts of time sitting. I recently read we'd all be more healthy if we got rid of our office chairs, but I doubt that will happen. I do try to limit sitting time and break it up with a walk or time on my exercise bicycle that sits nearby. If I don't do this occasionally, both body and mind become sluggish.

The same happens to my laptop. If I use it continually and don't take steps to "Clean My Mac," it gets sluggish. Over-use of some programs causes too much information to plug up and fill the "cache," which is the computer's trash can. Most newer programs empty the cache automatically, but some older ones require my doing it manually. Some places sell a program to clean the laptop and get rid of stuff no longer needed. A tech friend says those don't all work.

Like my computer, my life also gets plugged up with things that are not needed. Not necessarily things in my basement or garage, but thoughts I collect needlessly, worries about people, concerns still kept in my soul, or cares of the world about which I can do nothing, yet still haul around in my head. If I don't take steps to empty my personal "cache" regularly, those things will overflow and plug up my personal or spiritual life.

Personal and spiritual garbage only weighs us down. It needs to be removed, and our Lord offers a wonderful way. **"Come to me, all you who are weary and burdened, and I will give you rest,"** Jesus said in Matthew 11:28.

I try to do that regularly. My wife and I go to Him in our nightly devotions. I go to Him often in prayer during the day. Sometimes I need rest from the pull and draw of the world which whispers, *"Did God really say that?"* or *"Are you sure He is there?"* That sounds like Satan in the Garden, and it probably is. So I pray and think of a Bible verse or two, and the whispering goes away. Like Jesus in the wilderness. God empties my cache and my heart is light again.

What is your cache filled with these days?

NOVEMBER 24

Thanksgiving is close and each year I try to think of something new and special for which to give God thanks. This year I thank Him for His little surprises. My summer reading included a short book my sister gave me by Squire Rushnell called, When God Winks at You. It's a series of brief stories about people sensing God's presence through small events. The author says when small coincidences or events surprise or help you, those are "God Winks," signs He cares for you.

I had a little "God Wink" recently. I was having some tire work done in Colorado when a man and a young woman came into the store. They reminded me of a family from India I had known years before that had come from India to North Dakota with their two young children. They were Christians and became members of my church. I'd lost track of them after leaving that church.

I asked this man and woman if they originated from India. He smiled and said, *"Yes."* I explained about my friends and after a moment he said, *"I know that family. The daughter is married to my wife's brother."* The young woman said, *"I have a photo of her sister and daughter I can show you,"* and she produced one. She also said they were on Facebook, so I sent them both messages. The next day one responded.

Even more coincidental was that earlier in that week I had been thinking about that Indian family and wondered where they all were. The three of us at the tire store were glad for our conversation. It was a "God Wink."

"God Winks" are reminders that He is keeping track of us in this life, telling us He is near and guiding us through faith in Jesus. God never loses track of His children. We may do so in our busy life, but God never loses track of us.

It reminds me of a child's hymn, "I am Jesus' Little Lamb," which says in its first verse, *"For my Shepherd gently guides me, Knows my needs and well provides me; Loves me every day the same, even calls me by my name."*

Be on watch for any "God Winks" this week!

NOVEMBER 25

Thanksgiving Day is observed as an official holiday all over the United States of America. Historians say the first Thanksgiving Day may have been held as early as 1607, but the first recorded Thanksgiving meal and celebration was held in 1610 in Jamestown, Virginia. On November 26, 1863, President Lincoln established a national day of thanksgiving, urging all Americans to, *"Give thanksgiving and praise to our beneficent Father who dwells in the Heavens."* Amazingly, this decree was made in the midst of the American Civil War.

Jesus told a story showing one way people can give thanks for their blessings – by creating more. Three servants had been given money to invest. Two of them doubled the funds entrusted to them, but the third man did nothing with his. Not wanting to take a risk, he buried it.

You and I should wisely use what God has given us. He does not want us to become "money hoarders," hiding it under the mattress or burying it in jars. He also does not want us to be obsessed with it, counting it every day.

The third servant in Jesus' story didn't even want to touch the money. He seems afraid of the owner, like some people are afraid of God. It helps no one to bury or hoard God's gifts. They are to be used, whether they are money, skills or even our use of time. God has given us everything we have, so we should use it well, for our wise personal use or for the good of those in need.

We once planned a family thanksgiving and it snowed the night before so our invited guests couldn't come. So my wife and I invited people right out of our church line to come over, mostly people we knew had no family. Instead of six family members, we had six people from the church who otherwise would have had a meal alone. It was a truly memorable day in 1977, a long time ago.

How will you celebrate Thanksgiving? What would your perfect Thanksgiving dinner be like?

"Praise God from whom all blessings flow,
Praise Him all creatures here below." (from the hymn)

NOVEMBER 26

A teacher asked a group of people of mixed ages, *"What does Thanksgiving mean to you?"* One small boy said, *"It means a big dinner."* An older girl who was a student, said, *"Thanksgiving means a day off from school."* Some of the older people told what the day meant to them. A young woman who was an office manager, said, *"Thanksgiving means a day away from the office. I am at the office every day except Sunday, and I do appreciate, now and then, a day that is really my own."* Then a salesman spoke. *"Thanksgiving means a day at home. Last year I spent one hundred and sixty-nine nights away from home. I have three children. I would like to see them every day, but often many days pass and I do not see them. Thanksgiving week I plan to be at home."*

Each person in the group had an answer. Then the teacher spoke. *"You are all correct. Thanksgiving has a special meaning for me, too. It is the Harvest time and I have here a beautiful apple. What bright red color! Who mixed the paints, who handled the brush to give such color to this apple? It was God. He, in his infinite love and wisdom, has provided, through the unfailing laws of nature, for the growth, sweetness, coloring and beautifying of all the products of the fields. This apple is but one of God's many kinds of fruits."*

"Let us praise God," she said, *"that we all have a special and personal meaning for Thanksgiving. God, our heavenly Father, sends us every good gift. From his bountiful hand comes our daily and nightly mercies. We should praise him every day. But the day for the united chorus of praise is Thanksgiving."*

I give thanks for good teachers, like this one. She was not afraid of telling young and old of her faith in Jesus. Today many schools do not like people speaking of God or their faith. But if we are thankful, who should we thank for our blessings? The government? Luck? Fate? We have many precious blessings each day we live. They did not just happen, so we thank God, the Source of our blessings.

"Give thanks to the God of gods. His love endures forever." (Psalm 136:2)

NOVEMBER 27

I remember as a bachelor going to a church potluck while at the Seminary in St. Louis. My large fieldwork church had a reputation for great potluck dinners and invited everyone to bring some item to share. Now these people took their potlucks seriously. I think they warned the local grocery stores in advance so they could stock their shelves. Juicy hams, tender turkeys, incredible hot dishes and pecan pie. For the women and girls it was an unofficial cook-off, and for the men and boys it was an unabashed pig-out. No one went hungry there.

So what did I take? I was broke that day and took a half empty jar of Planter's Peanuts! But no matter. Someone ate my peanuts and I ate my fill. So did everyone else. I came there like a pauper and left having eaten like a king. Roast beef, mashed potatoes, gravy, salads, fried chicken, apple pie - you name it, they had it and I ate it.

You know what? God does the same for us every time you and I come to Him. We come with our puny little offerings that are nothing compared to the incredible blessings He gives. We bring Him the piddly and He gives us plentiful. We bring Him the puny and He gives us the powerful. We bring Him peanuts and He gives us paradise.

God is always like that. He doesn't look at what we brought. In fact, our offerings will get lost in the abundance of His goodness. For all our blessings on earth, we can only give Him thanks and praise. And it's only going to get better in heaven. He promises us that.

When you're young and "invincible" the world seems at your fingertips. Yet it's there only because of His grace and mercy. Whether you have a table full of food or a half-full can of peanuts, it is all from His gracious hand.

Jesus said, **"Blessed are those who hear the word of God and obey it."** (Luke 11:28) Both hearing and obeying God's Word can only be accomplished when we trust Jesus our Savior.

Have you ever gone to a potluck and forgot to bring something?

NOVEMBER 28

The story is told of two old friends who bumped into one another on the street one day. One of them looked forlorn, almost on the verge of tears. His friend asked, "What has the world done to you, my old friend?"

The sad fellow said, "Three weeks ago, an uncle died and left me forty thousand dollars." "Wow, that's a lot of money," the other replied.

His friend continued, "Then two weeks ago, a cousin I never even knew died, and left me eighty-five thousand free and clear." "Amazing! Sounds like you've been blessed."

"You don't understand!" his friend interrupted. "Last week my great-aunt passed away. I inherited almost a quarter of a million." Now the first man was really confused. "Then, why do you look so glum?" "This week," the man said with a whine, "I've gotten nothing!"

We are strange people, aren't we? We have an uncanny way of failing to recognize how blessed we truly are. Fifty wonderful things can happen to us and only one negative thing. What do we focus on? The negative.

It's in our nature—our sinful nature. We could all be chastised an hour for our lack of gratitude and we would certainly deserve it, wouldn't we? Ingratitude is a wretched sin. But will focusing on our failure to thank God make us grateful? No. What makes us grateful is the Good News that God loves us anyway, despite our sinful weaknesses, and that God forgives us in Christ. God's goodness does not depend on our response. It is just His nature to be good, and His love never fails, despite our ingratitude.

There is an old gospel hymn that comes to mind. "Count Your Blessings" by Johnson Oatman. It's based on the words in the 103rd Psalm, and it goes like this.

When upon life's billows you are tempest tossed,
When you are discouraged, thinking all is lost,
Count your many blessings, name them one by one,
And it will surprise you what the Lord hath done.

Be sure to count your many blessings today!

NOVEMBER 29

Today is our special day. My wife and I were married on Saturday morning, November 29. It was a wonderful day.

Our American prosperity is startling. To understand just how God has blessed America, consider this. If we could compress the world's population into a town of 1,000 people. Then, keeping proportions right, in this town there would be only 60 Americans – 6%. These 6% would have half the income of the entire town. They would have an average life expectancy of twenty years longer on average than the other 940 persons in the town. Those 60 would own 15 times as much as all of their neighbors.

They would eat 72% more than the maximum food requirements, while 100 of the other 940 would go to bed hungry each night. Those 6% Americans would own half of all the telephones in town. The poorest Americans would be far better off than the average of the other 940 people. 1/4 of the townspeople (including all the Americans) would be financially well-off. The other 3/4 would be considered poor.

How can we not see how God has blessed us here in America? He's even blessed unbelievers! And if we still want God's blessings around, maybe we'd better not exclude Him from so many things like we're doing. Like a Christian said when she was asked where God was during recent school killings, *"We've been telling Him He's not welcome in public for years, so why should we be surprised if He's not here any more?"*

But physical things are the not the biggest blessings. God has also given us eternal life through our Lord and Savior Jesus. People who don't believe in Jesus, no matter where they live, won't know the joy of heaven. So let's listen again to Psalm 67:1 - **"May God be gracious to us and bless us and make His face to shine upon us."**

Guess what, folks – He already has! Verse 2 continues, **"That Your way may be known on earth, Your saving power among all nations."** Now that's something we can all do, tell people of God's saving power. Count your blessings!

Do you have a wonderful and memorable day in your past?

NOVEMBER 30

> A letter came from their daughter in college:

"Dear Mom and Dad, by the time you receive this letter I should be out of the hospital. I feel so much better. But don't worry, I came through the accident quite well, only two broken bones, and they say the car is repairable. The other car can be fixed too, but that old man driving it was hurt pretty bad. Sure glad he had insurance. By the way, is my car insured?"

"But please don't worry. In the hospital I met the nicest man. He helped me so much. I just don't know how I can live without him, which is why he's asked me to marry him just as soon as I serve my 30 days in jail for alcohol possession. But please don't worry. I'm just so happy now that there is a baby on the way."

> Can you imagine receiving this letter? But there's more. The daughter's letter continues,

"Seriously Mom and Dad, I must confess the truth. There was no accident, I'm not in the hospital and the car is fine. I'm not engaged, there's no baby and I don't have to go to jail. But I did get 2 D's and an F this semester, and I just wanted you to hear that news in perspective to the really important things in life. Be home soon, Love, Jill."

Yes, everything in life is subject to the perspective of other things and events. What she described in the first part made the second part look almost unimportant. Yet it wasn't. In fact, her attempt to cover the truth was a sin.

We often try to minimize or justify our sins by saying, "In the big picture, this isn't so bad." Or, "It happens all the time, so no big deal!" Yet our sins are a big deal. They separate us from God and from each other. We can't excuse them just because other sins are worse.

A boy lied to his teacher and when she caught him in the lie, he denied it. She considered his denial was worse than the lie, so she punished him by his staying after school and writing, *"I will never lie again"* in his best cursive writing one hundred times. His hand was sore from the writing!

"Better to be poor than a liar." (Proverbs 19:22)

DAY BY DAY WITH JESUS
in
December
+ + +
DECEMBER 1

Burgers were consumed by tailgaters as the sun went down. Generators powered up tens of thousands of lights on floats decorated by organizations and businesses. Santas and reindeer, snowmen and elves, Disney, glitter and glitz lit up the night in bright array for the local "Parade of Lights."

Decorated golf carts on up to eighteen wheelers lined both sides of the town's main street, each awaiting its turn to go. Band members in flickering lights with twirler brigades were getting antsy. Organizers marshaled people here and there until finally the parade began. Lighted floats were a magnificent sight as they passed by thousands of people.

One float featured children and parents in front of a lighted manger scene. But it had a problem. Lights illuminated everything, the star, manger and wood candles, but no lights showed the sideboard signs telling who they were. The Holy Family was visible in the dark night, but who'd know who had put them there?

Someone came to the rescue. Producing two bright lanterns, a woman handed one to friend and pointed to the other side of the float. As they moved onto the street, each carrier shined her bright light on the sign that said, *"Trinity Lutheran Church Preschool."* The two sentinels showed the crowd who knew the real purpose of Christmas.

It's difficult these days to find much that tells us the true reason for CHRISTmas. The CHRIST child has been overshadowed by shopping, parties, Santas and blinking light. But if you look closely, you will still find some hearty CHRISTians shining their lights on the manger, showing the world God's eternal and holy gift.

"Let your light so shine that people may see." (Matthew 5:16)

DECEMBER 2

(Parade of Lights, pt. 2) Who guides your footsteps? Who directs your life journey? Who helps you stay on the right road? How do you know when to begin and when to stop?

The band entered the staging area, ready for its place in the Parade. A hundred students dressed in lighted uniforms marched quietly forward in formation, holding instruments smartly. Almost as one, they come to a halt on the side street, ready to move when called. Then the wait began.

The students held formation for a quarter hour before milling and whispering began. Adults urged them to stand, but the wait was long. The Drum Major tried to keep their interest, but as they waited, restless mumblings begin filling the night. Lighted uniforms dance in readiness, but time moves slowly in the wait.

Suddenly a snare drummer raps them to attention. **"BRAP! BRAP! BRAP!"** Within seconds all the bodies step into place. The drummer snaps into a cadence as the shuffling feet and lighted bodies sway gently forward.

Barricades are lifted and marchers move through to the ever-louder drummer, making a quarter turn onto the street. Suddenly, all drummers pierce the night with a loud, rapid cadence that sends chills into the crowd. The wait is over. It's SHOWTIME! The watchers proudly see their award-winning band lead the Parade of Lights on the streets.

Advent is a time of waiting, children for Christmas, workers for day's end, students for Christmas break, and Christians waiting for the Second Coming of their Savior. One day angels will announce the end of the OLD and start of the NEW. In that day the Divine Drummer will rap the world to attention, and all people, dead or alive, will know the Lord and His judgment have come

Until then, God calls us to wait. He'll tend to our needs, direct our paths and correct us when we fail. Today we live hopefully and joyfully, showing the world His love that was given to all in the Babe of Bethlehem.

"So be it! Come Lord Jesus." (Revelation 22:20)

DECEMBER 3

We are in the pre-Christmas season of Advent when we recall Jesus that came into the world was born in Bethlehem. While it's a time of preparation for His coming, we live between two advents, the first was His coming through human birth and the second, His coming on the last day.

Advent has been observed since 490 A.D. when Perpetuus, Bishop of Tours urged people to have special services. The Advent season can last anywhere from 22 to 28 days and is usually observed with solemnity. In Austria, Belgium, Netherlands and Germany, December 6 is St. Nicholas' Day and begins Christmas festivities. Shoes or stockings are set out to be filled with gifts for good children. Dutchmen watch as St. Nick steps off a ship in Amsterdam and later rides off on a white horse. The American Santa Claus arrives in the Macy's Thanksgiving Day Parade.

Swedish Christians begin Christmas observances on December 13, St. Lucy's Day. In traditional Swedish homes, a girl wearing a wreath of lingonberry leaves and lighted candles descends the stairway as all present sing carols. "Lucy" comes from the Latin word for "light" which is celebrated in the midst of their long dark winter.

Christmas is a time for people to help others in need. Letters that appeal to Christian charity pour into our mailboxes, and we must choose which ones to help. Our gifts become helping hands reaching out to the community, clothing the naked and feeding the hungry. We welcome strangers into our churches, or we visit nursing homes with gifts or Christmas songs.

Our gifts to others are also gifts to our Lord Jesus who provides for our needs and has said that whatever we do for **"the least of these,"** we also do for Him (Matthew 25).

What are your favorite charities this time of year? Are there ways to help those in need through your job or church or community?

How does giving gifts make you feel?

DECEMBER 4

The famous Christian pastor, Oswald Chambers, once wrote, *"It is not God's promises we need, it is God Himself."* What better time to consider this thought than during Advent, the time God gave us Himself in the Christ child?

There are all kinds of clever sayings for Christmas, *"Jesus is the reason for the season."* Or *"Christmas comes but once a year, and when it comes it brings good cheer."* Or *"Remembrance, like a candle, burns brightest at Christmas."* One I like is, *"God's presence is more important than presents."* But I have an idea that the amount of time and money we spend shopping for presents indicates otherwise.

As mentioned before, in some parts of the world, giving of Christmas gifts begins long before December 25. The people there say this allows them to have the rest of the month to focus on Jesus, not what's under the tree. Jesus is God's perfect gift to us.

Some famous people were born on December 25, such as actor Humphrey Bogart, hotel builder Conrad Hilton, Red Cross founder Clara Barton and singer Cab Calloway. But these and others born December 25 have all died. They are buried and gone, but Jesus is still with us. He never leaves us. He died on Good Friday but was raised to life Easter Sunday. Jesus who was born 2,000 years ago, still lives, in the hearts of His people, and also in real life.

Most all of us, especially children, may say we want God's presence, but we also want His presents. The best gift is one given without strings attached. Some may give a gift in return for one given, or a gift so that they might curry the favor of someone else, but God's gifts to us have no strings attached. Certainly He would like our gratitude for His blessings, but He gives gifts even to the ungrateful.

God gave us Himself in the child at Bethlehem. As Chambers wrote, *"...It is God Himself."* He is Immanuel, "God with us." So we sing the Advent hymn,

"Rejoice, rejoice! Immanuel shall come to thee, O Israel."

DECEMBER 5

During the season of Advent, Christians around the world light candles to symbolize Jesus, the Light of the World. Isaiah foretold that all nations would be blessed when they place their hope and trust in God's Chosen One who would come to save the World: **"Here is my servant, whom I uphold, my chosen one in whom I delight, and he will bring justice to the nations."** (Isaiah 42:1)

The candles on the traditional Advent Wreath have their meaning in four words often used by pastors in their Advent sermons: HOPE, PEACE, JOY, LOVE. The first two are purple or blue candles, the third is pink (for joy) and the last is also purple or blue. In some wreaths all are white.

HOPE: We have an inheritance reserved for us in heaven, a living hope that comes through the resurrection of Jesus from the dead. **"Praise be to the God and Father of our Lord Jesus Christ! In his great mercy he has given us new birth into a living hope through the resurrection of Jesus Christ from the dead."** (1 Peter 1:3)

PEACE: We will love life and see good days if we turn from evil and follow God obediently. **"They must turn from evil and do good; they must seek peace and pursue it. For the eyes of the Lord are on the righteous and his ears are attentive to their prayer."** (1 Peter 3:11-12)

JOY: Through Jesus we have incredible joy even if we have trials and our faith is often tested. **"In all this you greatly rejoice, though now for a little while you may have had to suffer grief in all kinds of trials. These have come to prove the genuineness of your faith."** (1 Peter 1:6-7)

LOVE: We can love one another with a pure heart because we have been born anew through the Word of God. **"So that you have sincere love for each other, love one another deeply, from the heart. For you have been born again, not of perishable seed, but of imperishable, through the living and enduring word of God."** (1 Peter 1:22-23)

What Hope, Peace, Joy or Love are you seeking this year?

DECEMBER 6

In Wellington, Florida, when someone stole the figurine of the Baby Jesus from a public nativity on the lawn of the community center for the second year in a row, they didn't follow a star to find him. Instead, they used a GPS tracking device placed inside the life-sized statue. Because the statue was valuable, the city gave permission for police to place a electronic tracking device inside the replacement figurine. When the Baby Jesus figurine disappeared again, Sheriff's deputies were led by the signal to the thief's apartment and arrests were made.

Instead of metal chains and padlocks to protect their valuable holiday display items, organizations were offered the use of GPS and security camera devices to protect mangers and menorahs, and seventy churches and synagogues responded. *"They took the family Jesus,"* said Gloria Herrera, a Catholic. *"How can anybody do that?"*

Difficult circumstances or personal losses can cause us to feel that Jesus has been stolen from Christmas. The commercialization of Christmas alone causes most of us to feel Jesus has been barred from His birthday celebration. How can we find Him again when everything seems to be working against Him at Christmas?

Like a spiritual GPS, the Bible can guide us to God's presence and love. The Bible tells us the Holy Spirit helps us in our weakness (Romans 8:27) and that God is for us, so who can be against us? (Romans 8:31) **"He who did not spare his own Son, but gave him up for us all—how will he not also, along with him, graciously give us all things?"** (Romans 8:32) The chapter concludes that nothing can separate us from the love of God in Christ Jesus. (Romans 8:38-39)

Whether we look for Jesus in a manger or in our hearts, we can be filled with joy because He has risen from the dead and lives and reigns with all His faithful people. That is where you can find Jesus now and every Christmas.

Focusing always on Jesus will keep us from losing Him.

DECEMBER 7

One autumn there was an international outcry that Sony decided not to release a new movie when threatened by a nation in the Far East. While debaters mostly sided with free speech, few people realized there had been a similar event a month before in the American Midwest.

Sioux Falls, South Dakota, annually holds its fall "Paint the Plow" event, in which students from area schools each year are invited to paint some of the city's huge snow plow blades with appropriate artwork. This year, however, the event became a battle after an atheist complained.

It was October and with Christmas coming, it wasn't surprising some Christian students decided to paint about Jesus. One plow showed the traditional red and white Coca-Cola logo but read, **"Jesus Christ"** and quoted John 1:14. The other plow blade displayed a cross and manger and read, **"Happy Birthday Jesus."** The artwork was by students from two area Lutheran Schools.

It also wasn't surprising that a local atheist complained to the city attorney that such things were inappropriate on city-owned equipment. *"That is a clear endorsement of religion, and it is on city property,"* he said. Score one for the Grinch! But the battle wasn't over.

Past students had painted religious themes on those plows, but no one complained. However, faced with a First Amendment battle, city officials told the schools to repaint their artwork. One of the Lutheran principals said there wasn't time, so the city could paint over it themselves.

Letters to the editor began falling like hailstones, so the city issued a statement noting this long-standing program had allowed students from all community schools to paint and design the plow blades. Since the students had broken no laws, so their artwork would remain in place. Score a win for Jesus and free speech! **"For unto us a child is born, unto us a Son is given."** (Isaiah 9:6)

Jesus is the Savior of all, even a Grinch!

DECEMBER 8

I made a change to an insurance policy and attempted to call the company to have them stop taking premiums from my bank account. It was a large national company, so I assumed they had enough operators to handle such calls. It took me four minutes to get through the prompts, but I expected this.

Then the wait to speak to someone began, 27 minutes the first time. During that time recorded messages said over and over, *"Your call is very important to us. A customer service representative will be with you shortly. We appreciate your patience."* Or, *"Thank you for calling. Please remain on the line, as redialing will only cause a delay."* Every minute without fail!

I saw a second customer service number, so I called that one and 17 minutes later did actually speak to a person. He took all my numbers and then said he was in a different department, so he would transfer me, and that someone would answer the phone right away. He was partially correct. A few minutes later a recorded voice said, *"Due to high call volume, we are unable to handle your call. Please call back later."* And they hung up on me. (Grrhh!)

We are now in the season of Advent, a time of waiting for Christmas, and also for the second coming of our Lord Jesus. Pastors tell us He is coming, but then urge us to wait patiently. Could it be God has put us on hold?

Yes, and No. Yes, we are waiting for a time we do not yet know, but No, He is listening and will not hang up on us. You and I will not talk to a recording, but we can talk to the Lord. He does hear us in our waiting. He forgives us our sins and reminds us the best is yet to come.

The younger we are, the longer the wait may mean to us, but the older we get, the more we realize our answer is at hand. Just remember, God will not hang up on us. He will answer our questions and needs in due time.

"Wait on the Lord. Be strong and courageous." (Psalm 27:14)

DECEMBER 9

Radio commentator Paul Harvey once told of an experiment involving a chimpanzee in which scientists were determined to teach it communication with humans. For fourteen years the project directors labored with this chimp, providing symbols and speech patterns to help it speak.

Finally, the day arrived when it seemed the chimpanzee was actually going to make a sentence. Word went out and scientists crowded into the room. They watched breathlessly as symbols were formed into words and words formed into a sentence. At last, the first message from the world's most pampered, most cared for and most patiently trained animal was about to come forth.

The scientists could hardly contain themselves as they pressed around the cage to watch the history-making sentence. What did the chimpanzee finally communicate? His three words: *"Let me out!"*

We people sometimes want to cry the same at whatever holds us in. A bad job, hospital bed, secret sin, troubling situation that won't go away, someone who makes life unbearable, or even when Satan himself seems to trail our every step. All these can lead us to cry, *"Let me out!"*

Some of us already know the cage of regret, or anger or bitterness. Others know the dark cage of addiction, crime, pornography or a skeleton in our closet that is rattling louder every day. Whatever our particular cage may be, our heart may cry, *"Let me out!"*

We can take courage because Jesus hears our voice. He is not deaf or silent to our cries. He who cried out on His own dark cross, **"My God, why have You forsaken Me?"** will hear our cries. Because He has been on earth like us, He will unlock our door, break our chain and release us from our prison if we ask Him.

Advent is here again, a time to prepare for Christ to come into our hearts. May our Advent prayer be blessed.

O come, Immanuel, and ransom all captives, including me!

DECEMBER 10

Carol and I decorated our house last weekend. We'd added a screened-in breezeway and now had room enough to put our big Christmas Tree brought down from Colorado by friends passing through on their way to Arizona.

In one box of decorations was the African Nativity set our daughter-in-law brought back for us many years ago when she went there to get their newly adopted daughter from the Democratic Republic of Congo. This ebony nativity has sleek, tall figurines we arrange on a small table and use a dab of "Elmer's Tack" to keep the figures standing up.

As we took them out of the box, I wondered aloud where the pieces should go. Without hesitating Carol said, *"Start with the baby. Put Him right in the middle in front, and the rest of the pieces will fall into place."* Considering this briefly, I said, *"Thanks. You just gave me a message. Put Jesus in the middle of things and the rest will fall into place."*

Can you see how it's true? As Christians we know this should be true, but it may be difficult to do on a daily basis. How difficult is it to put Christ first in our lives?

I often find it difficult. I like to take charge and do things my way, and this has helped me often in my ministry. I've learned this trait is a gift from God so long as I don't overuse it. I am often quite direct with God as to how I would like Him to answer my prayers and even right the wrongs in the world.

But God doesn't always follow my suggestions! He's smarter than that. It's easy to think I have most of life figured out, but then reality sets in and the world quickly looks different. Then Carol's advice really helps: *"Put Jesus in the middle in front and the rest will fall into place."*

Maybe that's what Jesus meant in Matthew 6:33, **"Seek first the Kingdom and His Righteousness, and all these things shall be added to you."**

May we all put Him in the middle of things this Christmas.

DECEMBER 11

Once again a school shooting raised its ugly and tragic head in Colorado. But this time it was more personal as I watched national media cameras zero in on Shepherd Of The Hills Lutheran Church, a congregation where I was pastor for eleven years. Cameras showed hundreds of youth being joined with anxious parents in the church parking lot, tearfully grateful to take their children home.

That weekend many stations carried a short clip on how the congregation ministered to the school youth and adults. I felt proud and grateful their pastors and people opened church doors to the shaken people and were seeking ways of providing spiritual counsel and answers to questions.

The answers are elusive, but the cause is simple. Evil and sin are gaining a stronger foothold in western culture. But what can be done about this obvious trend? How can we stop another angry child taking out his vengeance? A young adult legally owns a weapon, but turns a wrong corner in his journey. What can be done in a nation weary and callous at another tragedy? More political finger pointing? More defense of one's personal philosophy?

It's one thing to know the answer and another to do something about it. Homes need to be strengthened, and God needs to be honored, not denied. Schools need to teach basics rather than trends. People need more real face time and less tech time. Teachers need our prayers, and students need our good examples. Churches need to reach out and pews need to be filled with people honoring God.

We think we live in enlightened times. Who needs God when we've got technology? Forget sin and all this talk about evil! Youth need more choices, and schools need more money. We don't need God, just more education.

This time one of the first responders was a church and its pastors. They went into action, not with preaching but with living their faith in the parking lot of a Christian Church is where Jesus is King of kings and Lord of lords.

"Unto you is born this day a Savior" (Luke 2:11)

DECEMBER 12

Azariah set down the last stone of the day as there was no longer enough light to see and the temple floor was nearly finished. He was old, tired and wished for an end, an end to the day, an end to the project, and most of all an end to life in Babylon. The men of his crew trudged wearily to their quarters speaking few words even though it was the first time they could openly speak to each other that day.

"We cannot do this much longer," Mishael muttered as they walked slowly. *"How much longer will the Lord God have us suffer this exile?"* *"Only He knows,"* said Azariah, *"and He has not yet told us."* Kenaniah, the eldest said, *"The Scriptures say a Deliverer will come, so we must trust Him and wait."*

Azariah stepped inside his hut and smelled the aroma of food. Sitting down on the mat next to his wife Miriam and their two boys, he lifted his eyes heavenward and said, *"O God our Father, we thank You for this food that blesses our bodies. Come, Lord God and send Your Promised One. Save us, O Merciful God. Come, Emmanuel and end our exile here, amen."*

The year was 539 BC and in less than a year God would answer the prayers of His people. Cyrus the Great had already decided to let the Israelites return to their own land. But Azariah's prayer would be repeated over and over, sung in prayer throughout the coming centuries until Jesus of Nazareth, the Promised One, would be born in Bethlehem.

Yet this prayer would not stop there. Early believers in Christ would continue praying for His second coming, that He would again be their Emmanuel, **"God With Us."** In the eighth century AD, an unknown monk would write a Latin hymn, *"Veni Emmanuel,"* which would plead for Christ's promised second return. The song is with us today in the Advent hymn we love,

"O Come, O Come Emmanuel, and ransom captive Israel,
That mourns in lowly exile here, until the Son of God appear.
Rejoice! Rejoice! Emmanuel shall come to thee, O Israel."

"Even so, come quickly, Lord Jesus!" (Revelation 22:21)

DECEMBER 13

A small boy with his father was looking at a manger scene in front of a church when he noticed no baby in the manger. The boy asked, *"Daddy, where did Jesus go?"*

That's a very good question to ask these days. In 2008 the Veteran's Affairs Department ordered removal or covering of any sectarian religious symbols in its hospital chapels. Any crosses, menorahs, pictures of Jesus or Ten Commandments had to be removed or covered.

The regulation basically said all chapels could no longer look like chapels, which begs the question, *"Then why have them?"* If God must be barred from a chapel where people go to pray, what is the purpose of the chapel?

Ruth Graham, daughter of evangelist Billy Graham, was interviewed sometime after the terrorist attacks on America on 9/11/01. The interviewer on *The Early Show* asked her, *"How could God let something like this happen?"*

Ms. Graham replied, *"I believe God is deeply saddened by this, just as we are. But for years we've been telling God to get out of our schools, get out of our government and get out of our lives. And being the gentleman He is, I believe He has calmly backed out. How can we expect God to give us His blessing and His protection if we demand He leave us alone?"*

Her response was not just clever thinking, it was truth. If our leaders insist we neutralize religious public displays and eliminate all references to God, how can that make life better? When the proven commands of God not to steal, kill, defame or hurt our fellow man are removed from schools, what standards or rules are we replacing them with?

The answer, of course, is nothing. Young and old are told they can figure it all out without Godly references. With public morality degenerating through increasingly crude media and entertainment, how can we expect public behavior to improve? The little boy had it right. *"Daddy, where did Jesus go?"*

If we don't show Jesus in our lives, no one will know where He is.

DECEMBER 14

I am terrible at choosing gifts. Rarely can I think of something that would suit a person, so usually I give money. While that's not always bad, it isn't personal, and I do like my gifts to have meaning.

I was talking with a friend who referred me to a website that might help. It was a Christian-based site, so it had some good suggestions. Here are a few...

The Gift of Listening. No interrupting, no planning your response, just listening.

The Gift of Affection. Being generous with appropriate hugs, kisses and pats on the back.

The Gift of Laughter. Sharing funny stories and good humor. Your gift will say, "I love to laugh with you."

The Gift of a Written Note. Expressing in a brief, handwritten note your appreciation or affection.

The Gift of a Compliment. Sincerely saying, "You look great today," or "You're special to me" can bring a smile.

As we continue into this month, drawing closer to the blessed celebration of His birth, why not pass on the best gifts you've received. Share the fact that **"The gift of God is eternal life in Christ Jesus."** (Romans 6:23) Or John 1:12, **"To all who did receive him, to those who believed in his name, he gave the right to become children of God."**

Remind a friend or neighbor how grateful you are that, **"God so loved the world that he gave his one and only Son, that whoever believes in him shall not perish but have eternal life."** (John 3:16)

The best gift God has given us, besides our human life, is eternal life through Jesus. That's why Christians of all ages have found joy in the gifts they can share, cost-free gifts that bless so greatly. That may be why the Apostle Paul said to us in 2 Corinthians 9:15, **"Thanks be to God for His indescribable gift."**

The best gift ever was found in a manger.

DECEMBER 15

One Christmas Eve when I was a boy, my Dad asked if I would help him. It was after church and snowing and he wanted me to help him with something from our car. We went and unlocked our trunk that held a medium-sized box that was very heavy. Dad asked me to hold the trunk door open as he lifted the box and carried it a few cars down and put it in the trunk of my Uncle Paul's car.

"What is it?" I asked. "Plowshares," Dad said. *"Uncle Paul always lets me use his big tractor for fall plowing, so I get him a new set of plowshares in return. It's something we've done for several years."*

Uncle Paul was Mom's brother and for several years he was Dad's hired man. Back when Mom and Dad were first married, Uncle Paul was single and needed work, so Dad hired him for the normal pay of those days, which was room and board and little spending money now and then. Paul was there the day Mom and Dad were married, and he was there when the oldest three of their children were born. He always had a special place in our family, even after he was married to Aunt Esther and moved to her farm.

Gifts at Christmas are unique to those who give and those who receive. While the cost of those plowshares didn't equal the gift using a John Deere and plow, giving back new plowshares was a good way of saying *"Thanks."* That's what some Christmas gifts are for, to say *"Thanks."*

My mother had been Uncle Paul's baby-sitter when he was a boy. Despite her being only ten years old, she cared for Paul and Bill, each 6 or 7 years old, while their mother was washing or cleaning, or on rare days gone into town to the market. They came from Germany to America in 1912, glad to be citizens of their new homeland.

We are all citizens of two countries, earth and heaven. But the longer we remain on earth, the more it seems we are strangers here. When we leave here for our heavenly home, we will rejoice with more joy than we ever had here.

"They gave glory to the God of heaven." (Revelation 11:13)

DECEMBER 16

Duke University's basketball fans are sometimes called, "Cameron's Crazies." Whenever Duke plays archrival North Carolina, the Crazies are given instructions something like this: *"This is the game we've been waiting for. Give it everything you've got – no excuses! Cameron Stadium should never be less than painfully loud tonight."* If you've ever been there or even watched one of their games on television, you'd know Cameron's Crazies take their cheering seriously!

Cameron indoor stadium seats ten thousand fans and is home to the Duke Blue Devils. It is named after Eddie Cameron who served at various time as Duke's basketball coach, football coach and Athletic Director for his 44 years there from 1928 to 1972. Built in 1940, it was the largest stadium in its day and cost a half million dollars. Over the years, Cameron has seen its basketball teams appear in eleven Final Four NCAA tournaments, winning five of them.

Their present coach, Mike Krzyzewski, has been at Duke 35 years and has won all five of those championships. Besides his fine coaching skills, the Duke fans, "Cameron's Crazies," are a large part of their success. They take their allegiance to Duke very seriously.

The songwriter of Psalm 100 took his allegiance to the Lord seriously. **"Shout for joy to the LORD, all the earth."** he said, **"Worship the LORD with gladness and come before him with joyful songs."** (Psalm 100:1-2) The writer wanted his people to loudly express their praises to God because He was their mighty leader. He was the God of Israel who brought them out the land of Egypt, through the waters of the Red Sea and into a land **"flowing in milk and honey."** (Exodus 3:17) They would have health and wealth, so long as they followed the Lord and His commands.

May we worship and serve the Lord who has given us health and wealth during this blessed time of year. May our songs and shouts of joy resound because Jesus is born!

"The lord is good and His love endures forever!" (Psalm 100:5)

DECEMBER 17

On December 17, 1944, Lt. Hiroo Onoda left for the Philippines to join his fellow Japanese soldiers in fighting the Allies. Onoda was to lead his platoon in fighting, and he was ordered not under any circumstances to surrender or to take his own life. To the last man, he was to keep fighting the enemy. Lt. Onoda took those orders more literally than any commander could have given them.

When the Japanese surrendered on August 15, 1945, Lt. Onoda's refused to believe it and continued guerilla warfare, even when all his men were killed. In the ensuing years when leaflets were dropped saying the war was over, Onoda believed it a hoax and never came out of hiding.

Finally, in 1974, 51 year-old Lt. Onodo, lone survivor of his platoon, came out of the jungle and surrendered. He was pardoned by Philippine Pres. Marcos for killing 30 people and wounding 100 others during his personal war. It took Lt. Hiroo Onoda 30 years to believe WWII was over.

When Jesus said, "It is finished!" His work as Savior was over. Some of His disciples didn't believe it, but in the coming weeks He showed Himself alive to hundreds, including His own disciples, and all those were witnesses to His resurrection. They didn't all believe, so it took the Holy Spirit's coming at Pentecost to breathe life into His faltering followers. Without His resurrection, we would have no hope for heaven and there would be no Church. **"If Christ is not raised, then your faith is futile and you are still in your sins,"** said Apostle Paul (1 Corinthians 15:17).

Christmas is not just a festival in a long winter, nor is it the christianizing of a pagan midwinter festival. It is recalling that Jesus was born of Mary and knowing He truly is the Son of God whose forgiveness sets us free. Christmas is our reason to have courage in the midst of life's struggles. It is proof God loves and accepts us. God loves us just the way we are, and He helps us change for the better.

Christ the Savior is born - Hallelujah!

DECEMBER 18

(This story may or may not be true. It was first printed by Rev. Howard Schade in 1954 and has been often re-printed. If you have read it, it is worth reading again.)

A new pastor and his wife were assigned to reopen an old church in Brooklyn which was badly in need of repairs. They arrived in October and decided to have all repairs made before their opening service on Christmas Eve. They repaired and stained the pews, plastered and painted the walls, and were on schedule until a rainstorm caused the roof to leak and a large piece of plaster to fall off the front wall behind the pulpit above the pastor's head. What a mess!

The pastor cleaned things up the best he could and headed home. On the way to his car he noticed a sidewalk sale and there he found an ivory white crocheted tablecloth with a large Cross in the center. He bought it and hung on the church wall to cover the damaged plaster.

Back at the church it had started to snow and the pastor saw an elderly woman miss her bus. He invited her inside to wait for the next one. When she saw the tablecloth, she walked to the front and asked, *"Where did you get that?"* The pastor explained. She asked him to see if the initials, "EBG" were stitched on it - her initials! She had owned this cloth.

Before the war she and her husband were forced to leave Austria when the Nazis came. He was going to follow her, but they were separated and never saw each other again. The pastor offered to take her home and give her the cloth. She accepted the ride, but said for him to keep the cloth.

The Christmas Eve service was almost full, and at the end an older man sat staring at the tablecloth on the wall. He sadly told the pastor it reminded him of one he'd bought his wife years ago. But they'd been separated by the war.

The pastor asked if he could take him for a ride, and they went to the same house where the pastor had taken the woman a few days before. He helped the man climb the stairs to the woman's apartment, knocked on the door, and witnessed the greatest Christmas reunion he would ever see.

What a reunion it will be for us all in heaven! Praise God!

DECEMBER 19

Newgrange is a 5,000 year old burial ground in Ireland. It is famous today for the Winter Solstice illumination which lights up the passage and chamber inside at sunrise. It was built by members of an ancient farming community during the Neolithic period around 3200 BC. This makes it older than Stonehenge and the Egyptian pyramids.

The site consists of a large circular mound with a stone passageway and interior chambers. The mound has a retaining wall at the front and is ringed by engraved stones. There is no agreement about what the site was used for, but it has been speculated that it had religious significance since it is aligned with the rising sun, and the sun's light floods the chamber on the day of the winter solstice.

Some believe it was a place where ancient people went to struggle with dying, since it is situated so a beam of light would move through the chamber for 17 minutes each day from December 19 to December 23, the shortest days of the year. Some believe it served as a powerful symbol of the victory of life over death.

Ever since mankind's fall into sin according to Genesis chapter 3, death has entered into human history. It is one of the great inevitable experiences and for many people their chief source of fear. Sometimes people try to explain the mystery in their own way.

St. Paul wrote in Romans 5:17, **"If by the trespass of the one man, death reigned through that one man, how much more will those who receive God's abundant provision of grace and of the gift of righteousness reign in life through the one man, Jesus Christ!"** Despite mankind's fall into sin through Adam, because of Jesus we need not fear death. He conquered death and gives us hope for eternal life.

Christmas usually concentrates on the birth of a baby, but Christians also rejoice in what the Baby did when He came here to be our Savior.

Why do you rejoice at this time of year?

DECEMBER 20

If you look carefully at just about every Christmas nativity set, you will probably find a man looking over the shoulder of Mary as she looks at her child. That man is Joseph, appointed by God to care for her and the child.

After the Christmas stories in Matthew and Luke, we don't hear much about Joseph again, only when Jesus was left behind in the temple as a twelve year-old boy. If we didn't know better, we might think Joseph was just an incidental person in the story, a bystander only necessary to make up the family.

But Joseph played a strategic role in the story of salvation. If he had disobeyed the angel's command to take Mary as His wife, the entire mission would have changed, putting salvation at risk. Joseph was taking a risk when he accepted Mary as his wife after learning of her pregnancy. He easily could have chosen a harsh penalty for her, and it would have changed everything.

But Joseph stayed the course with Mary. He heard and obeyed the angel, and because of that he is given a unique and God-pleasing position in the story of salvation.

Most of us may think we are insignificant compared to the major players of this world, but all of us are loved by God. Each one of us is the reason Jesus came into the world. As one teacher told her class, *"If you were the only person in the world, Jesus would still have come to die for your sins and give you a place in heaven."*

Who knows what all God has in store for us in life? One person becomes a mighty leader while another is his lowly servant. But then the mighty leader falls and the servant takes over. That's what happened to Joseph in Egypt. He was in prison, then released to become second in command over the whole country. Joseph trusted and obeyed God and was granted a unique place in history, like Joseph.

"Joseph son of David, do not be afraid to take Mary home as your wife, because what is conceived in her is from the Holy Spirit." (Matthew 1:20)

DECEMBER 21

There is a story about Joseph's cradle. It goes like this:

They left their home, the new cradle still rocking on his work table. The aroma of fresh pine had filled the room as Joseph had patiently fashioned the sturdy cradle at night, using the same chisels and saw he used during the day.

Joseph wiped the tears from Mary's cheeks and shut the door behind them. "It'll be okay until we return," he told her, as he roped their belongings to the donkey's back.

"Can't we wait a few days? The baby could come any time." Mary didn't want to leave their home. "We've waited as long as we dare." Joseph said. He was ready to get on the road. "We must leave today or we won't get to Bethlehem in time for the census. I'd be arrested."

"But the cradle, Joseph," she pleaded. "I want the baby to have something nice." "It'll stay behind." he said. "In no time the baby can rock in it when we return."

But they did not return as planned, not for many months until after they had gone to Egypt to avoid Herod's soldiers. When they did return to Nazareth the next year, they found their small home occupied by strangers. "Why are you here? What happened to our things? Where is the cradle?" Joseph said. "The house was empty, and we are your cousins, so now we live here. The cradle? We sold it. No one said we couldn't, and you weren't here."

Joseph went to a judge who said it would take time to get his house back, so for the third time he had to find Mary and the child a place to live. There was an empty small house by the synagogue, and in the back he found the cradle, abused and damaged. But it was now too small for the child, so Joseph repaired it and soon there was need of it again, for Mary was expecting another child.

The boy Jesus never slept in the cradle, but after they were back in their rightful home, He rocked his brother James and later His sister Miriam in it. **"He came not to be served but to serve, and to give his life for many."** (Mark 10:45)

Did you have a cradle when you were a baby?

DECEMBER 22

In 2010, a 63 year-old man made the "find" of a lifetime. David Crisp of Wiltshire, England, was hunting with a metal detector in a field near the city of Frome when his device gave a funny signal. He dug down with his shovel and found an astonishing collection of 52,000 Roman coins from the 3rd century AD, a period barely touched in most history books on Roman Britain.

"The joy of metal detecting is that you never know what you will find," said Mr. Crisp, who has been sweeping those fields for twenty years.

The coins were in a huge metal pot and weighed more than 350 pounds, the size of two grown men. The coins were made of debased silver and bronze and had a lower value than those of gold or silver. But by English law Crisp was entitled to one half their value which netted him over $250,000. *"I always live in hope, but didn't expect to find something like this."* He said with a smile.

This time of the year we think of the Magi who came looking for the child born under the special star they saw in the sky. They, too, came expecting to find someone remarkable, but had no idea it would be the Son of God and Savior of the world.

The Apostle Paul told the people of Colossae that he came to tell them of Jesus, **"so that they may have the full riches of complete understanding, in order that they may know the mystery of God, namely, Christ, in whom are hidden all the treasures of wisdom and knowledge."** (Colossians 2:2-3)

Many years before the writer of Psalm 119 said to God, **"I rejoice at Your Word as one who finds great treasure."** (Psalm 119:162) I wonder if there are many people seeking treasure who might consider looking for them in Holy Scripture. The truths of God there must be sought with faith and hope to find the greatest treasure of all, the Lord Jesus who came into the world at Christmas.

What kind of treasure would you like to find?

DECEMBER 23

"How Far Is It To Bethlehem?" is a lovely Czech carol I learned as a student singing in my High School choir. Its first verse is:

> *How far is it to Bethlehem? Not very far.*
> *Shall we find the stable room Lit by a star?*
> *Can we see the little Child? Is He within?*
> *If we lift the wooden latch May we go in?*

When we visited Israel I asked our guide how far it was from Nazareth to Bethlehem, the route Mary and Joseph took when they went for the census. He told me if I was in Pennsylvania, it's about 9 miles and takes about ten minutes by car (I hadn't realized there were two towns in that state with those same names).

But if you're in Nazareth of Galilee, he said, it's about 80 miles. And if you're travelling by donkey with a pregnant wife like Joseph was, he said it would take about a week, mostly walking through the Jordan valley. It would be shorter going through Samaria, but no God-fearing Jew would consider that way, since it meant going through a country considered inferior to the Jews.

And when they finally got to Bethlehem, he said, they had no advance reservations to stay, so all in all, the journey would be a far cry from the comfortable bus ride we took that lasted perhaps two hours. Speed limits in Israel rarely are above 50 or 60 miles per hour. It is a small country.

The journey for Jesus was longer. He had come from His Father's right hand in heaven to earth where He took on our humanity and was stretched on a cross to die. When He was buried in a borrowed grave, His journey was still not over. He conquered death, left the grave and walked among people again until He finally ascended back to heaven in glory, back from where He came.

But even that is not the end, for one day He will come again in judgment. If you are taking any trips this Christmas season, reflect on the journey Jesus made for us.

He is King of kings and Lord of lords!

DECEMBER 24

Grace Ditmanson Adams is a retired nurse who wrote an interesting little work titled, "ASK Childhood Experience and Health." ASK stands for American School Kikungshan, which was one of the major schools for foreign children in China and which was especially well-attended by children of American Lutheran missionaries in central China. The school operated between 1914 and 1951.

As a young girl Grace travelled with her parents in the late 1920s through inland China. She wrote about the crowded conditions in some of the places they stayed overnight. They were very unhealthy accommodations filled with people coughing, sneezing and smoking. Additionally, babies were crying and children complaining, so her family had to be content to put their bedrolls on the board beds in a large room with all the rest of the people.

One very snowy night they came to an inn that was full. The innkeeper expressed regret of having no room, but then said, *"Please, follow me."* He led them to a side room used to store straw and farm equipment, and there they slept peacefully in a quiet place of their own.

Nurse Adams later wrote that whenever she read about Mary bringing forth her firstborn son and wrapping Him in clothes and placing Him in a manger because there was no room in the inn, she saw the experience quite differently. The innkeeper was not uncaring, and having a place in the inn would have been a much poorer accommodation, especially if Mary had given birth there. The privacy they had in the stable was surely far better than the crowded inn would have been.

Inns at that time were often segregated, one for men and one for women. Knowing of her coming delivery, Joseph could not have allowed Mary to stay in such a place. Even though it was among animals, God provided for them a far better place. We, too, would do well to see how He provides for us in better ways than we might think.

"She laid him in a manger, because the inn was full." (Luke 2:7)

DECEMBER 25

Mary's delivery of her first child was anything but idyllic. The sentimentality which centuries of Christian imagination have given us surely covers the reality of the silent night and the day which followed.

It's usually assumed that Joseph helped her deliver the child, but that would not have been the case. Strict Jewish rules prohibited men from assisting women in childbirth. Galilean woman, even those who were young, prided themselves in self-birth, so the young wife Mary would do the best she could, while Joseph would do only as much as he was allowed to ease her pain that night.

The day following would not have been restful, despite their location. Joseph needed to find food and would have sought a better place for them in the days to come. People other than the visiting shepherds would have come and gone, feeding animals or taking them out and bringing them in as needed.

Mary's Christmas was certainly a time of wonder. It is for every mother who sees and cares for her firstborn. Many questions would have come, and she may have asked Joseph to bring another woman to the stable for help and advice. She also may have wondered how she was adequately going to mother the new infant the angel had called Immanuel, *"God With Us."* Mary must have asked herself many times, *"Who is this child and what will His future be?"*

Today, two thousand years later, each of us needs to ponder similar questions, *"Who is He and what will my future be with Him?"* The importance of His birth, His life, His suffering and death, His resurrection, and His promise to return is of greatest importance to us all.

Take time today to ask God to help you know and appreciate what He has done for you in providing you a personal relationship with His only Son. Give thanks Mary and Joseph have given you a glimpse into the face of God.

"Mary pondered all these things in her heart." (Luke 2:19)

DECEMBER 26

I've written several short stories trying to capture the mood of what it might have been like the first Christmas, about the Inn Keeper, Shepherds and others. I even tried writing a story about the donkey, but it was too silly. But what of Mary and Joseph's first little house and the man who rented it to them after the child was born?

"Could we stay in the small hut in back, my wife and I?" The young man stood at his door. "We've just come from Nazareth." "Have you coin to pay?" asked owner Jacob. The man held out his hands, large and calloused from work. "I have some coin and will work for the rest, or help with animals, make repairs, any work. My wife has just given birth, and we need a place," he pleaded.

"That was you we heard of," said Jacob grinning. "A stable's no place for you now." The young man's face brightened. "You will have my first wages," Jacob looked him over carefully, then said, "The house is yours, but I will see money the first day you work. Times are busy and I have no time for charity." Both men nodded and grasped arms firmly. Joseph had a house!

Days passed and late one night a caravan made its way to the village well, halting there. Camels knelt and riders climbed down. Easterners they were, and wealthy. You could almost smell their money in the fine garments, brass and silver chains and servants. They were Magi, learned Persians, and worn with travel.

They spoke greetings at Jacob's door but looked past him as he came out, beyond to the small house where the new couple now lived. Though no moon, the tiny dwelling was bathed in starlight, and the visitors seemed anxious. "That's their home," Jacob said and walked with them. One of them tapped at the door and spoke greetings. The young wife said she was alone, her husband not yet back from his labor. They all bowed low as she let them enter...

Was this how it might have been? We all have our own vision. God had sent Gentiles to their doorstep, a portent of all whom the child had come to save. And the visitors came with needed gifts. The Savior and His parents were blessed.

"We saw his star when it rose and have come to worship him." (Matthew 2:2)

DECEMBER 27

How many Magi were there? Christmas has some interesting traditions that capture our hearts. There is a quaint story by Henry Van Dyke (1895) about a "Fourth Wise Man" (assuming they numbered three), a Persian priest named Artaban, who had intended to travel with the other three. He sets out to meet them with his treasures for the child, a sapphire, a ruby, and a pearl of great price.

However, he stops along the way to help a dying man, which makes him late to meet the other three. Since he couldn't cross the desert with only a horse, he sells one of his treasures to buy camels and supplies for the arduous trip. He commences his journey but arrives in Bethlehem too late to see the child, for His parents have fled to Egypt.

While there, Artaban saves the life of a child at the price of another of his treasure gifts. He travels to Egypt and other countries, searching for the new King Jesus for years, all the while performing acts of charity along the way. After many years, the "Fourth Wise Man" is still seeking the man Jesus and arrives in Jerusalem just in time for His crucifixion.

There he spends his last treasure, the pearl, to ransom a young woman being sold into slavery. He is struck in the head by a falling roof tile along the route where Jesus is carrying His cross, and is about to die penniless, having failed in his quest to find the Lord. Then he hears a voice, **"Inasmuch as you have done it unto one of the least of these My brethren, you have done it unto Me."** (Matthew 25:40) Artaban, the "Fourth Wise Man," dies in a calm wonder and joy, knowing his treasures were accepted, and he had finally found his King.

No matter whether such stories are legends, humanity has been captivated by the true story of God's love shown by people who have been touched by Jesus. The conviction that Jesus is the Savior of the world moves over two and a half billion today worldwide to worship Him as their heavenly King, born in Bethlehem.

May you be among those who kneel in your heart at the manger.

DECEMBER 28

Much time is given during the Advent and Christmas seasons to hearing the words of the Old Testament prophets. Especially do we hear the many words of Isaiah as he predicts the coming of the Messiah, His forerunner, His suffering and the comfort He brings to the people of God.

The world right now needs comfort and good news. This time of year needs the salvation of our God. Life can be difficult. At some point, most of us have wondered whether God is still in His heavens or not.

Where is God in my trouble, we may ask? Where is He in my illness? Where is He with all the injustice or suffering or war or evil that is raising its ugly head through beheadings, bombings, brutality and abuse in this world? If God is still concerned about the world, how can we take comfort with His apparent lack of caring?

One Old Testament prophet often overlooked is Habakkuk. His prophesies are more positive than most. In chapter 3:18, he wrote, **"Yet I will rejoice in the Lord, I will be joyful in God my Savior."**

Habakkuk had not had an easy life. He had seen the rapid decline in Judah's morality and lack of obedience to God, and it bothered him greatly. Yet He was even more bothered because he knew what God was bringing to his immoral people. The wicked nation of Babylon was going to punish Judah harshly, and this should have caused Habakkuk to weep, like it did Jeremiah.

Habakkuk chose instead to rejoice. **"Yet I will rejoice in the Lord, I will be joyful in God my Savior."** He had learned to trust God knowing what was to come. He was the prophet who most clearly understood the Gospel, as he wrote in 2:4, **"The righteous shall live by his faith."** Despite all that looked so wrong with the world, Habakkuk would not despair but express a faith that also brings joy, no matter how bad the world may seem.

Lord, give us peace on earth and good will towards all. Amen

DECEMBER 29

An event often overlooked at Christmas was the order given by King Herod to slay all Jewish male children two years of age and younger in Bethlehem. Since this town a few miles south of Jerusalem was quite small with probably no more than 1,000 residents, the number of infants Herod's soldiers killed might number two dozen or so. Jewish families encouraged large families as signs of God's blessings. The deaths of these boy children would have been a terrible, wrenching blow to both Bethlehem and its surrounding villages.

Innocent people have often paid the price for greed and power. At the International Slavery Museum in Liverpool, England, one can see the devastation of generations of enslaved men women and children. The price innocent people have paid for greed is horrific, and yet theirs is not the only cost. Engraved in one wall of the museum is a profound observation made by Frederick Douglass, former slave and anti-slave crusader. It reads, *"No man can put a chain about the ankle of his fellow man without also finding the other end fastened about his own neck."*

In the act of dehumanizing others, we dehumanize ourselves. Thus, in the act of killing innocent people, we are killing ourselves. Herod died a terrible death mere months after his brutal order. He who had lived such a powerful life had become so fearful in his old age of a baby becoming king that he would extinguish dozens of innocent lives that might threaten his reign of power.

Apostle Paul says in Galatians 6:7, **"Whatever one sows, that will he also reap."** Herod sowed jealousy, fear and murder, and in the end reaped a most horrible death for himself. Our sinful words and actions will always reap consequences. May our world's leaders and their followers today never forget this, and may they choose freedom and life instead of slavery and death.

"Let us not grow weary of doing good, for in due season we will reap, if we do not give up." (Galatians 6:9)

DECEMBER 30

During the final days of each December, journalists and newscasters look back to review the significant events of the year. Whether successes or failures, triumph or tragedy, they list what they believe has had the most impact on the world and nation. Thus they recall powerful people, natural disasters, good or bad economic news, deaths of various well-known people, as well as how leaders of the world have done their jobs.

I have preached many New Year's Eve and New Year's Day sermons, and all have centered on a review of the past year, together with a spiritual outlook and hope for the year to come.

Another overlooked Old Testament prophet is Micah who wrote in Micah 6:8, **"What does the Lord require of you but to do justice, and to love kindness, and to walk humbly with your God?"** Forty-plus years ago a prominent Christian radio preacher, Dr. Oswald Hoffmann, preached a sermon, *"What does the Lord require of you, Mr. President?"* This sermon came right after President Richard Nixon had been re-elected. Dr. Hoffman used the words of Micah 6:8 as his text.

Realizing now what was revealed at the Watergate Hotel in the following months should have made that sermon memorable. Dr. Hoffman received some criticism for that sermon because he was said to "mix church and state." But I always have wondered what those same critics may have thought when the crimes and misdemeanors of the President came to light and led to his resignation.

"What does the Lord require of you but to do justice, and to love kindness, and to walk humbly with your God?" With the end of this year so close at hand, may you reach out to the Lord in prayer with faith and hope, that you and all mankind may **"do justice, love kindness and walk humbly before God."**

May God give you joy as you do justice, love kindness and walk humbly with God!

DECEMBER 31

The pilot wasn't sure what to do. He wanted to make another swing past the target to see if the clouds had lifted so he could drop his bomb load, but his navigator said they were nearing the limit. If they flew longer, they'd not have enough fuel left to make it back to the air base in England.

"Captain!" the navigator shouted, *"It's now or never. We have to turn around or we'll never make it. We're at the point of no return."* The Captain paused a moment and made his decision. *"We're going around again and dump this load. I think the clouds are lifting."* *"But we won't have enough to make it back!"* the navigator shouted back. *"No matter, we're going for it, and God help us!"* said the Captain as he banked his plane towards the target again.

In a similar way, people at the end of the old year are at a point of no return. We can't go back and change anything about the old year. We can only look forward to the new year that is to come, and pray God's help for what will happen in it.

Sometimes the target for the new year is our health. It's worse than it has ever been, but we trust God for the future. Sometimes it's a shaky marriage, but we want it to continue, even if it seems hopeless. Sometimes it is a wayward child who passed point of no return long ago. We can only hope the future will bring a miracle for him.

In Deuteronomy 11:7 Moses reminded his people of **"every great act of the Lord which He did."** After four decades in the wilderness, they were ready to enter the Promised Land. It was a new land and a new year. There was no going back to Egypt. So he said, **"The eyes of the Lord are always on it, from beginning of the year to the very end of the year."** (Deuteronomy 11:12)

Today we are on the brink of a New Year and must once again trust God for what is before us. His faithful care will extend to every day the New Year will bring. We can count on Him to live up to His promises. Trust Him for that!

Merry Christmas and a blessed New Year!

Rev. Robert L. Tasler

The author is a native of Windom, Minnesota, and a career ordained pastor in the Lutheran Church-Missouri Synod. A 1971 graduate of Concordia Seminary, St. Louis, Missouri, he has served parishes in North Dakota, California, Utah and Colorado. Now retired, he and his wife Carol divide their time between Colorado, and Arizona. He has authored several other works, electronically and/or in print, including his highly successful devotionals, DAILY WALK WITH JESUS and DAILY WORD FROM JESUS which can be seen with all his published works on his website: http://www.bobtasler.com/. Thank you for reading this daily devotional. If you liked it, please tell others about it.

Made in the USA
Columbia, SC
20 May 2017